Definitely a must read for souls seeking a jo
courage, and self-discovery wrapped in the
— Tracey Callender

This book, *d.i.y. zen and the Art of Gentle Emotional Transformation*, is a powerful, gutsy, and humorous read, filled with valuable tools and practices to transform your life. With a clear, strong, authentic voice that is captivating and wise, Gary's impeccable honesty and wisdom will liberate and illuminate you. The 33-Day Workbook invites you into a personal freedom and mastery healing journey. Take this book and run! Use it to set yourself free from the bondage of self-limiting emotions and behaviors.
— Dr. Rev. Debbi Brown-Adams, Minister at Unity of Sun Lakes
Ministerial Leader & Teacher, The Center for Soulful Living

Gary Niki's book, *d.i.y. zen and The Art of Gentle Emotional Transformation*, is a must-read asap. I will certainly keep one of my copies on my nightstand. I highly recommend this tool as the one to use, like a Swiss Army Knife, whenever Life Happens.
— LMB CBL, USA

Gary's life-changing book is something you need to keep on your nightstand. Profound, powerful and simple to use, his work is deep and connected. Reach for it all the time to keep you peaceful and grounded. I've known Gary many years and whatever issue you are dealing with he's the healer who can support you. This book will make a difference in your life!
— Jill Lublin, International Speaker, Publicity Strategist and four-times
Best Selling Author, JillLublin.com

Joy and caring jump off every page of *d.i.y. zen and the Art of Gentle Emotional Transformation*. Gary Niki's authentic writing style, combined with his deep experience in the field, make this book a gem. Packed with wisdom, the book offers simple techniques for moving with grace through a range of life experiences — from everyday stressors to major traumatic events.
— Alicia Korten, Award-winning author CEO, The Culture Company

Gary is a master at leading us to new ways of living a fuller, happier life through his book *d.i.y. zen and the Art of Gentle Emotional Transformation*!

— D. Janie Guill, Consciousness Raising Coach

Gary Niki literally brings lifetimes of personal growth, development, wisdom, and enlightenment into every arena that he enters. His book *d.i.y. zen and the Art of Gentle Emotional Transformation* is no exception, exploding with practical information that will serve everyone that it reaches. We are leaving an era of theories, philosophies, and advice. Gary's book demonstrates the leading edge of consciousness through pure life experience, example, and incredible testimonials. Be assured though, the power of Gary's message will resonate with you and stay with you through your own personal development and growth. Gary is a "gifted giver of blessings" and you cannot be acquainted with him or his work without being blessed exponentially!

— Dr. Joshua Kai, Author of the three-time award-winning,
   best-selling book, *The Quantum Prayer: An Inspiring Guide to Love, Healing, and Creating the Best Life Possible*

d.i.y. zen and the Art of Gentle Emotional Transformation arrives at a time when humanity could really use an authentic, loving, powerful avenue for repairing - both in our individual lives and in the collective. With Gary Niki's practical mystic mastery, you will receive invitations, guidance, and wisdom with which to deeply lean into and grow forth. His blend of keen insights, captivating anecdotes, and raw self-reflection in his book, along with transformative practices in the accompanying workbook, will provide assured, positive alchemy in the life of anyone who authentically participates with his rock-solid brilliance in the artistry of self-loving transformation.

— Rev. Kate Rodger, Ph.D., Institute of Modern Wisdom,
   Founder and Director

Gary gives us simple tools in his book *d.i.y. zen and the Art of Gentle Emotional Transformation* that immediately start raising our energy and thus, our ability to act. Change your energy, change your life!

— William G. Chrystal, Congregational Minister and Author
of numerous books including *Hamilton by the Slice* and *Niebuhr Studies*

Reverend Gary Niki is a person of great vision and integrity. His commitment to serve the Human Condition as a Healer and a Teacher is exemplary and he brings these through his book *d.i.y. zen and The Art of Gentle Emotional Transformation*. The "Mystical Samurai", with a Yoda presence, has created a book and workbook of immense importance toward embracing the commonality of The Divine Energies to permeate all things. Practical use of these forces, in ways and with terms for everyone, is the core of his work. I am honored to be his friend.

— Rev. Dan Chesbro, Sanctuary of the Beloved – The Order of Melchizedek Author of *The Order of Melchizedek: Love, Willing Service and Fulfilment* and *The Gospel of Thomas: A Spiritual Interpretation of The Age of Aquarius*

Gary is ultra-sensitive to others and their healing/empowerment journey or evolution. Through his facilitation and teaching, he is thereby able to intuitively know just how to encourage your natural path of growth and expansion, with kindness and great empathy.

— Krystan AlecSandRa Bray, CEO and First Ministering Priestess at Ormes Temple Spiritual Life Science Education Center

Highest praise for *d.i.y. zen and the Art of Gentle Emotional Transformation!* This book is a must-read for anyone who has experienced trauma or suffering and has a desire to be free!

Rev. Gary Niki is a gifted healer and teacher who has perfected the art of gentle emotional transformation and has taken it to the next level. With the strength of a powerful, disciplined Zen Master, and the tenderness, presence, and patience of a Spiritual Midwife, Gary lovingly guides the reader out of pain and trauma and into a place of peace and absolution. With grace, love, and an elevated perspective, Gary helps us to identify our emotions and bring honor to what we feel, so we can finally transform and be free.

The simple techniques and tools that Gary shares with us in this book and workbook are powerful beyond measure! Prepare yourself to be pleasantly surprised by how much you transform in a very short time. And stay with it! Healing often comes in waves and it's great to know that you have this wonderful toolkit to help you every step of the way.

Thank you, dear Rev. Gary Niki for all your love and contributions to humanity! You are a gifted soul and a true blessing to the Earth and her people. Your book is fabulous! And I'm really excited to recommend it to my clients.
— Rev. Angela Mandato, Licensed Massage Therapist, Board Certified

So, you can imagine when someone tells you that they can help you heal an emotional issue in less than three minutes, the natural reaction is to be skeptical. That was my initial reaction when Gary Niki mentioned the 'Put Your Fingers On Your Forehead' technique to me from his book *d.i.y. zen and the Art of Gentle Emotional Transformation*. I am always up for good entertainment so, why not? Gary proceeded to ask me to think about a frustrating, negative or emotional situation. I chose a work situation that has been stressing me out for three months and that was totally out of my control. I placed my fingers on my forehead and followed his instructions. About three minutes later, I felt one hundred percent neutral about it. I am writing this days after the situation and I am still neutral. It is a non-issue. I can move forward with confidence and ease!

Please, please, please do yourself a favor and learn this technique, NOW! Don't waste your precious energy or time. Do this. It works. I promise!
Peace and Love!
— Carrie Pascoe, Project Management Professional

Gary Nobuo Niki has given us a beautiful gift in his new book, *d.i.y. zen and the Art of Gentle Emotional Transformation*. Gary has wisely shared his own story, using it as a springboard to helping his readers create positive releases and changes in their lives. His stories are heartfelt; we all identify with them. The power of the two methods of release that Gary then lays out in his book are not only clearly demonstrated, but also he has included powerful testimonial stories from his clients that strongly support the effectiveness of these beautiful techniques. In addition, Gary has included a 33-day workbook that will help the reader solidify these techniques by integrating them into real life experiences. Treat yourself to a wonderful journey of transformation.

> — Donna J. Bauman, Ed.D., Works with Visionary Art, Photography, Watercolor and Pottery. Served as the Vice President of Washington DC's World Peace Institute and as the Executive Director for the Center for Soulful Living.

In this well-written and easy to understand do-it-yourself book by Gary, you, the reader, will get practical tools and techniques that will teach you how to overcome the debilitating effects of ongoing stress and trauma in your life. I applaud Gary for having overcome some difficult situations in his own life. He writes and shares stories from his personal journey and experiences. I highly recommend this book to anyone wanting to help themselves live a more stress-free and fulfilled life.

> — Dr. Kenneth Harris, Author of *Synchronicity-The Magic-The Mystery-The Meaning*; Founder of the Mind-Body Wellness Center and the former director of the Waldwick Wellness Center. doctorkenharris.com

In a time when people feel so overwhelmed with stress, anxiety and worry, Gary comes along with simple, easy to do techniques that anyone can do themselves and with long-lasting results. Through stories of his own experiences and his expertise as a disaster relief team member and energy worker, Gary's *d.i.y. zen and the Art of Gentle Emotional Transformation* book plus workbook are here to meet you where you are, and help you step by step if you are willing to engage in the work. It may appear to be simple at first yet I believe you will find it life changing if you keep an open mind.

At the time when Gary shared his book, I was thinking about how to help people over the initial shock of learning they will be losing their beloved pet soon. "Put Your Fingers On Your Forehead" made perfect sense to me. As I talk to people on the phone, they are often too emotional to tell me what they really want from a session. 'Breathe' is my go-to tool and now I have been given another. I was listening to *Evolve Your Brain* by Dr. Joe Dispenza at the same time as I started to read this book. In it, Dispenza explains how we have sensors in our bodies. Two of the strongest sensors are in our lips and our fingertips. OMG I thought! This is why Gary's "Put Your Fingers On Your Forehead" works so well. The frontal lobe of the brain is where we hold stressful emotional images. Way to go, Gary! You followed your instinct, doing what you observed to work, and shared it. I will be referring this book to my clients to read more about the techniques.

    — Lesley Nase

    Author of *Who Paints the World*, Holistic Healing Facilitator, Speaker, Animal Communicator, Moonspinners Enterprise LLC

D.I.Y. ZEN

AND

The Art of Gentle Emotional Transformation

GARY NOBUO NIKI

D.I.Y. ZEN

AND

The Art of Gentle Emotional Transformation

The last photograph of Dad and me, December 17, 1982

Dedication

This book is dedicated with love, blessings, and good energy to ALL Humankind! Yes, it is dedicated to US!

WE are ALL part of Divine Love and One with Divine Light.

WE are ALL sharing planet Earth TOGETHER!

Special Dedication to my dad, Carl Nobuo Niki
(July 5, 1915 – June 3, 1983)

He was a great zen kinda guy who never treated anyone he met like a stranger, greeted everyone with a warm smile, deeply loved his GOD, family and friends. He treated everyone with dignity and respect. All in all, he just got it!

And Dedicated To…

The magnificence of our Divine bodies and how wonderfully made we truly are!

No matter what our spiritual, religious, or personal beliefs are, we must admit that our bodies have an innate wisdom to automatically start healing ourselves without us consciously doing anything.

With my deepest and profound gratitude! Thank you!

Aloha! & Mahalo! (Thank you!)

Gary Nobuo Niki

PUBLISHING

Published by:
Capucia, LLC
211 Pauline Drive #513
York, PA 17402
www.capuciapublishing.com

Paperback ISBN: 978-1-945252-92-1
eBook ISBN: 978-1-945252-93-8
Library of Congress Control Number: 2020917712

Cover Design: Ranilo Cabo
Layout: Ranilo Cabo
Editor and Proofreader: Penny Legg
Book Midwife: Carrie Jareed

Printed in the United States of America

CONTENTS

D.I.Y. ZEN

PART I

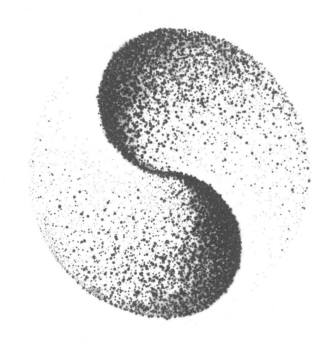

AUTHOR'S NOTE

Thank you for picking up *d.i.y. zen and The Art of Gentle Emotional Transformation*! This book has been a work in progress for the last 22 years and the three techniques that I share with you certainly are not new or my own brilliant invention. They are simplified, modified, re-discovered, re-developed, solid, tested and don't require any proving on my part or anyone else's, except your own.

I think of this book and workbook, as a "do-it-yourself" (d.i.y.) guide or manual to a system with a set of simple techniques and tools that have worked for me and several thousand individuals from five years old to 95 years old. They come from all backgrounds, including students, volunteers, teachers, business, industry, government, first responders, medical, public safety, military and war veterans. Many have gone through tough stuff, post-traumatic-stress (PTS), and critical incident stress debriefings (CISD). They survived and were able to move forward in their lives feeling more positive and changed, while starting to experience some zen on their own life path!

"Life is way too short to be miserable!"
— *Carl Nobuo Niki*

My Dad always came up with pieces of wisdom that I called his "Carl Niki-isms", which he would share with me to teach and make his point while I was growing up.

There were times I didn't get it or I wasn't sure what he meant! However, when I was brave enough to admit to him that I didn't understand, he would immediately stop what he was doing. He would smile and say, "Son, let's sit down right here and

I will tell you what it means to me so that you may understand it, too." He would always take his time to make sure I understood the importance of the lesson.

My dad always talked to me and demonstrated how important it is to be a good man who lives a happy, positive, joy-filled, best life right now.

Reflecting back half a century later, what I realize now is, doggone it, maybe he was just his own 'happy and practical zen master kinda guy' and I never knew it or couldn't fully appreciate his wisdom until now!

My dad used to tell me, "Son, we won't get out of this life alive and no matter who you are, we're all born dying and that's the way it goes. However, what matters is the time that we have here on planet Earth and for us to live the best life possible, no matter what happened to us. We are here right now and as long as we are alive, we can do a re-start from this point forward to live our best life from now on!"

What does that 'best life' look like?

I have no idea and I certainly don't know what it is for you.

What I do know is that throughout my 57 years on this Earth, I have never, ever met anyone who had a perfect life without any pain; suffering; trauma; doubts; fears; problems; losses; wounds; scars; disappointments or upsets both emotionally and physically.

No matter how "good" someone looks on the outside, we may never know what is really going on inside of them or what they live with and experience every day.

Over the last four decades, I've had the privilege of meeting so many amazing individuals from around the world, in all walks of life with heart-stopping and shocking stories of what happened to them. Many of them would say to me, "I was very fortunate," or, "How lucky I am to even be here!" And, "I am happy to be alive!"

There are also countless inspiring stories in books, movies, television and on the internet of incredible individuals that have made it through alive, living their best life right now.

I believe that, as humans, we are all similar with our own feelings, hopes, dreams, and desires. Digging down, we are more the same than we are different. While working in disaster and emergency management, public safety, anger management and a multitude of healing energy modalities, I have discovered countless individuals with the courage to be alive, to survive, then to thrive no matter what happened to them! Over and over, person after person, I would think with gratitude, wow, isn't it amazing that they are still here and none of them ever quit or gave up! They made it through to the other side of what happened to them and they're able to share their story of inspiration with us! Hey, maybe they found some zen in their own life.

The cold hard fact is, life here on Earth can be challenging, complicated and difficult! If you or a loved one have ever suffered or is suffering now outwardly or in silence, then my hope is, this book and workbook could be what you've been looking for to assist you on your journey.

> *"Son, the definition of crazy is doing the exact same thing over and over, expecting different results! Stop! Search for and do something different!"*
> — *Carl Nobuo Niki*

Over the last 33 years, I've been on my own quest to find what works for me. A dear teacher, LeRoy Malouf, in his eighties told me his experience and said, "After going through hundreds of training classes and modalities, I can tell you that everything works for numerous people and nothing works on everyone, so keep searching to find what works for you and your clients." I have found what LeRoy told me to be so true!

With that said, I hope that the simple "do-it-yourself (d.i.y.)" techniques shared in this book will be some of the tools that serve you as you explore your path to becoming as happy, healthy, whole and complete as is possible.

NOTE: There is a **Glossary** included in the back of this book. For early clarification of the word *"zen"*, **"zen-Zen-ZEN"** and for the purposes of this book, I use **"zen"** in lower case, **NOT** tied to a Religious or ZEN Religion, Zen Buddhism, doctrine, long time traditions, Buddhists, Sutras, schools, literature, organizations, dogma or beliefs. *To me it's the "zen" my dad lived, demonstrated and the way he was: aware; focused; mindful; spiritual; centered; present; attentive; meditative; calm, cool and collected; relaxed; peaceful; quiet minded; clear; self-aware; balanced; inner harmony to be himself.*

Please approach the book and workbook with an open mind, work through it slowly, take your time and, as with zen, experience it for yourself.

If it works for you, please consider sharing what you have learned, to make a positive difference in the lives of others.

Again, thank you very much for picking up *d.i.y. zen and The Art of Gentle Emotional Transformation!*

My deepest appreciation, best wishes, with lots of love, blessings and good energy!

Mahalo! (Thank you!)

Gary Nobuo Niki

FOREWORD

by Dr. Patricia Carrington

Why, I wondered as I began to write the foreword to Gary Niki's book, am I writing this at all when I routinely refuse to write forewords?

Actually, I had volunteered all on my own to write the foreword to this book immediately after I had read most of the prepublication copy that Gary had sent to me. Why had I done this?

The reason was that I had realized that the new "stress management" method using the two clearing techniques that this book introduces has a powerful potential to help the ordinary non-technical people of this world who encounter any sort of trauma in their lives. *d.i.y. zen and The Art of Gentle Emotional Transformation* is written for every one of us to use in times of crisis, or in fact whenever we are facing any traumatic or deeply distressing incident.

I was convinced that I had to tell as many people as possible about it because this book could, on occasion, literally be a life-saver because of the calm levelheadedness it engenders. The book enables a traumatized person to face intense life challenges, large or small, with an unusual inner balance from the clearing.

The fact is that most books in my field, although some of them contain self-help techniques of outstanding value, are not generally "good reads" as the saying goes. They are apt to be too technical in nature or too dry and detailed to hold my interest for very long.

But, to my surprise, Gary's book was different from these others. In fact, I couldn't put it down. I love stories and Gary's book was filled with accounts of his unusually exciting career as a disaster management and public safety worker during which, at the sites of the incidents and disasters where he worked, he was able to develop two amazing stress management/trauma dissolving techniques that he tells us about in these pages. He does so in such a down-to-earth and conversational manner that when reading his descriptions I felt as though he and I were chatting together across a table. In other words, I discovered that the book is wonderfully human…

I have long been involved in psychological research and, because of my work in the energy psychology area with my books, training methods, and Internet teleseminars etc., and in particular because of my experience in research, I know the intricacies of controlled studies and respect scientific proof, so I expected to encounter a lot of this kind of information in the book.

But when I picked it up, there was none! I found myself reading a book that contained an entirely different sort of research than what I was accustomed to. It was not from scientists studying stress, but from the "fighting front" itself, where the problems actually occur. It gave us an immense amount of what is called "anecdotal evidence", showing the effectiveness of the simple energy-based techniques that involves the use of acupuncture meridians to counteract the effects of trauma. The data upon which this method is based was recorded firsthand by a former leader and trainer on major disaster response operations and in daily life from many individuals.

Right away I asked myself, will Gary's *d.i.y. zen and The Art of Gentle Emotional Transformation* method with his "Put Your Fingers On Your Forehead" and "The Energetic Action Process" techniques take the place of such highly effective stress management methods as Dr. Joseph Mercola's Energy Tapping and Meridian Tapping Techniques (MTT) or Gary Craig's Emotional Freedom Techniques (EFT) or Dr. Roger Callahan's Thought Field Therapy (TFT) or Tapas Fleming's Tapas Acupressure Technique, (TAT) or the many techniques developed by Donna Eden of Energy Medicine, or of other respected energy-based methods that are now being used to transform the lives of millions of people?

The answer was clear. This easily learned and down-to-earth method does not take the place of any existing technique. Rather, it shares aspects of these other energy-based techniques in a uniquely simple and practical manner.

What is particularly interesting to me is the fact that he discovered the effectiveness of the "Put Your Fingers On Your Forehead" technique independently from the work of these outstanding pioneers. By the time he wrote the book, Gary had himself investigated many of these existing energy psychology techniques personally and was heavily influenced through the work of his teacher Virginia Dunstone and her teacher Dr. Roger Callahan, and by the chiropractic discipline of Applied Kinesiology as developed by Dr. George Goodheart Jr. (Goodheart, in case you don't know of him, was the "father" of muscle testing as a diagnostic tool, which Gary teaches so simply and masterfully in this book).

His attention was called to this method when, during his many incidents, disaster responses, traumatic situations and then on television and movies he noted thousands of times traumatized people spontaneously clasping their hands to their foreheads when they were faced with the shock of disaster. This seemingly almost instinctive human gesture seemed to lessen the overwhelming effects of their intense emotion. It was an effort to help themselves.

These distressed people, however, often clasped their fingers or hands to their foreheads in a rather disorganized fashion to try to cope with the overwhelming emotions they were experiencing. The result was that they could not easily replicate the effects of this gesture for clearing. Exploring this further, Gary discovered that in many instances all they needed was a little instruction to allow them to use this natural method systematically, in a way that would allow them to calm down amazingly in only a few moments and be able to talk and think rationally and become, in a practical sense, functional, and then to use the techniques in the 33-day workbook to address the deeper, more in-depth issues.

It is these firsthand experiences which led to the development of the "Put Your Fingers On Your Forehead" and "The Energetic Action Process" techniques that are presented to you in this book by means of real-life stories.

So that you will know why Gary Niki was qualified to have made these observations, here is a little about his background. During his career he served on local, state, federal and tribal emergency management and disaster relief operations, all of which subsequently led to major positions in the field of disaster response work in the United States. Working in public safety and for the American Red Cross as a Disaster Manager he had the opportunity to informally use his "Put Your Fingers On Your Forehead" technique many times with teammates, friends and people who were facing unimaginable fear and trauma, and then see it quench that upset and fear in a very short period of time.

He used it on himself at first, then with his friends, family, and clients. He then applied it when appropriate while working in emergency management, public safety, investigations and as a disaster response manager. He used it when he was at crash scenes; when houses were burned down or destroyed and at times their inhabitants weeping hysterically, unable to function or dazed, and in numerous other intense situations that he describes in the book.

He also found that he could use it to aid the rescue workers in the emergency crews. As he worked in the field on large-scale national disaster relief operations and as a leader, he assumed a multitude of official roles right in the middle of the disasters themselves, including during the tragedy of the World Trade Center in New York City in 2001 and Hurricane Katrina in the southern United States in 2005. At these major sites, he saw some of the top disaster health and mental health workers in the world, who had been deployed to these sites from hundreds of diverse agencies and locations, facing unimaginable challenges because the damage being created was so monumental. The workers in the field needed help themselves just to continue coping and responding, regardless of the wide range of devastation they were experiencing in doing their jobs.

At these sites, Gary began sharing the "Put Your Fingers On Your Forehead" technique with some of his fellow workers and other agency colleagues. Many of them were able to get positive results rapidly from this simple technique and soon "swore by it". The traumatic events became cleared and neutralized for them at the time, although frequently it took many repetitions of the method to accomplish a complete clearing because the impact of the disaster had been so deeply embedded in their minds and bodies. This book is the result of persistent work in the trenches, so to speak.

Interestingly, I have learned that Gary wants assistance to find a way and the funding to make electronic and hard copies of his book and workbook available to rescue workers, first responders, disaster responders, emergency medical workers and military veterans from all countries of the world who have experienced traumatic situations and who are unable to purchase a book for themselves. This is how deeply he is inspired by this method's power to help, and I know that this is the way many of you will feel when you use it for yourself.

Gary developed "The Energetic Action Process" for deeper clearing work and he also developed *The Energetic Action Process 33-Day Workbook* (which presents an entire workshop on stress management in workbook form). He has generously incorporated it as part of this volume.

He has also included the "Awful-Distressing-Stuff List" as he calls it. It is filled with traumatic emotions and feelings that have affected hundreds of individuals that he worked with. So as not to leave you with only clearing out the negative things, Gary also included the "Positivity and Empowerment List" for you to use after all of the clearing work to ensure that you are strong to the positive items.

I don't think forewords should be too long, however, I felt it's important to have told you all that I think you need to know about this stress-trauma-relief method. It is now time for you to explore it for yourself. I hope you will find this adventure as meaningful as I have.

Patricia Carrington, Ph.D.
Associate Clinical Professor of Psychiatry, Rutgers
School of Biomedical and Health Sciences, Piscataway,
New Jersey. Originator of the EFT Choices Method

In Loving Memory of My Dear Friend:
Dr. Patricia Carrington (July 1, 1924 ~ October 19, 2019)
Thank You Very Much for all of the love, friendship, wisdom, insights,
assistance, guidance and encouragement that you gave me over the years on
getting this book done and out to the world! Love you, miss you!
THX GARY…

INTRODUCTION

I'm on a mission and journey to make a positive difference on our planet by sharing simple, natural tools and techniques that empower us to help clear out the negative unwanted thoughts, words, feelings and emotions that do not serve us or promote our happiness, freedom, peace, and calm for the highest good of our body, heart, mind and spirit of zen.

This book *diy zen and The Art of Gentle Emotional Transformation* stems from this commitment.

We are not here together by accident. I know that this is by Divine Grace, GOD (whoever He or She or It may be to you), The Blessed Divine, God, Lord, Jesus Christ, El Shaddai, Jehovah Jireh, YHWH, Mother Earth, Father Sky, Grand Mother Moon, Grand Father Sun, The I AM, Your Higher Power, Divine Providence, The Universe, The Highest Self, The Great Spirit, The Mighty I AM Presence, or by YOU choosing to be here with me through this book.

Hey, if life here on planet Earth was always smooth, kind, nice and easy then maybe we would all naturally be zen and sitting somewhere with a quiet mind, happy, calm and meditating. If that were true, I certainly wouldn't have written this book. You wouldn't be reading it or even looking at it right now and we wouldn't be here sharing this moment together!

Today, I'm sure that even with all of the changes in awareness and training at schools, work sites, Social Media and all of the anti-bullying, anti-harassment, etc., I still know that every day there are millions of individuals around the world that are suffering right now, this very minute as you are reading this book. Yes, Right Now! This Very Minute! Someone Somewhere Is Suffering!

Like many people who have been living life for a while, I got here through what I call 'Stuff'. For me, it showed up in the form of a lot of pain and silent suffering from grade school bullying, to teenage and early adult life stress of one thing after another: failing marriage; my dad dying; going through divorce and bankruptcy, and at the same time losing everything; feeling hopeless and ready to kill myself; changing jobs; feeling miserable and lost; being a stressed-out work-a-holic, and on and on through my mid-twenties. So yes, I've been through some stuff in my life as most of us have.

And, like millions of others, I never told my parents, teachers, coaches or anyone that I was being picked on, teased and beaten up at school and on the bus. I just sucked it up. I suffered in silence so that I wasn't a wimpy, whiney, cry baby, tattle-tale. I was so ashamed and embarrassed, I could not tell anyone what was happening at the time and I had no idea what to do except suffer in silence, endure and deal with it!

I believe that as Humans we are all similar and, in digging down, we are more the same than we are different.

This was driven home for me in the later 1990s and early 2000s while serving as a diversity instructor for government agencies and non-governmental organizations. I would tell my participants that we are able to divide up the individuals in this classroom in a multitude of ways to show how different we are without even talking about the biggies: race, color, creed, ethnicity, age and sexual orientation.

Of course, they would kinda laugh, smirk and say, "yeah right". Some of them would actually look at me and laugh or smirk with some sort of disbelief and shake their heads until I physically divided them up in the room by big city vs small town, socioeconomic background, education, left vs right-handed, life experiences, on and on.

Yes, they were kinda surprised and once I had their attention, I would say, "We are more the same than we are different!"

I would tell them, "And if you don't believe it, think about this, we humans may pee (urinate) differently, however, we all eat and release (defecate) the same way!"

That would get them thinking, their gears grinding, minds spinning and their heads nodding in agreement and realizing that, yes, on many levels, we humans are the same. In doing our jobs as responders, we are here to assist and serve those who have experienced loss, and trauma, and survived disaster situations or events. While we are helping them, we serve with dignity and respect because we are the same. The difference is, this time we are the responders that are here to help them to make it through!

Over the years working as a responder, I have discovered countless individuals with the courage to be alive and to survive, then to thrive no matter what happened to them!

Over the last two decades, I have sought out lots of positive books, tapes/CDs/DVDs, self-help programs, guides, helpers, teachers, leaders, groups, organizations, technologies, tools, modalities, and techniques that would help me deal with the challenging experiences I faced with the lingering painful thoughts, feelings and emotions that accompanied them. I have learned, practiced, worked with and benefited from all of them. Some I continue to use today. However, I found that many of them are very detailed, with an extensive process, or they require a certain amount of time to get through them properly. That is extremely good and appropriate for those specific tools, modalities and techniques to work effectively. While they all work well in their own right, what I've found in an emergency or disaster situation, or immediately after a traumatic experience, is that we may not have the luxury of time or a quiet space to do some of their techniques properly.

For any techniques or methods to be effective, they must be capable of being used by anyone immediately and naturally after an incident of this type. Then, after the immediacy of the event is over, these techniques may be used to help the individual with their ongoing, longer or past thoughts, feelings and emotions.

One of the reasons I have written about the techniques I use is because they are very simple to use and they've had quick, positive results throughout a multitude of situations and events. These are not limited to disaster situations but may be situations such as anger management, building or recovering self-esteem, saving your life or someone's that you care about, getting past bullying and harassment on every level, belief systems, family issues, sexual trauma, religious or political persecution along with any other thoughts, words, feelings, emotions or beliefs that may have negatively affected and weakened us in the past.

All of these techniques are simple and non-invasive. They have a foundation in the natural wisdom contained within our own bodies and the body's innate ability to heal itself, and you are able to use them immediately on your own and by yourself.

The first technique I present in this book is "Put Your Fingers On Your Forehead". At first it may sound too simple and impossible however, I have found this technique to be natural and work in countless traumatic situations, whether a shaken driver at the scene of a vehicle crash or accident; a person who has suffered an assault or the loss of a loved one; someone coping after a disaster event or for an individual who feels paralyzed with fear.

By putting their fingers on their foreheads, staying with and experiencing the distressing thoughts, feelings and emotions that arose, these people and countless others were quickly able to release them and started to achieve a state of increased calm and clarity within minutes.

The second technique I discuss is the "The Energetic Action Process". By identifying the troubling emotions being experienced and then using a series of short statements or little mantras accompanied by energetic clapping or drumming motions on the sides of the hands, debilitating feelings and emotions can be cleared or released. Again, it may seem hard to imagine that something so simple could really work however, I have found this technique to be effective in any of a number of situations I have faced in my own life and also in the lives of thousands of other individuals.

The last technique I cover is the "The Art of Muscle Testing", also known as kinesiology. While it's certainly not new, I have found that muscle testing can be used to great effect in conjunction with "The Energetic Action Process". I provide two lists to work with to assist these processes: "Awful-Distressing-Stuff List" and the "Positivity and Empowerment List".

I have found many times that after doing a bit of clearing work on ourselves, we may come to a point when we just don't know what else is weakening us or what we are feeling. However, we know something is still stuck there. By using "The Art of Muscle Testing" our body can confirm that there is still something that is weakening us and we just don't know what it is. That's when we are able to go to the "Awful-Distressing-Stuff" List to search through and possibly find out what this is and what to work on next.

By testing the strength or weakness of our muscle/energy while thinking about a particular event, or after making a negative statement, or even while just thinking about a word describing an emotion, we can discover whether we are strengthened or weakened by this stimulus and therefore identify what the truth may be for us. Yes, it is possible for our thoughts, words, feelings, emotions and actions to physically and energetically strengthen or weaken us immediately on many levels! Just feel the energy of them!

Once we've identified what has weakened us, we are able to use the techniques to start processing and clearing them out. Then, through muscle testing, we have an opportunity to test again to determine through physical demonstration to ourselves that we have, indeed, cleared, released out or at least be on the way to healing our condition.

Another reason I have selected these three simple techniques for presentation in this book is that many individuals, like me, have happily discovered them to be secret therapy or secret self-therapy. Why? Because we have found that using them to get cleared does not require us to tell anyone else what we were thinking, feeling, or experiencing at the moment of our trauma!

That's absolutely right, we did not have to speak out loud, tell anyone lots of history or offer any explanations or defenses in order to be set free from thoughts or feelings that have kept us in bondage; chained to past experiences that weakened and negatively affected us throughout our lives.

My hope and desire for you is that this book will inspire and motivate you to take action for yourself and your loved ones!

You have the opportunity right now to help yourself, by learning, practicing, experiencing, identifying and starting to clear out stuff that no longer serves you, and to become strong to positive words and energy.

Even if you use just one of these techniques, I am certain that you will experience profound results while gaining insights!

You have the opportunity to step up as the leader in your family, circle of friends, workplace or community and by sharing what you've learned with them you may help them in ways that you can't even imagine right now. You may even help someone save their own life.

I have also included in this volume *The Energetic Action Process 33-Day Workbook* to help you use and anchor these simple techniques for yourself by practicing them. The workbook also provides a private space for you to record your results. Together, the text and the workbook provide one simple and natural system of transformation and clearing.

The last tools included are the "Awful-Distressing-Stuff List" and the "Positivity and Empowerment List".

Please consider the "Awful-Distressing-Stuff List" as a Power Tool. I consider it as an eclectic, pain-filled, non-conventional list that was collected from over two decades of working with individuals by writing down the thoughts, feelings, emotions, events and statements that have been worked on and cleared by hundreds of brave people.

Please go slowly while you work with the "Awful-Distressing-Stuff List". Like any power tool, it would be good for you to get used to it while you go through the workbook, just like an operations manual. Take your time. Be your own detective and archaeologist while you investigate and dig through your life to identify what is coming up and ready to be released and cleared. You are about to take on the most important archaeological dig to solve the biggest mystery in and throughout your life!

Moving forward please remember the quote from my dad:

> *"...what matters IS the time that we have here on planet Earth and for us to live the best life possible no matter what happened to us. We are here right now and as long as we are alive, we can re-start from this point forward to live our best life from now on!"*
> — *Carl Nobuo Niki*

As you go through this book and workbook here are some of the important things to consider:

Always take care of yourself!
- ✓ Check in with yourself often and keep an open mind!
- ✓ Take your time

- ✓ Question everything
- ✓ Be patient with yourself
- ✓ Only do what is in your highest and best interest
- ✓ Put on your own oxygen mask first!

Sometimes, it does take multiple repetitions and multiple sessions to get results, especially if what needs clearing occurred repeatedly or if it has been holding on for years.

- ✓ Go slowly, check in and feel your own energy often!
- ✓ If something isn't working for you, stop and breathe.
- ✓ After re-starting, if it isn't working for you, stop and use one of the other techniques.
- ✓ After re-starting and something still isn't working for you, stop for this session, take a break and start again at another time.

You didn't get this way overnight!

You may be feeling stuck. If so, stop. Feel your energy.

It could take several micro shifts before a big one occurs. That's OK, it took you your whole life to get this way. The reality is that it won't all completely go away or change overnight however, a lot of immediate change and shifting most certainly does, so stay with it and do whatever it takes.

Life is way too short to be miserable! Keep going! It's a lifelong adventure and you are worth it!

Please remember always take care of yourself first, take your time, only do what is in your highest, best good!

Best wishes to you, Archaeological Detective! May you have the most empowering energetic discovery of a lifetime!

Aloha! & Mahalo! (Thank You!)

Gary Nobuo Niki

CHAPTER I

zen, Tools, My Dad and Me

Writing this book caused me to look back over the first half-century of my life and to do a lot of things beginning with "re": re-flecting, re-looking, re-viewing, re-examining, and re-understanding who my dad was, how he got there, the wisdom in his lessons, what he taught me, the way he taught me, the pain and joy of being Human and how he lived his own zen life. All of those "re"-words apply to me discovering who I am in zen.

Was my dad zen? Did he know zen? Did he study zen? Did he teach zen? Did he live zen? Did he end up zen?

Hmmm! The answer is, "I don't know." Maybe he was and maybe he wasn't. What I do know is that he certainly didn't start out being zen!

My dad was born Carl Nobuo Niki on July 5, 1915, in Las Cruces, New Mexico on his fathers' farm, to George Nobuo Niki (Japanese) and Conacha Luna (Mexican).

Most of what I know about my dad's early years is still very sketchy to me, mainly because he would not talk about his dad at all, except to say when I asked, "He died when I was five and I grew up in a pool hall where my mom worked after we moved from the farm." Apparently, my dad had to grow up quickly. By six years old, he was a shoeshine boy at the pool hall, made his own money, bought his own clothes, helped his mother as best he could.

Being born in 1915, he grew up through the stock market crash, the Great Depression, and the big soup kitchen era. When he talked about being a kid, however, he always said with a big smile that he had lots of fun and a good life!

Growing up in a pool hall, my dad would be there helping his mom. When he wasn't working with her, or shining shoes, he was shooting pool. "I shot pool from the time that I could barely see over the table and I loved it!" he would say. He became very good at it and, from his and my Uncle Sandy's stories about them in their twenties, I know my dad was a crack-shot pool hustler who would whistle then yell his invitation or challenge to play, "Nine Ball anyone in the house!" Most of the time, he would win.

Uncle Sandy (James Sandy Hirano) was full Japanese and my dad's best friend. They eventually ran a pool hall together and had no idea that on my dad's second marriage to my mom they would become real family, brothers-in-law.

Uncle Sandy was a very smart, kind, soft spoken, peaceable kinda guy who didn't like or want to fight. However, he told me that my dad, even though he was always smiling and friendly at first to everyone, was always ready and willing to fight, to jump in and stand up for or defend someone.

From Uncle Sandy's stories about my dad's early life, I gathered that he was certainly not zen, even though on the outside he was always a smiling, happy, friendly guy to everyone. Uncle Sandy said, "If someone ever crossed your dad, hurt or insulted one of his friends or customers, then look out! He became a ferocious, angry tiger that would beat the crap out of them and literally drag them out of the pool hall by their feet and throw them out into the street!" We were all surprised to hear that story!

My dad just sat there, smiled, laughed and waved his hand at Uncle Sandy. Then, Uncle Sandy said, "Hey Carl, remember the time that guy in the pool hall threatened to cut me with a broken bottle when he lost the poker game?"

My dad just shook his head and Uncle Sandy said, "I was just sitting there. The guy was lit up. He jumped up, broke a bottle, yelled and waved the broken bottle at me. Your dad came out of the back with his Kendo stick. He got in between us and when the guy started swinging the broken bottle at him, your dad broke the Kendo stick over the guy's head, dropped him, and kicked the broken bottle out of his hand. He dragged him out by his feet and threw him into the street! Then, your dad came back in, and with a big smile, told everyone, everything was taken care of, they were safe, and could go back to playing cards and shooting pool. He went on like nothing happened." All my dad said to us was, "That was a long time ago. I was just young and dumb back then." Then he looked at me and said, "That was stupid, son, don't be like I was back then. Be smarter than me. Learn to be wise, peaceful, calm and zen!"

During World War II, my dad was working somewhere industrial. I don't know what it was or what he did. I do know he was somewhere in California. Then, on December 7, 1941, the Japanese bombed Pearl Harbor in Honolulu, Hawaii and life would never be the same for him.

Even though my dad was an American Citizen born in the United States of America and only half Japanese, his dad was a naturalized citizen born in Nagasaki, Japan. My dad was still considered Japanese. His name was Niki and on his birth certificate his race was listed as Japanese, like his father. He was soon arrested and taken to the Japanese Internment Center in Fresno, California.

He stayed interned in camp for six months. When the government needed individuals for the war effort, he stepped up and became a United States Merchant Marine. He served through the rest of the war on a ship overseas.

My dad never talked about what happened and never seemed to be upset or bitter about it. However, I guess he must have seen and experienced some bad stuff because he would never speak about it other than to say, "I served my country loyally and did my duty and my job, that is it." Then, with a smile, he would change the subject to something happy or at least more positive.

My dad had two families. First, he was married to my Big Bro John's mother. They had four more children and went through what he told me was a horrible eleven-year marriage that ended up in a very hostile, bitter divorce. She got custody and my dad was not able to see his five children. He chose to pay their child support through the Clerk of the Court back in the 1950s to show that he did pay on time.

My dad and my mom were married in 1954. My mom had a miscarriage sometime early after that and I was born eight years later in Las Vegas, Nevada when my dad was forty-seven years old and my mom was thirty-one. About two and a half years later my little sister was born. My mom and dad were a great match and certainly best friends. Looking back, I'm certain there was no one on Earth that my dad trusted more than my mom and I'm sure that was a large part of his zen life.

When I grew up and started to drive, my mom taught me how to drive a stick shift smoothly. She said that you have to be calm, cool and collected when driving and even if you get mad or someone gets mad at you, do your best to be calm. "Someday," she said, "your life may depend on it." Then, she told me two stories about how much my dad had changed. In the early 1950s, she was riding with my dad and something happened and a guy in another car honked his horn at them, yelled, then held up his middle finger and flipped them off. She said, "Your dad stopped the truck, walked over to the other car, grabbed the guy through the window and punched him. Then walked back to the truck like nothing happened and we drove off! I was so scared!"

Of course, I was surprised. I thought she was kidding me! Then, she said that a similar event started, only this time she grabbed his arm, hung on to him and said, "No, don't get out, I'm scared. Let's go!" She started crying. Apparently, that totally shocked my dad and he closed the door and drove away. This time when they parked, my mom told him that she could not handle that kind of behavior at all, and if he wanted her to stay then he would have to change. When I asked her what happened, she said, "Your dad sat there quietly for a few minutes staring at the steering wheel and then he said, 'I apologize. I'm sorry that I scared you, and I will never, ever do that again!'" Again, I was surprised and asked her what happened after that. My mom said, "True to his word, it never happened again and even when he was angry or upset he kept his word, let it go. He would smile and drive on and whistle to his favorite songs on the radio." That does sound kinda zen to me…

Sometime during the late 1950s, my dad became a Mason and joined the Masonic Lodge. He became a Master Mason and a Shriner. As I grew up and asked him about being a Mason, he would say, "Son, all I can tell you is that it's about honor; being of good conscience and good morals; love of GOD; devotion to humanity, family, brethren and my country. I do my best to live up to that every day!" Again, out came the big Carl Niki smile and the conversation was done.

My dad worked for Bonanza Air Lines in Las Vegas, Nevada. In the mid-1960s Bonanza moved to a brand-new hanger built for them at Sky Harbor Airport in Phoenix, Arizona. We moved to the middle of the desert in Paradise Valley, where there was nothing except for cactus, brush, rattle snakes, horny toads, ants and a lot of dirt roads. We had a lot of fun times together as a close happy family.

He worked for the airlines over 27 years, through lots of changes from Bonanza, to Air West, Hughes Air West and lastly, Republic Airlines, before he retired. He loved airplanes, jet engines, mechanical work, fixing and making things with his hands.

One early Christmas, Santa brought me an "Erector Set." It was amazing and I was thrilled. My dad was excited about it, too! We opened it up, and it was my first introduction to using real tools to build real projects. It had gears, nuts, screws, and little motors, along with mini wrenches, screwdrivers and pliers. That was the official start to my lessons about how important it is to use the proper tools for the job and that it is equally important to take care of them, keep them clean and in order, organized in my toolbox.

The first time I ever remember hearing about zen outside of family and inner circles was at my dad's retirement celebration event. They roasted or teased him about several things! My dad had an Airframe and/or Powerplant Certificate, issued by the Federal Aviation Administration (FAA). Like pilots, there are rules for certification and regulations, which must be abided by for use of their license. He was an A&P licensed mechanic, machinist, welder and a sheet metal man.

The first roast I remember was when one of the leaders stood up and said, "Everyone knows that Niki is a picky, perfectionistic, anal S.O.B. extremely focused on making every jet engine he worked on purr. He wasn't happy or satisfied until it did!" Yes, he loved building jet engines and everyone howled, laughed and shouted out, "Yeah, that's Niki alright!" with a cheer and thunderous applause! My dad stood up, bowed, smiled and said, "And fortunately none of the ones that I worked on ever crashed or went down on my watch!" Again, there was thunderous applause and cheers. Then, one of his colleagues talked about how creative, inventive and perfectionistic he was with all tools, especially his own. God forbid if you borrowed one of his and didn't return it clean and in the correct location! Everyone clapped, cheered and agreed. Then someone yelled out, "He sure loves his tools!" Someone shouted, "How many of us still have and use the 'Carl Niki Specials' today that he made for us and got the awards for?" Most people's hands went up, including some of the bosses, because my dad modified, invented and made special tools to use on the different airplanes to make their work smoother and more efficient.

This went on and on about my dad. Then, one of the big bosses stood up and said, "I've known and worked with Niki for over twenty years. Even during the Airline Strike when we were out walking on the strike line and picketing and someone fired off some gun shots at us, he never lost his cool or his head. He brought us coffee, patted us on the back and said as they took off, 'We'll be okay. Let's keep on going,' while he smiled and whistled away! He was always so happy and zen no matter what happened! Thank you, Niki, we're going to miss you!" Again, a lot of them clapped, cheered and started whistling for my dad. He just smiled, laughed and waved. Then someone stood up and said to my mom, "Thank you, Kay. We know that you made his life happy because he really did smile and whistle while he worked. In any case, you should have seen the huge grin on his face at quitting time when he would say, 'I'm going home to Momma and the kids. See you guys tomorrow!'" Everyone stood up, clapped and cheered for my mom.

Then, they shocked and surprised my dad by presenting him with a complete set of custom-made Jack Nicklaus Golden Bear Golf Clubs that they arranged like a Japanese Rising Sun flag, attached to a huge cardboard sign with everyone's signatures and goodbye messages to him, along with boxes of balls, a golf bag and cart! They really got to him and I think he almost started to cry. Then, in his Carl Niki style, he stood up, waved and let out his signature whistle that could snap anyone to attention. Then, he said, "Thank you all very much. I love all of you and I have enjoyed every minute that I worked with you!" He raised his hands and said, "Now, let's eat!" Of course, he said all of this with his great, big Carl Niki smile! I have to admit my dad was one heck of a character!

When I was growing up, my dad and I were best friends. We worked together on projects. Little did I know that all of the initial training he gave me when I was a kid with the Erector Set, about appreciating and respecting your tools, would go on to serve me greatly throughout my entire work life and while we were building hot rods and four-wheelers before he died. He was an amazing man to watch, learn from and be around. I'm sure that if he was asked about being wise, enlightened, awakened or zen, he would just laugh and say, "I'm just a regular kind of guy."

Throughout the later part of his life, he was joy-filled, positive, upbeat, loving, relaxed, calm, aware, and intuitive. He was a focused listener and an extremely present, generous kinda guy! He was happy, looking forward to the next family adventure, before he died quickly and without suffering on June 3, 1983 at an emergency center in Phoenix, Arizona. When I got there, the doctor told me his last words were, "Hey doc, it's kinda hard for me to breathe. It's like an elephant is sitting on my chest. I just have to catch my breath, I'm sure I'll be OK." Then, he took his last breath and laid back on the examining table and passed peacefully, fully graduating Earth School in his own zen kinda way.

My book publishing coach, Christine Kloser, told all of us at her amazing Live Author Breakthrough Event, an event specifically for transformational authors and writers, including authors-to-be like me who are learning about the process from start to finish and what's required to complete and publish our book, to remember that in writing our book we get what we need for our own healing and transformation when we write! Also, most likely we will be doing a lot of re-writing before it's ready to publish and be the book we wanted to publish, not just some book that we wrote and published. I was a total newbie to the "real" book publishing world and what it takes to successfully get a book published.

You could say that I didn't have the first clue about any of it! Seriously, I must have thought all I had to do was put pen to paper and start writing, and magically it would become a real book all on its own! Christine was so right and at the event her words made a huge impact on me! Initially, I joined The Christine Kloser Trainings: Transformational Author Experience (TAE), The Get Your Book Done (GYBD) Program and direct one-on-one coaching with Christine. All of it was a huge eye-opener for me with a whole bunch of technical and detail stuff about the publishing world that I didn't even know about! As Christine was coaching me, she had me read and re-read the manuscript feedback from Julie Clayton, the assessment editor, and then read and re-read out loud all of my re-writes and corrections over and over. It did affect me and thanks to Julie for her powerful editorial/editing insights and feedback and to Christine Kloser for her incredible coaching, insights and guidance the book that you are holding has finally become the book that I wanted to write and publish. Actually, it's only through the book publication process that I have realized just how much I learned from my dad and to truly appreciate all of his teachings and lessons, while honoring just how zen he really was!

Yes, it's hard to believe he died 37 years ago. I still miss my dad! Nevertheless, today in 2020, over a dozen years later I'm not crying like I was in 2007 while writing the main story part of this book. Maybe over the past decade, without knowing it, those lessons have helped me to become zen in my own way, too. Maybe my dad was right and it really is "do-it-yourself" (d.i.y.) zen.

Thanks for always being there, Dad! Love YOU Man!

My zen Dad at work, Master Mason and Shriner

Us before a Shriner event; Dad receiving an award in Las Vegas.

Masonic Officers Oasis Lodge 41, Las Vegas, Nevada (1960s)
Dad, on the upper far right, was a Master Mason and the Chaplain.

Dad and Mom

My mom is certainly one of the main influencers that helped my dad to become as zen as he was!

Dad; "Sparky" — Jameson Spark O'Luck; Mom; 1958 in Las Vegas, NV

PART II

CHAPTER 2

Life On Earth Is Not Easy and We Are Not The Only Ones!

Personally, I believe that if anyone tells you that life on Earth is easy, they are either a liar or a virgin – a life virgin that is, and they're eventually in for one heck of a shock or reality check.

It would be hard for me to even imagine that anyone living on this planet for more than a couple of years would not go through some sort of pain or the challenges of being human.

We have all been there, done that, or are on our way to experiencing it! So, if you are feeling like you are the only one who feels angry, hurt, shamed, insecure, messed up, broken, deficient, no good, depressed, and lost, take heart.

We really are more the same than we are different. We feel the energy and we are NOT the only ones either!

Most of us have at least had some of that going on, and I am certainly no exception. HA! Maybe we've been the poster children for it and just didn't know it!

I'm sure that while we are in the middle of the 'STUFF' especially at a young age, when it happens to us we may think or feel that we were the only one.

Seriously, as a school kid I thought that I was the only one!

Hey, now, decades and a couple thousand people later I can flat-out guarantee you that I wasn't the only one and neither are you!

For me, it first showed up in the form of a lot of pain and silent suffering from grade school bullying. As a little kid, I was picked on, harassed, bullied, beaten up, and even peed on (urinated on) literally, just for being Japanese. Some of the bullies and tormenters used to say or yell, "Hey Jap! Remember Pearl Harbor!" when attacking and humiliating me. If that wasn't bad enough, then there were sports in physical education (PE). Of course, being skinny, small and uncoordinated, I was picked last for any of the PE teams.

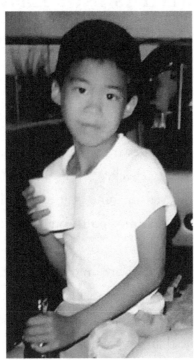

Little me in the 1960s. Of course, I got picked on and bullied in school.

Needless to say, these experiences left me feeling very sad, hurt, humiliated, weak, rejected, unwanted, unaccepted, shamed and angry. These feelings left me without any self-confidence for a period of time. Even after I learned some simple karate (empty hand martial arts) techniques from family and I could better defend myself, I still felt shamed, insecure and angry. I felt that way into my teenage years. Then, in my early adult life, I felt stress from one thing after another (getting married, death of my dad, marriage failing, changing jobs, working several jobs to make ends meet, going through divorce and bankruptcy at the same time as losing everything, and not even having a car or a place to stay after all of that). I was feeling hopeless, extremely angry and ready to kill myself. Feeling miserable and lost, I was a stressed-out workaholic. This continued on and on through my mid-twenties.

In all of the chaos of the early 1980s, I am still grateful to Mary Burmeister, who taught Jin Shin Jyutsu to my in-laws. It was the first Healing Energy process that I experienced and learned during that time. It helped me physically as I went through a lot of big life changes on many levels. These included multiple jobs many times over the years, several of them at the same time just to survive. It's amazing what can be done in a 24-hour day with little sleep! Some of these jobs ranged from an offset lithographer; graphic artist; technical illustrator; photographer; auto mechanic; body and fender repair man; automotive painter; construction; labor, mixing cement and assisting brick masons; wall-papering; painting; hanging drywall; lawn mowing; landscaping; calligrapher; martial arts, self-defense and roller skating instructor; skate guard, and disc jockey to learning and working security, investigations, bail bonds, and public safety; serving court orders/documents; teaching personal self-defense and crime safety seminars. These led to sales, marketing, motivational speaking and training, and at the end of 1989, qualifying for my own private investigation agency license.

That was mostly the 1980s for me. I was usually a happy, smiling, friendly, huggy kind of guy, at least on the outside. That was the mask that I worked very hard at wearing every day, however, looking back, inside I was still very angry, sad, scared, and an emotional train wreck. All of that was going on inside me without me even knowing it. I was completely clueless, shut down, and in denial.

So yes, I've been through some STUFF in my life as most of us have. Fortunately, I found some effective techniques, modalities and tools to help me clear out and free myself to release those deep, dark, buried fears, hurts, thoughts, feelings and emotions that were unconsciously still running my life over a decade later!

Some of the most simple and effective of these lifesaving tools and techniques will be shared with you in this book!

Please note that there are other tools, techniques, modalities, methods, groups and organizations that may be mentioned however, due to lack of space, they are not explained and taught at all, or in any depth, within this book. They, though, have certainly helped me on my journey.

One of them is Co-Dependents Anonymous (CoDA). Basically, Co-Dependents Anonymous, is a 12-step program and a fellowship of individuals whose common purpose is to develop healthy relationships. Their only requirement for membership is to have a desire for healthy and loving relationships. CoDA also helps with addressing the painful emotional and interpersonal relationships from the past.

As destiny would have it, a friend of mine was a paralegal at one of the law firms that I worked for. She was making copies and one of them was an informational flyer for a CoDA meeting that she supported.

When I picked up the flyer on the copy machine and went to hand it back to her, she said, "That's okay. Keep it for yourself or give it to someone who can use it." So, I stuck it in my briefcase and promptly forgot about it.

A couple of weeks later, I was driving in downtown Phoenix traffic and had to slam on my brakes. Of course, my briefcase flew off the front seat and exploded on the floor. I had to pull over into a parking lot to reorganize its contents.

Yep! You guessed it. There was the CoDA flyer again. The flyer contained information with patterns, characteristics and questions about what a person may be feeling at the time and explained how someone could be a 'Codependent' and not even know it. There I was reading it, sitting in a parking lot on the side of the road and going through the questions and bullet points like these:

- Think they can take care of themselves without any help from others.
- Mask pain in various ways such as anger, humor, or isolation.
- Do not recognize the unavailability of those people to whom they are attracted.
- Have trouble setting healthy priorities and boundaries.
- Are extremely loyal, remaining in harmful situations too long.
- Judge harshly what others think, say, or do.
- Refuse to give up their self-will to avoid surrendering to a power greater

than themselves.

I was sitting there, surprised, saying, "I feel like that and that and that. Hey, maybe I am Codependent!"

I ended up going through CoDA in the mid-1980s and received a lot of benefit from everyone there on multiple levels. This is how CoDA operates, in the group's own words:

> *CoDA follows the tradition of anonymity. We as members are not identified, we remain anonymous during meetings and only use first names. Any information we share at meetings is not discussed outside that meeting to ensure everything we shared is held in strict confidence and trust of that group.*
>
> *Each CoDA meeting is about us being able to freely share our thoughts, feelings, and experiences. The ground rule is that everyone is silent when one is sharing and no one asks questions.*
>
> *The rule is called "no cross talk" or referring to another person or their sharing when it's our time to share. We only speak about our own experiences and no one else's period. Some of the meetings go around the room and we can share in turn. Others are free form, where people share as they are moved to.*
>
> *We can share about any current issues in our life or issues that we are dealing with and no one has to share if they do not want to share!*
>
> *At the end of the meeting, the whole group stands for a prayer. We hold hands. It's usually 'The Serenity Prayer', well known in all 12-step programs and no one is required to recite any prayer they find objectionable.*
>
> *NOTE: It takes a lot of courage for us to admit there is an issue or a problem and even more to take action to seek help.*

The few things that I listed above were just the tip of the iceberg. They were the start of a huge group of life-changing experiences that ended up opening the doors for me to discover many other books, teachings, tapes, techniques, tools, modalities, groups and organizations that positively impacted my life. After working my program for about six months in CoDA, the members helped me on different levels to clear out some of the major issues I have mentioned that haunted me since childhood.

What was most amazing to me was that I did not even know why I was acting, doing, and feeling like that! Talk about not even having a clue! HA! Some detective! Oh well, thanks to CoDA starting it off for me, along with a whole lot of other positives on my journey, a few decades later I am much happier and extremely grateful that I can laugh at myself and appreciate all that I've gone through to get here today.

During a hard and struggling part of my life, when I needed him the most, my dad, Carl Nobuo Niki, died suddenly on June 3, 1983. He was my best friend, mentor, confidante, life coach, leader, teacher, and a great father. He certainly taught me many important things that I still use and teach today.

About two months before my dad died, he called me and said, "Son, come pick me up and take me to lunch. I want to talk to you." At the time, I really didn't think too much about it because I would regularly take my dad to lunch or for rides. We went to one of his favorite Mexican restaurants. Even though this lunch started out just like all the others, it is one that I will always remember and it certainly made a huge impact on my life!

After we finished eating, my dad got a strange and serious look on his face and asked, "Son, are you happy?"

I don't remember what I said. He then said, "I want you to be happy! Life is way too short to be miserable or unhappy. If you aren't happy in your marriage, get out. If you are not happy with or don't agree with your religious beliefs, change to something you do believe in. Don't waste your life. I'm proud of you, you turned out to be a good man and a hard worker. You deserve to be happy and always remember, find the job you love and you will never work a day in your life."

Today it's more than three and a half decades later. Those words still ring in my ears and mind, along with the memory of the seriousness of my dad's face, that turned into a great big smile that was the Carl Niki trademark as he said, "I've had a good life, a wonderful family and I love you very much. I want you to be happy, Son!"

To this day, I don't know whether he knew he was going to die a few weeks later or not. Over the years, I have recalled a story from the Bible about a patriarch who, shortly before he died, gave his blessings to his son and how much that impacted and guided the son during his lifetime. The same has been true for me. That talk over lunch with my dad is still impacting me, guiding and shaping my life.

My dad's death hit me hard and years later, thanks to CoDA and the wonderful people of Co-Dependents Anonymous, I was able to have a safe place to begin to address his death and many other profound losses.

During the last few years of my dad's life, every time he would talk about the event of his death, he always told me over and over again, "Son, Don't Cry. Be strong for the family. Take care of your mother and sister. You are the man of the family, you must be strong and do not let anyone in the family, including yourself, see me after I die! Even now, I remember seeing Grandma Concha (his mother). That still haunts me to this day and I don't want that for any of you! I am to be cremated, period. Do you understand, Son?" My response was always, "Yes Sir, Dad. I understand. I will be strong for the family. I won't let you down. I promise!"

Over thirty-six years later, in retrospect, that was actually a really bad promise for me to make, and the advice my dad had given me about being strong for the family and not crying or showing emotion was not helpful. It was one of the few times my dad told me something that hurt rather than helped. However, at that time I was determined to honor his wishes, so I kept my feelings stuffed inside after his death and never cried.

> *Wow! Even now in 2007, 24 years later, while writing this at the Merrifield Silver Diner in Falls Church, Virginia, I had another piece of emotional pain surface about what I just wrote and I had to stop, put my fingers on my forehead, and experience the pain and cry a few tears! At this moment, I am so grateful that I have this simple and effective technique in my tool bag. Again, it worked for me and now I am smiling as I continue to write!*

In CoDA, they say, "Keep coming back, it works." I never knew anything about the 12-step programs before I went to my first CoDA meeting. At each meeting, there was a member who generously shares their story with the whole group. Then, after the large group, everyone breaks up into small groups of various sizes and everyone is given the opportunity to share if they are so inclined.

Interestingly enough, the first two times that I attended, I really did not relate to the main speakers and did not say or share anything meaningful with the small group members. True to form, they would say, "Keep coming back, it works." After two meetings, I was already saying to myself, "Yeah, yeah, I'm fine. I don't even know why I'm here! I have it together and I'm certainly not as messed up as some of 'those people!'" (HA! How totally clueless I was at that time! I was extremely hurt, scared, lost and caught in, "I don't know and I don't know that I don't know!") In retrospect, I was an emotional train wreck and a mess, without a clue of how hurt, injured, angry, and wounded I was! I was in some state of extreme emotional shutdown and in intense pain without any means or tools to use to help me cope from day to day. Worse yet, I did not even understand what was happening to me or why I was feeling that way.

The saying, "the third time's the charm" came true for me at my third CoDA meeting. I'll always remember with the deepest appreciation and gratitude the events of that night. The main speaker that evening was a firefighter, and he started talking about the death of his dad.

All of a sudden, I felt my insides start churning as this man freely shared his true feelings, and his story unfolded. I remember he said, "My dad was my best friend and we built boats together. I saw him the night before he died and was grateful that I hugged and kissed him before I went home, because it was the last time I saw him alive."

At that point, I almost lost it! That man was telling my story. I'm in Public Safety; my dad and I built hot rods and four-wheelers; he was my best friend and I hugged and kissed him the night before he died! Oh, My God, that sliced me to the bone.

It took everything I had to keep my composure!

As destiny would have it, there were over 100 people at this meeting and the only open seat anywhere was in the small group where the main speaker was sitting.

For certain, that was the last place on Earth I wanted to be. I moved around from group to group, asking if there was an open seat for me to be in their group. Everyone kept pointing to the main speaker's group, saying, "They have an open chair and they are waving at you to join them." Being the strong, self-assured kinda guy I was at that time in my life, I was looking for the nearest exit to escape through without appearing to be, or to show the inner sniveling wimp that I truly was! Again, as destiny would have it, the only exits were right by the main speaker's small group. So, not wanting to appear like a total wussy, I walked up and thanked them for asking me to join their group and sat down 'trying' to look strong, poised, and confident. Reflecting back, I'm sure the only person I was fooling was myself!

To this day, I don't remember any of their names, however, I still remember what the group looked like and the stories of the four people who shared before it was my turn. Each one spoke about the death of someone close to them and how it had impacted their life.

I felt the sheer terror rising inside of me, realizing it was going to be my turn soon and wondering if I would be able to be strong enough to hold it together to just get through this and get out of this group. At that moment, I made a pact with myself that if I could get through it and keep my composure, not embarrass or shame myself, I was done with CoDA forever, and I would never, never, ever, ever go back!

All of a sudden, it was my turn and I felt that I had to share something! I almost said I would pass, then inside I thought, 'No way!' That would be wimpy, and I'm tougher than that! So, I took a deep breath and I can still hear myself say, "I lost my dad several years ago, and I never cried over him. I was strong for the family, and I'm fine. I pass it over to you." I motioned to my left for the next person to speak. (Yes, I was F.I.N.E. an acronym for: Freaked out, Insecure, Neurotic, and Emotional!) Yeah, I was FINE!

Nobody said anything for what felt like an eternity. Then the main speaker leaned forward and said something like, "I'm sure you're fine and as a rule, we don't ask any questions of each other, but can I ask you a question?" Trying so hard to hold my composure and keep my pride up, I said, "Sure, go ahead and ask me anything, I'm fine." He simply asked, "What did you feel when your dad died suddenly like that?"

To this day, I still do not recall what happened from that moment to when I came out of the deepest crying that I have ever experienced. When I regained my senses, I was soaked from tears, as were the men and women who had been holding and supporting me through that episode. I clearly remember one of the women who had been closest to me with a blouse and skirt that were soaked through, along with a man whose pants were soaked, and a couple of others who were wet from my tears.

It felt like it had gone on for hours. The group told me it had only been about four or five minutes of solid crying with an ocean of tears. They kindly gave me tissues, napkins and handkerchiefs. When I could finally speak, I said, "I don't believe this! I am so ashamed and embarrassed!" Immediately, almost in one voice they said, "Stop! Don't say that or feel that way!" Then, the main speaker said, "You are going to be okay, and someday you will be helping someone just like yourself. You will be able to give them the love, caring and support that we gave to you tonight."

That is most of what I remember about that night in the small group. When I was ready to leave, a number of them kindly stopped and gave me a hug, took their time, checked on me to make sure I was okay to drive. I was okay and for the first time in years I felt a huge weight lifted off of me.

As I was driving home, I actually felt myself smiling, really smiling for the first time since my dad had died! That was the start of me getting a whole new lease on life!

I stayed with Co-Dependents Anonymous for the next five and a half years, I also worked through *A Course In Miracles* in a group for over a year while attending several CoDA meetings a week in different locations and cities. (This book by Helen Schucman, (1976) is a curriculum for anyone seeking spiritual transformation. The premise is the greatest miracle is the act of simply gaining awareness of love's presence in your own life.) The last three years, I was the CoDA State Coordinator and I went to different groups and shared my story with them. Numerous times, I had the honor of being there for others, just like when I needed the support, love, and caring of those dear people who were there for me that fateful night when I finally cracked open, fell apart and needed them at that CoDA meeting in

Scottsdale, Arizona.

That was just the beginning of my self-help, self-healing quest and journey. While in CoDA, a number of my fellow members shared their recommendations with me about the different books, trainings, workshops and therapists that helped them. One of the amazing therapists was Sally-Jo Walters, a hypnotherapist and Gestalt therapist. Sally-Jo worked with me through a number of the Gestalt therapy processes. These went well for me over the years as I was practicing, learning, growing with my work on myself through CoDA and other modalities. She also helped coach me to become the CoDA State Coordinator. I will always be grateful to Sally-Jo for helping me through those dark times in the mid to late 1980s.

As is life, it became time for me to leave CoDA and find new modalities, tools, trainings and ways to help myself.

Reflecting back over a quarter century ago, had I not left my Co-Dependents Anonymous Group, I probably would not have been introduced to Virginia Dunstone and her Psycho-Neurology and Psycho Neurological Repatterning training workshop. I most likely would not be sharing the simple natural tools and techniques that I write about in this book and workbook with you now, either.

CHAPTER 3

Letting Go, Lost, Searching and Finding Tools For Me

While I was growing up, when warranted, my dad would tell me, "Son, you have to know when it is time to move on from people, groups or organizations and that's okay, even if it hurts! At first, the loss is hard and painful, however, in the long run you will realize that it was most likely for your benefit." Of course, my dad was right again.

I left CoDA after five and a half years. Although it was an ending, and a painful one, it did not come about the way I thought it would happen.

In retrospect, it was an important ending, while starting me on the next path to being where I am now...

Over the years, a lot of people asked me, "Why did you leave CoDA, especially after all of the benefit you received and the five-plus years you invested in the program?" For a long time, I did not want to tell anyone why I chose to leave because I did not feel I had a right to be hard core and honestly express my true feelings about what happened.

Okay, it is time to be brutally honest about my feelings at that time.

*(Reflecting way back then, of course all of this is on me and only
about me, and certainly not about any of the wonderful and dedicated
CoDA members!)*

I had been attending CoDA meetings for more than five years. I had received a lot of benefit and had some huge breakthroughs during that time. I was stunned, though, at what would be my last meeting, to hear several individuals telling almost their same story. This was especially true of one of my mentors whose narrative about his spouse and relationship was the same as he told five years prior, when I first got to CoDA. Actually, there were several members who had told their same stories verbatim for five years as well. I could almost tell their stories from hearing them again and again. All of a sudden, it hit me. Wow! Was I going to end up like that or would I do whatever it took to change within myself, and make a shift in my life that would very likely cost me my CoDA mentors, sponsors, and friends?

When it came around to my turn in the small group to share, I just sat there silently for what felt like years and looked at each of the six members. My mentor, who had just told his relationship experience, broke the silence and asked me if I was okay.

I remember saying, "I don't know, I just don't know." Then they all simply encouraged me to speak up and share.

My mentor said, "Just say what's going on for you and be blunt and honest, don't hide."

"Fine," I said. "Let's put the ugly monster out on the table right now and talk about it." I looked around the group and said, "You have been my mentors and sponsors in CoDA for over five years and tonight three of you have told the exact same story that you told when I first started, and it hasn't changed at all! You are still in the same dysfunctional relationship with the same nasty person and nothing has changed except now I can tell your story almost as good as you can! Over the years, most of you have certainly called me out on my actions and behaviors for reality checks. Okay, now I am doing that to you. You are my mentors, and you are as screwed up as I was. You know all of this stuff, some of you are like founding members of this organization. Don't you get it? Aren't we supposed to be healthy enough to change ourselves and move forward instead of wallowing in the muck, mire, and negativity?"

I remember being pretty upset while voicing my point of view.

After I was empty and had nothing else to say, one of my mentors (actually the one I respected the most) looked directly at me and said something like, "Okay, that was certainly blunt and direct!" Then with a smile he said, "Hey, quit holding back, tell us how you really feel!" Then in the spirit of the true leader he was, he said, "You are right, I am still in a screwed-up situation, and I am still telling the same story that I told way before you got here. The only difference is that over five years have gone by, and I'm still stuck in this and you have certainly moved on." He stopped, took a deep breath, let it out slowly, then he stood up with a smile, held out his hand and said, "Okay, grasshopper, take your pebble and go. It's time for you to move on from our group, and it may be time for you to move on from CoDA completely." Then, he gave me a big, huge hug, a pat on the back and hearty handshake. The rest of the small group also stood up, hugged me, and shook my hand. Several of them said that I had grown up and that CoDA had certainly worked for me, as we said our goodbyes.

I got into my car, and, sitting there, I remember feeling totally stunned, not knowing what to think or say. I felt like I had been hit right between the eyes with a big stick. I also knew on a gut-feeling level that my mentor was absolutely right. It was time for me to move on and do something else. Now that I had this huge realization and confirmation that it was time to move on, I got scared and felt unsure, alone, and lost. I did not have any idea what my next step was, let alone where to find it. For me, this state of not knowing what I was supposed to do was a very uncomfortable time in my life.

What I knew for certain was that there were two things I was really good at. First, being a total workaholic. Second, being a good detective and a zealous researcher, and I could dig like a motivated archeologist. I started by studying every self-help book, seminar, workshop and tape program that I thought could fix me or make me feel better.

So, that's what I did after CoDA. I followed a bunch of authors' advice, and tried umpteen methods, technologies, modalities, tools and techniques. Some of them worked for me and some didn't work for me (which was certainly no fault of the brilliant authors, trainers and developers). It was that I was unable to grasp, understand, or put into practice their teachings, instruction and concepts at that time.

During the late 1980s and early 1990s, I felt like a Ronin, a Masterless Samurai, wandering around surviving and searching for "Do" (the way or path), while reverting to the two things that I did best.

By November 1989, I had put in over 6000 hours of investigative work and qualified for my own Arizona Private Investigation Agency License. On January 8, 1990, NIKIDO (the name of my private investigation agency) was officially licensed #1001665 and operational.

In Japanese, NIKIDO "Ni-Ki-Do" means "Two-Spirit-Way." At that time, I did not realize how prophetic that name would become for me. I had always resonated with being Japanese and was always drawn to the black and white Yin and Yang symbols.

Yin and Yang: Usually shown black and white as swirling complementary forces interacting together and forming a dynamic system with balance between the two opposites. A part of each element is in the opposite section to maintain harmony and balance.

There I was with my very own Private Investigation (PI) agency and I was feeling pulled in two directions: as a workaholic business owner working 16 to 20 hours a day, seven days a week, and as a searcher looking for whatever would fill the empty cavernous hole that I felt inside me. Of course, all of this was going on while I was attempting to put on a good front, displaying, "I am okay. I am successful. I am competent and in control of my life." I was actually feeling lost, incapable, and unsure of what to do next.

"So, what did you do next?" you may ask. I did the only thing that I could think of at the time. I shut down as many feelings and emotions as I could and dove headfirst into work! I was attempting to block or stop the emotional feelings that I didn't know what to do with and what I certainly did not want to deal with. And yes, sometimes it did work for me.

All the while, the interesting and challenging thing for me was that the Two-Spirit-Way kept haunting me. I kept feeling a pull or push to attend to my brokenness and I still didn't have the first clue or any real idea what to do about it.

Not knowing what to do, I went back to being the detective and I started investigating myself by asking questions of myself, hoping to somehow get enlightened or at least a glint of what to do next. Then, one day, when I was driving, all of a sudden I could hear one of my teachers and business mentors from the early 1980s (the great Dan S. Kennedy) saying loud and clear inside my head, "Keep coming up with ideas. Most of them aren't worth a tinker's damn, but if you keep thinking up ideas, you will find a couple that will make you some money or solve your problem! Even a blind pig can find a truffle or two, so don't quit. Keep going!" As usual, Dan was right, so I started asking for answers, insights, and guidance from the Universe and my Higher Power.

At that time in the early 1980s, I did not have a good connection, belief, or relationship with GOD. In fact during that time, truthfully, I hated GOD! Growing up, I always considered my mom to be very religious and I did not have the same belief systems as she did. After my dad died, one day it came to an explosive head with my mom and we had it out. Even though it was a tough experience for both of us, it was quite necessary! As my dad said to me, "If you are not happy with or don't agree with your religious beliefs, change to something you do believe in." Moving forward, the Higher Power that was shared with me, in CoDA was all that I could relate to and was my stand-in for GOD, the Highest Power or Energetic Being that I could believe in and connect with. I started asking my Higher Power over and over again for help. Then, all of a sudden, people and information just started to show up and come to me, seemingly out of nowhere, to help, assist and guide me.

That period in my life was quite a blur! To this day, I don't know the exact timeline, however, it was a very powerful time for me on my transformational life journey.

Somewhere in the early 1990s, my mom and I attended The Sedona Institute with Hale Dwoskin as our trainer. He is the author of the best-selling book *The Sedona Method*. Through his awesome facilitation and caring manner, we started on an exciting journey of healing our relationship and opening up the opportunity for us to talk and relate from a totally different perspective. Through that, I started to discover the real Gary Niki and got a whole new mom! After that, true to her word, she never attempted to push her religious beliefs on me ever again. We actually became close friends. We even had our own mom and son book club, where we would discover and share positive self-help books with each other, and then have fun, enlightening book and life discussions together.

Then, we went through Holographic Repatterning training with Chloe Wordsworth and her sister Lyndis. Through their workshop facilitation and teaching processes, Chloe and Lyndis helped me break through and clear out some of the events from grade school that had seriously impacted my life. Interestingly enough, I was not even consciously aware of how much some of that had negatively affected me over the years.

After that first Holographic Repatterning training, I felt much clearer and freer to move forward. I continued training with Chloe and Lyndis, all the while searching for the next learning experience.

Then, a life-long family friend and awesome Holographic Repatterning practitioner, Alyson Reid, told me about and introduced me to the work of Virginia Dunstone and her amazing training called Psycho-Neurology with her Psycho Neurological Repatterning training workshops.

I truly had no idea what to expect. Alyson told me Virginia was great and advised me to be open to whatever happened in her workshop. On the day of the training, in Gary Niki style, I showed up early and sat in the front row, right side, first seat off the middle aisle. Once the all-important seat was chosen, I started looking around as people arrived. Of the 180-plus people that attended, I was surprised to see 20 to 30 that I recognized from my business and personal life.

On the way to the training, I had decided that I was going to participate full out, no matter what happened! The training started, and Virginia Dunstone turned it on! She was intense, funny, serious, candid, and real. What really captured me was that she was a great speaker, truly motivated, passionate, and enthusiastic! As I remember it, she told us some of her life story and how she arrived to be in front of us, sharing her Psycho-Neurology and how it positively worked for her and her clients. Virginia's enthusiasm was contagious. She then asked for a volunteer from the audience to be muscle tested. My arm shot up and she pointed to me. Before I knew what happened, I was up on the stage with her. She asked me if I knew about muscle testing and kinesiology.

(I'll talk more about this later. Muscle Testing is basically a technique where you may test your muscle strength to find out if a thought or statement strengthens or weakens you.)

I said, "Yes, I do."

She said, "Good, hold your arm straight out from your body, palm down, and push up toward the ceiling and resist me."

My arm stayed up strong as she pressed down on my arm.

Then she told me, "I am going to do something and your arm will become weak."

She moved her hand downwards in front of me and pushed my arm. To her surprise, it stayed strong. She did it again, and it stayed strong. The look on her face was priceless! I told her that I used a simple martial arts energy technique to keep from being weakened by the down sweep movement, and that I had learned years before how the downward sweep movement was used in martial arts to cut through the energy and weaken an opponent.

Virginia laughed and said, "Okay, let's try something with you using your technique and we will see how it works."

I said, "Okay, I'm ready."

She pushed on my arm. It was strong. Then, she said, "While holding your technique, think 'My name is Bob' and resist as hard as you can." HA! Now it was my turn to be blown away! She pushed on my arm and it fell so fast that I really whacked myself hard on the thigh. I'm sure I said something like, "No way!" I must have looked stunned like a deer in the headlights! Then we did it again with the same results!

Virginia said, "Now just be normal and don't try or do anything else."

I said, "Okay," and we went through the muscle testing with me saying, "My name is Gary." My arm was strong. Then we did it with me saying, "My name is Bob." My arm went weak. She did the same with me saying, "I am male," versus "I am female," then doing the down sweep and up sweep movements with her hand, all of it working exactly as the natural laws would have them work, the down sweep weakening me and the up sweep strengthening me.

We had a good connection on the stage, and after the muscle testing Virginia asked me if I was happy.

I said, "Of course, I'm happy!"

So, she said, "Good. Hold up your arm and we will test that."

Oh well, just as you guessed it, I whacked my thigh again as my arm went down.

Then, she asked me, "Are you angry?"

I said, "Not me. I'm not angry."

HA! Again, I totally did not have a clue. Oh yes, she pushed on my arm, first with one hand, then with both hands. I'm sure she could have stood on my arm and it would not have gone down! As I was standing on stage with her, looking out over the sea of faces in the audience, I was stunned that my arm was so weak when I said, "I am happy," and just a moment later it was so strong when I said, "I am angry." I remember thinking, Okay, now what? I thought I had been doing pretty good, at least on a conscious level, even if I was still searching and feeling a little lost or unsure of what to do next.

Then, while I was feeling stunned, Virginia said to me something like, "That's okay Gary, now that we know what has been weakening you and what you are neurologically 'off' for, don't worry. We can clear it out, reverse it and you will be alright." Hey, at least she gave me some hope!

The rest of the day was a blur and totally amazing! Virginia shared story after story of the wonderful, life-changing successes that her clients and students achieved with Psycho-Neurology. She brought up multiple people on the stage, just like me, for demonstrations and enlightenment provided through muscle testing and using her Psycho Neurological Repatterning techniques to clear out stuff.

The day went by very fast and all the while my mind was racing about all of the possibilities for me to clear out from my past the negative events and emotional blockages that were affecting my life decades later.

Virginia Dunstone powerfully and positively impacted my life with her Psycho-Neurology and Psycho Neurological Repatterning training. Wow! She rocked my world and my belief systems!

Thank You Very Much, Virginia Dunstone!

After extensively working with the techniques I learned in Virginia's workshop, on myself and hundreds of individuals, I re-developed what I learned into simpler tools. These I hoped could work for me and others as a true "do-it-yourself" (d.i.y.) process in the middle of immediate trauma, emergency or disaster situations. I was still able to measure the emotional levels before and after, through the full potential of muscle testing, however, the muscle testing process was not necessary for myself or anyone to use in the event of an immediate traumatic incident or emergency situation in the field. Now, over two decades later, you are reading about these d.i.y. tools in this book and maybe you will be able to imagine how they have helped thousands of individuals, and how that may be able to assist you, too.

In Virginia's workshop, she gave us a twenty-three-page 8.5 x 11 inch handout (that I still have to this day) with a couple of lists of emotions to work with, and told us to work slowly through the lists by muscle testing to see what came up for us. Then, we were to use the techniques in the handout for clearing out any of the negative emotions or statements that we were strong for.

Yes, several times she told us to take our time and, "Do it slowly over the next few weeks or month. Just don't do it all at once."

Right away, I knew that I had a lot of STUFF that was still haunting or bothering me over my entire life, and I knew I had a lot of work to do on myself!

Did I listen to Virginia? What do you think? Of course, I didn't listen. I went home, and, that evening, I muscle tested and cleared everything on the list and felt wiped out and drained from big time overexertion, and mental and emotional exhaustion!

Please remember, clearing work takes a lot of energy. Yes, your own energy!

One of the keys to doing any type of clearing or energy work is to take your time, do it slowly and responsibly.

Yes, over the last forty-plus years I have certainly had to "learn some lessons the hard way" as my dad would say!

Please learn the easy way or the simple way! That means learn from my mistakes. Don't be clueless like I was and do too much when starting to use and experience the tools in this book.

Moving forward, please take everything in this book and workbook slowly, step by step, and by doing so, become your own best friend, archeologist and detective.

Once you've read through the stories, the techniques and lists, and understand how to use the power tools I describe, I recommend that YOU become your own detective and archeologist digging through your life, taking your time methodically to go through the *Energetic Action Process 33-Day Workbook* included in this edition.

Take it one day at a time, stopping to ponder and question yourself all the way through your process. Save yourself some grief by learning from my mistakes and the hard-earned insights that I've gained from my own healing journey.

I consider this a lifelong journey that you are embarking on, just like the one I'm on. Remember, it's your life! Take your time! It's your own marathon. It's certainly not a sprint race, and You are worth it!

Even after using these techniques for years on myself, and even though I had probably cleared "anger" several thousand times (I do it on myself with every person or group that I share it with), I still had a stubborn, specific issue of getting angry while driving in heavy traffic on the I-495 beltway. This is the highway that runs through parts of Maryland and Virginia, encircling Washington, D.C. It seemed that no matter how many times I cleared the terms anger/angry or variations of anger/rage/road rage, although I was certainly better and a lot less angry, there was always something under there just waiting to get me riled up!

I decided to take my own advice and started investigating and asking the Universe, my Higher Power and GOD for the energy, insights and guidance to identify exactly what this was about, along with the wording to effectively clear out, free and release me from this issue.

After about a month of inquiring, I was driving into Washington, D.C. and listening to one of my favorite self-help guru's CDs, Wayne Dyer, when I heard him say the words, "angry thoughts." All of a sudden, I felt like I was hit between the eyes with a big stick! I had to skip back the CD and listen again. (I actually skipped back and listened multiple times to be sure I heard it.) This insight and wording were exactly what I was searching for to clear and release. Amazingly, I had listened to that CD over 30 times! I didn't recall ever hearing these words, let alone realizing that they had made any real impact on me until that exact moment, when my internal light switch was turned on and I finally got it, while driving without any incident.

Sure enough, I confirmed through muscle testing that the words "angry thoughts" were exactly what I was searching for. Then, by using "The Energetic Action Process", I was able to successfully clear them out.

The results were both emotional and physical. I now feel totally different while driving in traffic throughout the Washington, D.C. metropolitan-area! Just for clarification, I still do get irritated and frustrated while driving the beltway and in other Washington, D.C. Metro areas, due to traffic, weather, clueless and texting drivers, etcetera. However, it has become less and less an issue for me, and I have not been or felt extremely angry as I felt before.

Now that I have shared these examples with you, maybe you can see that we are all on a lifelong journey to discover ourselves and identify how we are affected by words, thoughts, or memories that may have specific emotional impact on us. Rest assured that we can clear out even the emotional pain we have felt from the words that were said to us by some of the most important, influential individuals in our lives, including our parents, siblings, best friends, lovers, spouses, teachers, religious leaders, employers, colleagues, and fellow organizational members.

In this book, I share stories of real people (some of their names have been changed to respect and honor their privacy) who wrote to help others through real life situations. They have had a positive life outcome by using the very simple techniques described in this book. These could help you see how you might benefit from doing the work on yourself using the "Put Your Fingers On Your Forehead" technique along with practicing with the other simple tools in "The Energetic Action Process" technique while working through *The Energetic Action Process 33-Day Workbook*.

From time to time, someone will ask me how or why this works. The truth is that I don't have a clue! I really don't know the scientific reasons why putting your fingers on your forehead works. What I do know is that it has worked for me and several thousand of my fellow human beings who have used it.

The way I explain how it works for me is through what I call "the VCR concept" (Video Cassette Recorder-VCR). Yes, it's old school now, just like me since the DVD, Blu-ray and DVR came out. Hey, where did the time go?!

Let's say you have a movie that you recorded on your video tape and now you want something else on it, instead. You do not throw out the video cassette tape, you simply record over it by pushing the play and record buttons, and the old movie is erased by the new movie.

In a way, this has been my experience with putting my fingers on my forehead. It's not that I don't or can't remember what happened; of course, the incident didn't just magically disappear, "Un-Happen" and then was erased from my memory! Certainly not! Actually, I could clearly remember the incident or experience, however, what I have found is that the original hurt, shock, upset and power of the initial impact or traumatic feelings had been neutralized!

This occurred by simply putting my fingers on my forehead and reliving the situation with as many of the original emotional feelings as I could bring back. By doing this, they would become less and less intense, then clear out to the point that I would have trouble recalling the feeling and impact of the full trauma. It was as if it magically became neutral without either good or bad, up or down, high or low feelings. This is what inspired me to write about and share my experiences with you and to open up the possibility of hope and freedom for you now so that you can quickly change your life, literally by your own personal action. It really is d.i.y. empowerment and processing.

Because we are here on planet Earth together in Earth School, I believe that we are here to learn whatever lessons that we may require to be the best that we can be!

We are here to live our best life right now as happy, healthy, whole and complete as we can be and, if necessary, let's take my dad's advice and do our own "re-start" right now.

PART III

CHAPTER 4

Our Words Have Power! And Our Thoughts Do, Too!

Another point that I believe is important for us to cover, before we get into the specifics of the techniques, tools and modality detailed in this book, is the impact and energy of our own words, spoken or unspoken, and thoughts about ourselves and others.

Here are some stories and examples for you to ponder and think about:

My mom instilled her dad's wisdom into us children

My grandfather, Tamachi Mataga, known as Poppa within the family, came from a line of Samurai ancestors. My mom always told me to, "Watch what you say." She said that Poppa would often tell her and her younger brothers a saying in Japanese that means:

> *"Think before you speak. Watch what you say. You can cut your tongue out with a sword and never be able to take it back."* —Tamachi Mataga

Wow! What an image! Seriously, that simple and profound statement became a point to ponder for me and all of us. Over the years, my mom would retell that same story to me and my little sister whenever there was a situation that warranted it.

As a result, my grandfather's saying made an impact on me. I would even think about it before unloading on someone with a well-armed verbal tirade!

The truth is that after I let someone have it with both barrels verbally (of course, I'm not perfect and I still did it many times), I could hear my mom telling me what Poppa had said and I would feel a knot in my stomach.

I knew that what I had done was not good, kind, or energetically positive. Reflecting back, lashing out at people verbally felt bad even when I was a little kid!

"Thank you very much Poppa for that powerful lesson and others from Mom. I still remember them and share them with my clients, colleagues, students and participants today!" THX GARY

Our words are powerful, they carry either hurtful, weakening energy or positive, strengthening energy.

Let's stop for a moment or two. Think back and run through your life. Assess how words have weakened or disempowered you, and strengthened or empowered you.

✓ Has criticism ever dragged you down?
✓ Has praise ever built you up?

For me, the bottom line is that the frequencies of all words are powerful, energetic and, most of all, may have a physical, mental, emotional, spiritual, or neurological impact on all of us in human form.

I believe knowing and understanding this may motivate us to take a look at our words beyond what my grandfather believed and to start asking ourselves, "If the spoken word can have such a profound impact on me as a human, what impact do my silent words, thoughts and phrases have upon me via my mental, internal dialogue that just runs in the background, constantly talking to my subconscious mind 24 hours a day, seven days a week?"

Looking back over the last 50 years, I know that it's possible for us to be our own worst enemy, critic, and persecutor without even being aware of it.

Why are we unaware of this, or in my case, was I so clueless?

In my case, I believe it's because, at that time in my life, I didn't know that I was using my own words against myself in such a powerfully negative way! Interestingly, even without my awareness, the negative things that I had been saying and thinking to myself over and over had dug themselves deep into my subconscious mind and neurology.

Lessons from Dan S. Kennedy

Only by looking back in retrospect do I realize that is why, no matter the amount of positive affirmations that I used and as much as I would repeat, repeat, and repeat, at that time they would only work for a short period of time. Then, I would spiral down even lower, while thinking to myself, "HA! What a loser. You can't even believe in yourself and you know you're not good enough! Yeah, just keep 'trying' and you'll get even lower next time."

That thought process and mind-set haunted me during the 1980s. I would self-deprecate and berate myself even when I gave a good speech, talk, lecture, or training class.

After presentations, lots of people would come up to me and generously tell me how much they learned from it or enjoyed and appreciated it. All the while they were graciously giving me positive feedback and appreciation, I would be saying in my head to myself, Oh, if only you knew how I really screwed up. I didn't deliver the story the right way; the punch line was off; I forgot to say stuff that I knew was important, and I'm just not good enough to be up here in front of all of you to deliver (whatever it was). If only you knew me, you wouldn't say these nice, wonderful things and then, how in the world could you gladly pay me, not to mention invite me back or be here a second or third time?

Unfortunately, in the early days of my professional public speaking career, I would actually tell people some of the above garbage, crap and stuff that I just shared with you.

One time in the early 1980s after observing me doing the above stuff, my mentor Dan S. Kennedy called me into his office after one of my talks and everyone left. He said, "What's the matter with you? These people are paying you and giving you positive feedback and you are saying stupid things like that? Stop that right now!" I said, "Dan, that's what I really feel inside! What am I supposed to do?"

Dan was brilliant at coaching and figuring out what each person needed. Then, he taught what was necessary for them. In my case, he knew to teach me by demonstrating. "You be the appreciative client and I will be you," he said. Then, he asked me to come up and thank me for a great talk, so I did. He, with a big smile, simply shook my hand, then lightly squeezed my right arm with his left hand and said, "Thank you!" Then, again with his left hand, he would kinda point at me and say, "See you next time!"

Of course, I didn't get it at that moment and I'm sure he knew it because he said that we would practice it together.

It took at least half a dozen times of Dan correcting me, and demonstrating, with a smile, the correct response for me to do it and say it exactly the way he said it and did it, and for me to get it!

Thanks to the great Dan S. Kennedy, I got it and never forgot it!

I still remember the first talk that I did after his coaching. I felt like a different guy and responded the way he taught me. I was smiling, shaking hands, thanking people, beaming in the afterglow of positivity and success as they walked away and later returned for another event.

That was 36 years ago. Dan made me realize that I was the only one who had the power and ability to change myself.

He especially put his emphasis on the importance of me "Doing vs Trying". Just like Master Yoda in the *Star Wars* movie working with Luke Skywalker, Dan's teaching and guidance was a powerful reality check that certainly made me do the work for myself back then and that is what I'm asking you to do for yourself right now.

Yes, I had to stop, look closely at myself, test and follow the guidance I was given. It helped me to start to re-set and re-shift my thinking and mind-set forever. To this day, I'm still grateful to him and I remember and use his lessons with my clients today.

Thank you very much Dan S. Kennedy for believing in me when I didn't or couldn't do it for myself! THX GARY

don Miguel Ruiz, one of my great teachers

In the late 1990s, while continuing on my search for positive and life enhancing tools, I found don Miguel's book *The Four Agreements*. It rocked my world, belief system and my thought processes forever on multiple fronts!

Of course, I immediately dove in headfirst, reading it straight through in one sitting! Interestingly, before even getting into the actual Four Agreements, don Miguel said:

> *"To be alive is the biggest fear humans have. Death is not the biggest fear we have; our biggest fear is taking the risk to be alive — the risk to be alive and express what we really are. Just being ourselves is the biggest fear of humans."*
> — *don Miguel Ruiz*

Yes, back then reading that stunned me! Now, over 20 years later, I still reflect back on his words, especially when I think about how powerfully our words and thoughts affect us.

Ever since I read about don Miguel's Four Agreements they have been burned into my mind. To this day, I still regularly reflect on them and how their wisdom shows up throughout my life.

The Four Agreements:
   #1 *Be impeccable with your word.*
   #2 *Don't take anything personally.*
   #3 *Don't make assumptions.*
   #4 *Always do your best.*

I'm not able to go into them right now, however, as you continue reading this book and then go through the workbook, please think about them and how they may apply in your life! I highly recommend that you read *The Four Agreements* by don Miguel Ruiz and dig into it like I still do now and did back then.

Fast forward to 2010, I was fortunate to have the privilege of two days in a private, small group in Washington, D.C. with don Miguel Ruiz and his son don Jose Ruiz!

don Miguel Ruiz and The Four Agreements with Gary Niki

don Miguel Ruiz and The Four Agreements; don Miguel Ruiz, Gary Niki and don Jose

On the first day, there were thirteen of us and don Miguel told us that a lot had come to light since he wrote *The Four Agreements* in the late 1990s. He talked to us about some of the insights since then, about all of us being a piece of love and a piece of light.

Then he talked about his new book with don Jose, *The Fifth Agreement: A Practical Guide to Self-Mastery.* The Fifth Agreement is: Be skeptical, but learn to listen.

The first day, I brought all of my books and CDs for him and don Jose to sign for me and they graciously did! After class, I went to the closest Barnes & Noble bookstore and bought every single don Miguel and don Jose book they had. The next day, I brought the books for them to sign for my friends and clients. On the second day, we were able to literally sit at the feet of The Masters. It was amazing to be in their presence and experience masters who are following their own teachings from *The Four Agreements.* They were impeccable with their words and didn't make assumptions.

In 2013, at an event in Washington, D.C., I was very happy and excited to see don Miguel again, meet don Miguel Jr. and Heather Ash Amara.

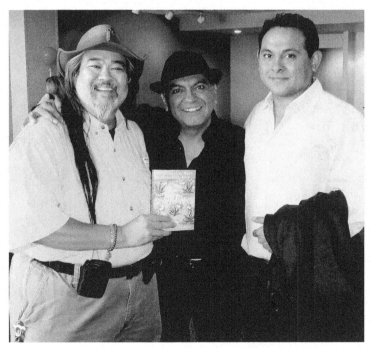

Gary Niki with don Miguel Ruiz & don Miguel, Jr.

don Miguel Jr. with Gary Niki

Heather Ash Amara and Gary Niki

They were all amazing speakers and teachers as they shared their wisdom and insights with us. I'm reflecting back over the now Five Agreements, and ask that you please keep them in mind as you realize how powerful your own words and thoughts are, both inside yourself and outside of yourself in your world.

The Five Agreements:
#1 Be impeccable with your word.
#2 Don't take anything personally.
#3 Don't make assumptions.
#4 Always do your best.
#5 Be skeptical, but learn to listen.

Thank you very much don Miguel Ruiz, don Jose, don Miguel Jr. and Heather Ash Amara! THX GARY

My top six 20th Century authors, whose books and recordings demonstrated to me the power of our words and thoughts:

✓ Florence Scovel Shinn (1871-1940)
- *The Game of Life and How to Play It* (1925)
- *Your Word is Your Wand* (1928)
- *The Secret Door to Success* (1940)
- *The Power of The Spoken Word* (1945)

✓ Joseph Murphy (1898-1981)
- *The Power of Your Subconscious Mind* (1963)
(And way too many other works to list here)

✓ Catherine Ponder (February 14, 1927 -)
- *The Prosperity Secrets of The Ages* (1964)
- *The Dynamic Laws of Healing* (1985)
- *Open Your Mind To Prosperity* (1971)

- *The Prospering Power of Prayer* (1983)
- *Dare to Prosper!* (1983)
- *The Dynamic Laws of Prayer* (1987)

✓ Maxwell Maltz (1899-1975)
- *Psycho-Cybernetics* (1960)
- *The Magic Power of Self-Image* (1970)
- *Five Minutes to Happiness* (1967)
- *Thoughts to Live By* (1975)
- *The Conquest of Frustration* (1976)
- *The Search for Self-Respect* (1977)

✓ Neville Lancelot Goddard (1905-1972)
(way too many of his works to list here)

✓ Napoleon Hill (1883-1970)
- *Think and Grow Rich* (1937)
- *You Can Work Your Own Miracles* (1971)
- *The Law of Success* (1928)
- *Success Through a Positive Mental Attitude* (1959) *with W. Clement Stone*
- *The Magic Ladder to Success* (1930)

NOTE: There are hundreds of other amazing authors related to the power of our words and thoughts who have made a positive difference in my life and who I'm not able to even start to list here! After going through three home moves in four years, I had to downsize and let go of over a thousand physical books, cassette tapes and CDs. That was certainly a personal disaster! However, thanks to Kindle, EPUB, MOBI, Nook, PDF and Audible, I now have over a thousand of them in my eReader and audio player. Thank You Very Much to Teachers and Technology!

Point proven to the Anger Management class participants

Over the last 15 years, I have been an Anger Management facilitator for individuals on Court Ordered Probation, or recommended to my class by Public

Defender's Offices, Psychologists, Psychiatrists, Personal Defense Attorneys and Judges.

On week four of the five-week class, I share with my participants the techniques and tools in this book to demonstrate exactly how much energy and power their own words and thoughts truly have.

I do this to emphasize and prove to the class that they are physically either weakened or strengthened by the energy of their own words or, even more shocking and mind blowing to them, by the energy of their own unspoken, silent thoughts! This experience is priceless!

I'm sharing this class experience with you here because it punctuates the importance of this chapter, along with the power of using the techniques and tools in this book.

Eight years ago, I had sixteen participants in the class with a wide range of diversity. There were five women. From the very first class, one of the women, in her thirties, was very upset with the woman with whom she had had the altercation that led to her arrest, being put on probation and being court-ordered to anger management class. Now, here she was with us. She certainly was not shy about voicing her upset with, hate for and discontent about the other woman, along with using several expletives to describe her, including calling her a "Skanky C***" and a "Useless B****".

Surprisingly, the other women in the class were agreeing with her and throwing in the fact that they knew and experienced women like that, too! I think the men were too shocked and way too smart to say or react to anything as they sat there still and quiet, not even moving a muscle or looking around!

On week four, I always start with the muscle testing demonstration. I ask for a volunteer to be muscle tested. This time, one of the men volunteered. I went through the initial muscle testing demonstration on him first. Then, the same muscle testing with all of the class participants so that everyone is tested, experiences the muscle testing and knows it's for real. Then, I show them how their thoughts affect my demo volunteer and then each other. After that, I ask someone to think of a positive or happy thought and I muscle test them for strong or weak. Then, I have someone else think of a negative or sad thought and I muscle test them for strong or weak. Yep! Darn right their energy is zapped/weakened. It really works and blows their minds!

We spent about 15 minutes on demonstrating the powerful, energetic effects of their thoughts and words. All of a sudden, the woman who was upset in the beginning raised her hand and said, "Mister Gary, are you telling me that by me hating on that Skanky C*** and Useless B**** that it's doing something to me because of her?"

I thought, what an opportunity to emphasis the power and energy of our words and thoughts!

So, I paused, looked around the circle at everyone, then said, "Hmmmm, what do YOU think?!"

By this time, everyone was nodding in agreement. I said to her, "Great question! Now stand up and let's muscle test you and see what your body and energy have to say to us!" She shot up out of her chair with her arm out and said, "Let's see about this!"

I said, "OK. Think about your friend and let's test you." She snapped back, "She's NOT My Friend, she's a "Skanky C***" and "Useless B***" and I hate her!"

When she stopped talking, I said, "OK, show me some strength." Then, I pushed on her arm and it went weak. Down it went, hard and fast! The look on her face was priceless. She stepped toward me and said, "Wait, push on my other arm." We went back and forth, with her name strong, being male weak, then happy thought strong, then the woman weak. After about seven times back and forth, all of a sudden SHE GOT IT!

She literally screamed out, "OH, MY GOD! OH, JESUS! I felt that! Are you telling me that I AM SNARKING MYSELF? OH, JESUS! OH, MY GOD! Is that what you are saying?! I've been doing myself ugly all this time hating on her?"

Everyone sat there, silent. When she regained her composure, she looked at me and said, "Oh, My GOD, Mister Gary, I almost don't believe it, except you have proved it to me with my own body and energy going weak when I'm hating on that (long pause) woman!"

She just stood there in the middle of the circle with me, shaking her head. I said to her, "OK, what did you decide to do about all of this now that you felt your energy go out, get weak and now you know it?"

She looked at me, looked around at everyone and said, "Well, if I'm snarking and weakening myself, then I ain't never hating or thinking bad about that (pause) woman ever again!"

I smiled, said, "Big Time CONGRATS! YOU Got It!"

She smiled, took a long pause as she was breathing and letting all of it catch up and integrate. Then said, "Wait a minute, what about my momma, push on my arm!"

HA! It went weak and again she had her OMG moment! She said, "Oh, My GOD! That means I have to start watching and feeling the energy of everything that I'm saying and thinking about everything or else, huh?!"

I just smiled and said, "Yes, I believe that you are certainly on to something. What do you think?"

I looked around the circle and asked everyone, "And, what do you all think about that?"

They simply clapped and said, "Yeah, I felt it and got it, too!".

Our words and thoughts have energy and power over us in many ways, whether we are aware of it or not.

The truth is that our words and thoughts have energy and power over us in many ways. In fact, the negative thoughts we have about other people not only weaken those individuals, they also weaken our energy as well!

Remember, the words we speak, the words that are spoken to us, the thoughts we have about ourselves and about others all affect us both physically and energetically. We'll explore more about that later, however, you can be sure it is true and the best part is that you don't have to take my word for it. You can muscle test any of the words or thoughts for yourself anytime you chose, once you have learned the simple Art of Muscle Testing technique described later in this book.

I know that we have all experienced words and thoughts that may have been abusive and damaging to us.

Reflecting back, now I can only vaguely recall the sting of those negative words that I had been saying to and about myself before Dan S. Kennedy pointed them out to me. I am happy to say today, in 2020, they absolutely do not have any of the same heavy, negative impact on me. This is thanks to the *d.i.y. zen and The Art of Gentle Emotional Transformation* modality and the two simple techniques, "Put Your Fingers On Your Forehead" and "The Energetic Action Process." I have also voraciously used my detective skills on myself to become a dedicated archeologist to dig up and uncover by muscle testing both positive and negative words and statements that haunted me for more than 50 years. That's half a century!

Because we are here on planet Earth in Human Form, we exist. We are important, not because of what we do or how we do it or what other people think we are! We are important because we are here and we belong.

Let's get started doing the best that WE can do for ourselves right now, starting to live our lives with positive energy becoming Happy, Healthy, Whole and Complete!

WE ARE WORTH IT!

I think my dad would say, "Now that's becoming zen, Son!"

CHAPTER 5

How To Approach This Book and Workbook

After sharing the simple technique of "Put Your Fingers On Your Forehead" along with "The Energetic Action Process" with well over a couple of thousand people since the mid-1990s, I know it just works and it's simple! (I like simple!)

I am eager to share these simple techniques with you, too. However, before we go on, I want to make sure you understand that "simple does not mean easy"; "knowledge does not always equal power"; "practice certainly does not make perfect" and "put on your own oxygen mask first"!

(I will clarify these statements in a moment.)

I also want to ask you to please question everything, especially everything in this book and workbook. You certainly owe it to yourself to check out everything for yourself!

Become your own detective and archeologist. Dig deep into yourself to see, explore and investigate what resonates with you to determine what your personal truth really is. If you are uncertain as to what it is, use "The Art of Muscle Testing" technique described in this book.

There is repetition in this book and especially in the *Energetic Action Process 33-Day Workbook.*

If you are like me, I'm sure you are most likely thinking, "Okay, dude, why are you telling me up-front about all of the repetition that I am about to encounter in reading and working through this book and workbook?"

My response to you is, "Hey, great question. I would be wondering that myself, too." I just want to make sure you don't miss something or discount these techniques because of their simplicity. The strange fact is that "Put Your Fingers On Your Forehead" and "The Energetic Action Process" are so simple that, at times, it's hard to believe it can really work. Then it moves to, "Wow! It is so simple. Can it really work for me?"

Oh, yeah, I certainly had all of those thoughts in the beginning when I first learned about these techniques. Actually, I was amazed the first time and I am still amazed every time I share it with another person. Now it's 2020, about 24 years later, and it's still working!

The best and most important part of all of this is that you get to check it out and test it for yourself! It really is "do-it-yourself" (d.i.y.) and Secret Therapy or Secret Self-Therapy!

Remember:

Please question and experience everything in this book and workbook for yourself, especially if it is just a small glint of something that may relate to you or if it concerns you. If any of your experiences resonate with what is on these pages then I am reaching out to you!

Again, please do not let the simplicity of these techniques and tools get in the way of you making a positive difference in your own life, and the lives of your friends and loved ones.

Before we move forward, I will provide explanation and clarification of the following four statements for us to be on the same page and effectively move forward together:

1. Simple does not mean easy.
2. Knowledge does not always equal power.
3. Practice does not make perfect.
4. Put on your own oxygen mask first!

Simple does not mean easy.

Of course it doesn't! If it did, then everything would just simply happen without any work or effort at all. And that would be easy, just handled or fixed for us. Simple, on the other hand, means that the technique, modality, technology, tool, concept, or implementation is simple however, not necessarily easy.

Here is an example to describe or explain this point of view. Let's start with interpersonal relationships. (Oh boy, did I just kick a hornet's nest, stir things up? I hope so!)

If you have ever been in any type of relationship that ended in one way or another (good or bad, positive or negative), then you may be able to relate to the concept that simple certainly does not mean easy.

No matter what the relationship was at one time, when it ended it was certainly not the same. It could have been a childhood friendship at school; a friend from a social club, group, church, or work, or one of the "big ones" that involve family or marriage break-ups or separation.

If you were like me and have gone through the break-up of a marriage that ended in divorce and bankruptcy (as mine did in the mid-1980s), then you know, legally ending a marriage in the United States of America, specifically for me at that time living in Phoenix, Arizona, may be a simple "no fault divorce" process consisting of these steps:

(01) realizing the relationship is over
(02) filling out the required legal documents
(03) getting the documents signed by both parties
(04) filing documents with the courts having jurisdiction
(05) waiting for the court dates
(06) showing up at the court
(07) attending the hearing or proceedings
(08) speaking or testifying
(09) receiving the verdict or outcome
(10) getting a copy of the final determination by the court
(11) both parties receiving the official copies

(12) dividing up, turning over, picking up, or transferring property or
      animals (we did not have children or any stuff after the bankruptcy,
      it was considered by many very fortunate to have a fairly "simple"
      divorce). She even got my Dog!

Then, we went our separate ways, and the marriage was legally over after these twelve steps.

Now that you have experienced my "simple" 12-step divorce story, can you possibly imagine that it was "easy" for either one of us? (HA! Talk about being angry and upset!)

During my 57 years on Earth, to this day that is still one of the hardest events that I have ever had to go through. While many people may consider our divorce "simple," especially without divorce attorneys or children involved, I flat out guarantee you that it was not easy!

From my point of view "SIMPLE" certainly does not mean "EASY"! Hmmmmm, I think we all get it, 'nuff said!

Knowledge does not always equal power.

This is true especially when there is no "Practical Application" of "Correct Knowledge" to make it powerful.

Here is an example to explain this point of view. In the late 1990s, I was certified as a Fire and Life Safety Educator by the Arizona State Fire Marshall's Office, so I am going to use the example of effectively using a fire extinguisher to safely get out of a burning room and making a safe exit. Of course, these procedures would be a part of being trained to use a fire extinguisher effectively.

The knowledge and information part contains four simple steps that can be recalled with the acronym P.A.S.S., which means that a person would:

Pick up the fire extinguisher (and follow these steps)

✓ **P: Pull** the pin at the top. (This releases the locking lever to discharge the fire extinguisher's contents.)

- ✓ **A: Aim** at the base of the fire (to stop the fuel, not the flames)
- ✓ **S: Squeeze** the lever slowly so that the chemical agent will be released.
- ✓ **S: Sweep** from side to side. (By using a sweeping motion from a distance you can knock down the flames and escape.)

Now that you have the knowledge, and you know what P.A.S.S. means, let's say you and your friends are in a room with a working fire extinguisher and suddenly a fire breaks out. Good thing you have taken the training on how to effectively use or deploy the fire extinguisher and you have the knowledge of what to do to escape the burning room or building. So, you sit there looking at the fire extinguisher, knowing that you have the knowledge to deploy it effectively and save yourself and everyone else.

Now, the flames are getting higher and everyone is agitated and scared, saying "Save us. You know what to do!" You respond with, "Yes, I certainly do. All I have to do is use P.A.S.S. and get us out to safety!" By this time, the flames are even higher. People are screaming, "Do something to save us!" As you are sitting in your chair looking at the fire extinguisher, you say to them, "Of course, I know what to do. Knowledge is power, and I know that all I have to do is pick up the fire extinguisher, Pull the pin; Aim the nozzle; Squeeze the lever; Sweep the nozzle to knock down the flames and get us to safety. Hey, aren't you impressed? Knowledge is power, isn't it?"

Okay, enough already! My point is that without what I call "Practical Application" of "Correct Knowledge", absolutely nothing occurs! The people in the story, along with you, would burn up in the fire even with someone like you there with working equipment and the knowledge to effectively deploy the fire extinguisher.

Seriously, from my point of view as a long-time disaster manager, public safety and operations guy, knowledge alone does not and cannot do or accomplish anything without the practical application of that knowledge. However, with the practical application of correct and accurate knowledge, that can be very effective and powerful!

I hope you will stop and consider how you will use "Practical Application" while you are reading this book and working your way through the workbook.

OK, I think we all get it now.

Practice does not make perfect!

Wow! Talk about a true statement. Of course it does not!

This may be apparent to some of you, however, for others it may not be, so I am going to tell you another true-life story to show you why I know this statement is true.

When I was growing up, I would hear people say "practice makes perfect" again and again. Then, one day, I said that to my dad and he stopped me right in my tracks and said, "No, stop, Son! That is absolutely not true, get that out of your mind right now!" (My dad was a brilliant, insightful, practical zen type of guy with many life lessons.) He asked me where I had heard that saying, and I told him lots of people say it at school. He gave me his great big Carl Niki smile and said, "Sit down here, Son. I want to tell you why that statement is incorrect and not only is it untrue and why believing it can be detrimental to you and hurt you in the long run!"

He told me, "Son, the reason the saying "practice makes perfect" is sadly untrue, is that you can do or practice something the wrong way over and over again and in doing so, it will only make you perfect at doing it wrong. Then, you have to do a lot of hard work to break the habit or practice of doing it the wrong way."

He said, "I don't want you to have to learn this lesson the hard way, Son!" Then he said, "I want you to think back to when you were first learning empty hand or karate to form a correct fist. Then, the correct punch. Remember, Sensei (Japanese for Teacher) would show you the correct technique. He would have you do it while watching you intensely, then correcting your form each time, over and over until satisfied that you were doing it correctly. Only then would he turn you lose to practice on your own for a while, before returning back to you to re-correct your form. He would repeat these steps over and over again to make sure that you are doing it correctly.

"Son," he said, "the reason that the saying "Practice makes perfect" is so wrong for you is if Sensei let you practice punching the wrong way a thousand times, then you would be perfect at doing it the wrong way and then, to do it effectively and correctly it would take you a lot of time, pain and suffering to un-learn and un-do the wrong practice. Then, you would have to re-discipline yourself to learn it correctly and then practice again over and over again just to get back to the beginning."

Then, with his great big Carl Niki smile, he said, "I love you, Son, and I don't want you to have to go through life having to learn things the hard way like I did throughout my life. If I realize and see it, then I can help teach you from my experience and save you from some of the unnecessary pain and hardships in life that I went through."

My dad continued, "Here is the way that statement can be reframed, true and effective for you: "Perfect Practice can make you Perfect." Always remember, Son, when you take the time to correctly learn the basics of anything (from automotive repair to martial arts) and get the steps, movements, or techniques down correctly, then by following through with "perfect practice" you will be on your way to being as correct and perfect as you can be! At least by doing it correctly, you will be on your way to gaining mastery at that activity." Of course, he ended that lesson with his great big Carl Niki smile.

I think we all understand and get his message.

Put on your own oxygen mask first!

Growing up, my dad always taught me that I must be a responsible person and take care of myself first.

Then my dad told me, "Son, you must take personal responsibility for your own actions and take care of yourself first, then you will be able to help and take care of others as necessary or required just as I have done for you."

Having a dad that worked for the airlines, I was literally raised flying and grew up on airplanes most likely before I was born, or before I could even remember flying as an infant.

As I grew up, every time we would fly, my dad always told me, "Son, when you hear the attention beep of the 'Stews' or Captain to signal that an announcement is coming over the intercom, instantly stop whatever you are doing, listen carefully, pay close attention to their directions and obey them immediately because your life may depend on your paying attention, listening and actions someday!"

"Always pay attention to the Safety Briefing by the 'Stews' (in the 1960s it was Stewardess or Steward, now it's Flight Attendant). They are the most important people on the airplane!" my dad said.

I asked him what about the pilots and what about you? He smiled and said, "That's a good question, Son and I will tell you the pilot's job is to fly the plane: take off, keep it in the air, on course and land it safely. My job is to maintain the engines, the airframe and the mechanical parts of the airplane to keep them running and working smoothly, so they keep the airplane in the air. The 'Stews' are the most important people on the plane because they take care of all of the passengers, like us. They keep us safe and direct us, especially in an emergency."

The engines started to roar as the pilots began to push back from the terminal and then came the beep and the voice of the head stewardess came over the intercom. Of course, I instantly snapped to attention with heightened awareness as she spoke and her team demonstrated the seat belt, showed us the safety card and pointed out the safety lights on the floor and the emergency exits.

She said, "In case we lose cabin pressure, the overhead oxygen masks will come down, grab yours and make sure that you put on your own oxygen mask first, pull the straps tight and secure, then help your neighbor." She and her team were holding up the demo masks for us so we could see what she meant.

After the briefing and beginning the last safety check before takeoff, the head stewardess stopped to greet my dad and mom (they knew each other in Las Vegas, Nevada). She gave my little sister and me a cool plastic 'Wings' pin each. I asked her about the oxygen mask, and she handed me her demo mask to look at. She smiled as I handed it back and said, "Make sure your seat belt is on tight, young man."

After we were in the air, I asked my dad, "Why do we put on our oxygen mask first instead of helping someone else?"

My dad said with his most serious face and voice emphasis, "Son, this is one time you absolutely must Put On Your Own Oxygen Mask First BEFORE attempting to help anyone else including me, your mom or sister! If you don't take care of yourself first and put yours on first, you may not be able to breathe and then if you pass out you may die and not be able to help anyone else! Do you understand, Son? In an emergency, all of our lives may depend on you putting on your own oxygen mask first then helping us. You must take care of yourself first, period! Got it, Son?" He said this with his big Carl Niki smile. Of course my response was, "Yes Sir, Dad, I Got it!"

The older I get the smarter and more zen my dad gets!

Thanks, Dad! Many of my students, teammates, colleagues, employees, volunteers, business partners and clients have certainly benefited from your insights and guidance.

Your zen and wisdom still lives on!

More important things to consider before you start…

As you go through this book and workbook here are more important things to consider:

No matter what happened in your past, it is up to you to make your own choice and decision to take action right now to make a positive difference in your life!

Only you have the power, authority and ability to choose to start taking care of yourself from the inside out!

It is all up to you!

Always take care of yourself first!

- ✓ Check in with yourself and energy often
- ✓ Breathe! Breathe! Breathe!
- ✓ Take your time and go slowly
- ✓ Go Slowly!
- ✓ Question Everything!
- ✓ Keep an open mind
- ✓ Be patient with yourself
- ✓ Only do what is in your highest and best interest
- ✓ Put on your own oxygen mask first!

"Everything works for numerous people and nothing works on everyone."
— *LeRoy Malouf*

NOTE: As you are going forward using the "Put Your Fingers On Your Forehead" technique and "The Energetic Action Process" technique, sometimes it does take multiple repetitions and/or multiple sessions of these techniques, especially if the trauma, feeling or emotion occurred repeatedly or if it occurred years ago and now it is coming up to be addressed and worked on.

- ✓ If something isn't working for you, stop and breathe
- ✓ After re-starting and it isn't working for you, stop and use one of the other techniques
- ✓ If something isn't working for you, stop and breathe
- ✓ Restart again!
- ✓ If something isn't working for you, stop and breathe
- ✓ After restarting and it isn't working for you, stop and use one of the other techniques
- ✓ If something isn't working for you, stop and breathe
- ✓ After restarting and something still isn't working for you, stop for this session, take a break and start again at another time
- ✓ If something isn't working for you, stop and breathe
- ✓ STOP FOR THIS SESSION, TAKE A BREAK!!!
- ✓ Breathe! Breathe! Breathe!

You didn't get this way overnight!
- ✓ You may be feeling stuck
- ✓ There could be several micro shifts before a big one occurs
- ✓ That's OK, it took your whole life to get this way
- ✓ It won't all go away or change overnight
- ✓ "Life is way too short to be miserable." Keep going!
- ✓ It's a lifelong adventure and you are worth it!
- ✓ And so is zen, a lifelong journey and adventure

This is where you are able to start to take back your power, your control, your ability to make a positive difference in your life! It really is all up to you! You have the choice to start right now! Please do!

PART IV

CHAPTER 6

Put Your Fingers On Your Forehead

In this chapter, I describe the simplest of the three techniques covered in this book. This I call "Put Your Fingers On Your Forehead".

Demonstrating the "Put Your Fingers On Your Forehead" technique.

With children, demonstrating the technique.

Originally, the "Put Your Fingers On Your Forehead" technique was part of "The Energetic Action Process" techniques. However, after a lot of feedback from clients and guidance from colleagues doing their own energy work modalities and process, I have separated them out for individual discussion, practice and use. "Put Your Fingers On Your Forehead" is a simple and powerful technique that you can use on its own right now.

It's a great place to start learning about how to help yourself immediately.

"Put Your Fingers On Your Forehead" is a simple, quick, completely natural, and non-invasive process. It is definitely not new and you most likely have the original tools required. We have just re-discovered it in this day and age. It basically involves placing the first three or four fingers of each hand on your forehead – above your eyebrows – and keeping them there for a few minutes while you are experiencing the thoughts, feelings and emotions related to a current traumatic situation, or reliving a past event.

Demonstrating with children the hand placement for using the "Put Your Fingers On Your Forehead" technique.

If you are experiencing a current trauma, keep your fingers on your forehead until you begin to feel calmer. If you choose to clear the thoughts, feelings and emotions tied to a painful memory, briefly recall the event to conjure up or remember the thoughts, feelings and emotions associated with it, then "run through" the scenario – complete with thoughts, images, and emotions – while keeping your fingers on your forehead. I recommend starting with three times. In most cases, people find that by the third time the emotions have subsided greatly, if not completely.

Demonstrating feeling painful feelings and emotions using the "Put Your Fingers On Your Forehead" technique. NOTE: The more strongly that you can bring up and feel the pain and trauma the more it clears them out.

An alternative is to put your palms on your forehead in place of your fingers on your forehead. That has been proven to work equally as well. So, that's how it works! How and why? You may ask. I don't have those answers. What I do know is this is a natural process that humans have been using since the dawn of time.

Think about it, what do people often do when they see something horrifying, when they've suffered a loss, when they've received bad or sad news, or when they feel terrible about something they've done? They grab their head with their hands or they bury their face in their hands with their fingers on their forehead.

Basically, they simply put their fingers on their forehead.

You've probably done this yourself, and all of us have likely seen others do it — in person, in movies, and on television. People do this instinctively without even thinking about it.

Demonstrating feeling painful feelings and emotions using the "Put Your Fingers On Your Forehead" technique. NOTE: The more strongly that you can bring up and feel the pain and trauma the more it clears them out.

Demonstrating the "Put Your Fingers On Your Forehead" technique.

In my operations career, I've worked in emergency management, public safety, investigations, and as a disaster manager. In those roles, I've seen and worked emergency operations and disasters on many levels: local, county, state, tribal, federal — from local vehicle crashes, floods, storms, and single family home fires to large scale national operations including: the World Trade Center terrorism event at ground zero in New York City; the Rodeo Chediski wildfire in Northern Arizona and the scenes of devastation in Mississippi, Louisiana, and Alabama after Hurricane Katrina. In all of those instances, I personally saw lots of people putting their fingers or hands on their forehead after experiencing or witnessing distressing events, or receiving news about the injury or loss of their loved ones or property. I would guess that few of them, if any, had ever heard about putting their fingers on their foreheads. However, over and over I watched them naturally do it on their own as they cried and experienced their pain and grief in that moment. Those experiences convince me that this technique is natural and instinctive.

I can also tell you that my own experiences have shown me that this technique works! It has worked for me and for the friends, colleagues, clients, first responders and upset, traumatized citizens I have shared it with.

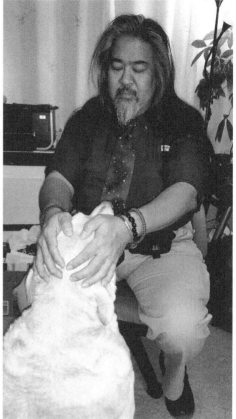

You may be able to help a friend or loved one, too!

To give you an idea of what is possible when you use the simple technique of "Put Your Fingers On Your Forehead" and experiencing or re-experiencing the situation three times or more when necessary, please continue on and I will share a few stories with you.

At the Scene of an Accident – Multiple Vehicle Crash

After learning the fingers on your forehead technique, I immediately started using it extensively on myself and friends. It also came in handy during my work in public safety, investigations, emergency management and as a disaster manager.

One of the first times I used it at a vehicle crash scene was in the mid-1990s. One of the drivers involved in the accident was very shaken up and could hardly speak about what had occurred. "It's okay to be upset and cry," I told her. "Just sit down here on the curb where it is safe. Now put your fingers on your forehead and feel whatever it is you are feeling right now. It's okay to cry. Just stay here, keep your fingers on your forehead, and I will be back to check on you in a few minutes."

After four or five minutes, I noticed that the driver was sitting calmly and looking around, so I went over to her and asked her to tell me what had happened. To the amazement of both of us, she calmly said – in list format – this happened, and this happened, and this happened, and this happened. She then stopped and looked at me in a puzzled manner and asked, "What in the world happened? What was that thing with putting my fingers on my forehead?"

Since I didn't have the time to explain about the technique right then, I most likely said something like, "Oh, no big deal. It's just an oriental thing." (Being of Japanese ancestry I could get away with that.) She said, "Oh, okay," and turned to walk away. However, she was very sharp and astute! She stopped, turned around and asked me, "Does this work for other things, too?" She nailed it and got me! I smiled and said, "It certainly has for me!" She got it and gave me a slight smile, turned and walked away.

I remember thinking, Wow! That worked great and it was fast! The shock was gone from the woman's face and she appeared much calmer, and actually smiled a little while waiting for the tow truck and for her ride to arrive.

I knew then that I would certainly use this technique again on the job. And yes, it worked time after time in a multitude of situations!

The house fire that affected a mother, her two young children and took the life of their beloved family dog

Of all of the times I have thought to share about the power of the "Put Your Fingers On Your Forehead" technique, the following situation is the one that always comes to mind first.

A call came into our Red Cross Chapter in Phoenix, Arizona where I was working as a disaster manager. The call was from the local Fire Department, requesting us to assist a client in their jurisdiction who had lost everything in a single-family home fire outside of the Phoenix area a week earlier, and who was still having a difficult time talking about what happened.

I went on this evening call with two of our on-duty Disaster Action Team (DAT) members. One was David French, a leadership volunteer member and friend who had personally trained me years before when I was a new volunteer, and the other was Catherine Christy, a new casework volunteer. David drove us to the client's residence, and just like the Fire Department said, it was mostly a shell, almost fully destroyed by fire.

We met the client (I'll call her Teri – not her real name) on the scene of the house fire; she was upset and shaken due to the devastating fire she and her children had experienced the week before.

Teri was not able to talk about what had happened without breaking into tears and crying. I asked David to start training Catherine on the damage assessment and documentation and let me sit with and talk to Teri. I gave her some water and asked her if she would be willing to do something very simple that had worked for me and others in the past when we had experienced trauma and fearful situations.

Being the brave person she was, Teri said, "Yes! I'll do it. What do I have to do?" I showed her by putting my fingers on my own forehead and asked her to do the same. I then asked her to start playing the situation through from the first thing she remembered (which was her daughter saying, "Mommy, my bedroom is smoking.") all the way up to the present moment, as the family continued to face the devastation and ramifications of the fire.

Before she started, I told her to play the events through one time and no matter what happened to not remove her fingers from her forehead until she got to the end. Teri looked at me, nodded, closed her eyes, and started. I looked at my watch. About one minute went by and she started crying. About four minutes went by and she stopped crying and put her hands down.

I gave her tissues and water, and she regained her composure. I said, "Don't say anything now," and asked her to put her fingers back on her forehead and re-play it through again.

She put her fingers on her forehead again, started the process for the second time, and again about one minute went by before she started to cry. This time she completed the process after about two and a half minutes.

When she stopped, I gave her some more tissues. She wiped her face then looked at me with a bewildered smile and told me that for the first time since the fire happened a week ago, she could think about it and not cry. I asked her to put her fingers back on her forehead one last time and re-play the same situation all the way through again. She stopped for a moment and said, "Seriously, over the past week, I have not been able to even think about the fire trauma without crying!" Again, she put her fingers back on her forehead to go through the process.

This time it was barely one minute and there was no crying or tears! After it was over, Teri looked at me and smiled. I asked her to tell me what had happened the night of the fire. She started talking in a calm and composed manner, and told me all that had happened, all the while looking a little surprised. I asked her if she was ready to talk to our caseworker. Teri said she was. She then calmly sat with Catherine and worked through the questions and information required to finish the paperwork and case file. David and I completed the damage assessment process for her to receive the initial assistance vouchers on scene for herself and her family.

We were finished and getting ready to leave when Teri asked if she could talk to me privately before we left.

Teri told me that one of her legs was injured when she stepped on broke through the burned floor. She cut the back of her thigh and this required stiches. She told me about another trauma to her family; their beloved dog died in the fire. Teri told me that her two children, a son of five and a daughter of seven, were having nightmares over the past week about the house fire and the "fire monster". She wanted to know if she could use the same "Put Your Fingers On Your Forehead" technique on her children to help them clear out their nightmares, and she asked how she could do it for her children.

I had never had anyone ask me that so I thought about it for a few minutes, then asked if she regularly held them on her lap. She said, "Yes, especially over the last week after the fire. They both wanted to be held a lot." I suggested she hold each one individually and tell them, "Mommy is going to hold you and rub your head for you." Then, while doing so, I suggested she ask them to tell her their story of the fire or fire monster. (Having her rub the children's forehead is simply to let them feel the rubbing and not ask or think about the fingers on their forehead.)

That was it, and I got back into the vehicle and we left the scene. As we drove away, I was wondering what would happen and how the "Put Your Fingers On Your Forehead" technique would work for Teri and her children. We had many more disaster response calls come in and I didn't have time to think about it anymore as we moved on to the next disaster response. About a week later, Teri came to our Phoenix office for follow-up casework and brought her children along. They looked happy as they ran up to me with big smiles and said, "The fire monster is gone!" Teri said that after she had used the "Put Your Fingers On Your Forehead" technique with the children as I suggested, they cried for the moment while telling their story and, happily, their nightmares went away that night. A week later they had not returned. This was by far the story that made the biggest impression on me. It showed how this simple technique could even be used with children to clear out specific, traumatic disaster-caused fear and nightmares.

Sometimes, the people I have shared the "Put Your Fingers On Your Forehead" technique with have taken the time to write about their experience and how this simple technique has helped them and how it may help someone else through their story. Here is one that I find particularly inspiring.

Releasing the Pain and Trauma of Incest, and the Loss of a Mother

As we all know, life is very stressful, but when you bring baggage from childhood and keep loading it with all the bad and uncomfortable circumstances from life, it gets heavier, making life unbearable at times.

I was taught the "Put Your Fingers On Your Forehead" technique and it helped lighten the load. By placing my fingers on my forehead and facing each problem, and learning how to release all the bad feelings, the load became lighter and lighter.

I am an incest survivor. There were times that I couldn't face the shame. I told my ex-husband and he was very supportive, but eventually it was one of the causes of our break-up. I thought I would never have a sexual relationship again. That way, I wouldn't have to deal with the shame.

Even two years of counseling did not help me as much as the "Put Your Fingers On Your Forehead" technique. I am now free of the shame and the feelings that came with me. I am now remarried and able to fully enjoy sexual pleasures.

When my mother died several years ago, I never cried. I was strong for my brothers and sister. But, every time I would talk about her, I could feel the tears start. I couldn't control my emotions. I still miss her, but now I don't have the tears. Just by placing my fingers on my forehead and feeling each emotion, I was able to cry in the privacy of my own home and finally found the peace and acceptance of my mom's death and accept it.

Life is too short to have to suffer with emotional and physical pain.

I never realized how much hurt I had hidden deep inside me.

Wherever I happen to be when an emotion from my past breaks through, I am able to stop and deal with the pain. It doesn't matter where I am — at home, at work, at the beach, or on a bus. The "Put Your Fingers On Your Forehead" technique can be done anywhere with positive results.

- Purposely Anonymous (South Carolina)

One experience that I think captures the profound power of the "Put Your Fingers On Your Forehead" technique is MJ's story about the loss of her beloved dogs, Molly and Smoke. This demonstrates how it can be used to help a friend or loved one over the phone, from a distance, to work through their grief.

Clearing the loss of her beloved dogs (actually her four-legged children) to being able to remember the joy

Smoke and Molly were my four-legged children, who were laid to rest within a few months of each other. Smoke was my ex-husband Russell's dog when I first dated him.

Smoke was my first experience of having a dog for a pet. I quickly came to love him and he became my instant companion, especially when my husband was gone working.

Shortly after we got married and moved to our dream house with a huge backyard, my husband came home with a cute black lab puppy named Molly.

He said the neighbor had found her along the side of the road and couldn't keep her. Molly became my instant daughter.

Our family was complete. Although we never had two-legged children, the dogs became our kids. They would go in the car with us, go camping with us, and even canoeing. Eventually, we put in a large swimming pool, and Molly would swim until she was so tired she could barely get out of the pool. Smoke didn't like the water and generally had to be pushed into the pool and supervised while he paddled to the edge to get out. Molly was a hit with the kids when they came over. She would lead them around the pool as they held her tail while she swam. I can still hear the giggles and see the happy look on Molly's face.

As fate would have it, the marriage broke up and my husband did not want to have anything to do with his "kids." I decided to move back to Wisconsin.

I didn't have much support in this new adventure and everyone told me, "get rid of the dogs." They wondered how I was going to find a place to live that would take two big black labs. I stuck to my guns and told everyone that I would never get rid of my kids. They were my comfort during the most devastating, heartbreaking time of my life.

I knew God would help me find a place.

I sold the house, packed a 26-foot U-Haul with a car carrier on the back for my Nissan Xterra and drove us all from Florida to Waukesha.

With a lot of prayer and perseverance, I found a house to rent there that had a fenced-in back yard. The landlord worked with me on having the two dogs. The place was filthy and a dump, but the price was right. As the weather began to change and the snow arrived, I recall the first time snowflakes fell from the sky and the look of wonder on my dogs' faces. They were smiling and trying to catch the flakes on their tongues, trying to figure out what the mysterious white things were that were falling from the sky.

We were forced to move in February when the landlord needed the rented house for a family member. But, with a lot of time, tears, and tantrums, I found a place just down the road. It would work. We lived there without many problems for about a year. I would take the dogs for walks and had orange reflective vests on them as we walked. These two peas in a pod would sit, fetch, and run in unison. We were the hit of the neighborhood, and Molly and Smoke would greet everyone we met along the way with happy smiles and wagging tails.

One day in September 2009, I noticed that Smoke was sleeping more and appeared to be in a lot of pain. His hip was bad now and he could barely stand up. I was so afraid and heartsick. Then, one day, I came home from work and Smoke was hurting so bad and was so lethargic that I knew it was time to take him to the vet. I was crying and scared and wasn't sure what to do, but I called and they told me to bring him in.

Molly was by Smoke's side the entire time while I wrapped him in blankets and carefully lifted him into the car. He was in pain and having trouble breathing. My heart was breaking and my eyes were so full of tears it was hard to drive.

The staff at the hospital were wonderful. I delicately put my boy on the cart, wrapped in his favorite Green Bay Packers blanket. I whispered in his ears and told him how much I loved him, and thanked him for watching over Molly and me.

He looked at me and I knew he loved me. I kissed him goodbye then. I did not want to be in the room when they took him away. When I left the hospital, I felt a deep sense of loss in my heart but a sense of relief that Smoke was no longer in pain. I called Gary, and he helped me to process the grief. He had me use his "Put Your Fingers On Your Forehead" technique. I did as I let all the images and emotions play out, like watching my life flash before me.

I cried for several minutes but also smiled and laughed throughout the first time through the process, Gary comforting and reassuring me the entire time from thousands of miles away.

I did the process several times and felt an incredible sense of peace when I finished.

This simple process of "Put Your Fingers On Your Forehead" allowed me to clear out the pain and be able to remember the good times with Smoke, rather than dwelling on the loss.

Little did I know that a few short months later I would have to repeat the entire process when Molly was sick and had to be put to rest.

Again, Gary and the "Put Your Fingers On Your Forehead" technique saved me from a debilitating grief.

- Mary Jo Spencer (Waukesha, Wisconsin)

Personally and quietly sharing Help for the Helpers and Emergency Responders ("Secret Therapy")

I have always been inspired at how something so simple can give relief quickly to a person who is hurting in the moment, and free them from the intensity of the emotional pain.

While writing out and recording the stories for this book, one of the exciting things I found about putting my fingers on my forehead and clearing out painful issues from my past was that, for me, this became "secret therapy." I did not have to tell anyone what had happened to me. I only had to identify the emotions that came up for me, then continue to clear them out and get relief – without sharing the traumatic circumstances that had occurred. That has been true freedom for me.

Reflecting back, since 1996, I had worked in the field on 25 large-scale national disaster relief operations and lots of small, medium and regional events. Over the years working disasters, I've been from the lowest Technician to an Assistant Director on the largest wildfire in the United States at the time and I've cleaned toilets on Shelters as a Manager along with a multitude of other roles in Training, Government Liaison, Voluntary Agency Liaison, Shelter, Public Affairs, Staffing-Disaster Human Resources, Mass Care, Logistics, Communications and Administration.

During my time on the ground in New York City responding to the World Trade Center 9-11 Disaster Relief Operation (DRO), I was deployed to the Training Function at the DRO Headquarters at Cadman Plaza in Brooklyn, New York. Being assigned to the Training Function meant that I would work a lot of roles there, from organizing the training forms, documents, manuals both physical and electronic versions, equipment, supplies and instructors to traveling out in the field conducting training and orientations in locations around New York City. In this capacity, I had interactions with all levels of Red Cross Disaster Workers, United Nations Translators and Government Agency First Responders. During that time, I personally experienced a wide range of emotions and feelings as you can imagine and, of course, I used the "Put Your Fingers On Your Forehead" technique to help myself clear out stuff and to be able to maintain a true positive, upbeat disposition while doing my work and serving our clients, fellow disaster workers and first responders.

I was asked many times by my colleagues and other agency partners, how I was able to be the "Happy Trainer" and have a real, positive attitude and upbeat smile while working in the fray of a large-scale terrorism event. I was working mega hours day-in day-out — at least 16-hour and sometimes 20-hour days. I was traveling to different locations via subway, bus, taxi and walking every day or night, depending on what was required to get the job done. As appropriate, I would share with them the "Put Your Fingers On Your Forehead" technique and that it obviously worked for me.

After I shared with the first few individuals, the word went around, and others would come up to me and say that someone told them that I was the "Happy Trainer" and I was helping myself with some technique that I showed to someone, it worked for the person that told them and they wanted me to show them what I was doing for myself. They hoped that it would work for them too. Yes, it did work for many, who were from all walks of life and all types of response jobs.

After returning home from the World Trade Center New York City 9-11-2001 Disaster Relief Operation assignment, I was right back to working many hours addressing lots of DROs of all sizes, including multiple floods and wildfires around Arizona and multiple single family home fires! I also assisted and worked with our Disaster Fund-Raising Team by speaking at events about the work we did in New York City and on DROs around the state. Yeah, we were busy!

Our Arizona Disaster Team started initial response to The Rodeo - Chediski Wildfire in mid-June 2002. This fire eventually spread over 468,000 acres in North-Eastern-Central Arizona. It was not controlled until July 7 and, at that time, it was the worst forest fire in Arizona's recorded history. Eventually, we had over two thousand Red Cross Disaster Workers on the DRO, from as far away as Hawaii, Alaska and New York City! We were all swamped. Everyone at our Chapter was working to support the huge DRO in every capacity. Bonnie Wright, our Chapter Chief Executive Officer (CEO), was even helping to bring us lunch and to serve us because our Chapter Headquarters' workers were non-stop answering calls, sending emails and communicating with the main DRO headquarters in Northern Arizona (NA) and the National Disaster Operations Center in Washington, D.C. On this DRO, I was an Assistant Director supporting the NA DRO, the Family Assistance

Center in Phoenix, the Government Liaison Officers, Public Information Officers, Fundraising Officers, Logistics, Mass Care, Staffing, Training, the other Support and Direct Service Functions. All this while continuing to maintain the local single-family fires, other wildfires and floods around the state that were still occurring at the same time! You bet at times I would be sitting at my desk using the "Put Your Fingers On Your Forehead" technique! Just like Bonnie our CEO, I wore multiple hats, filling in on anything that had to be done at the time. One day, my amazing Volunteer Partner Gary Ashkenazy, aka Gary A as we had two management Garys in the office, came to me and said, "We have a DRO Orientation that has to be done and I can't do it because I'm in the middle of Staffing and Logistics." I told him, "no worries I'll do it." It is interesting how everything works out. The orientation room was packed and one of the Staffing Volunteers was handing out the DRO paperwork. He said, "We are starting a little late, waiting for Gary A to do the orientation." As I walked in, I said that I was filling in for Gary A. The ones that knew me said, "Oh no, we're stuck with Gary N instead!" Everyone started laughing. I got to the front of the room and said, "Welcome to Arizona and thank you for coming to support our DRO. We need You!" All of a sudden, three men stood up and said, "Oh my God, it's the Happy Trainer!" Everyone turned around to see them and with huge smiles they said in unison, "We're from New York City, here to help you!" Everyone clapped and cheered for them and wanted to know what the inside joke was. One of them said that during the 9-11 relief operation in NYC, I was known as the Happy Trainer from Phoenix, Arizona. Interestingly enough, they actually put their fingers on their foreheads and smiled at me before they sat down. It was a great day and the little diversion of doing the DRO Orientation was a good mental health break for me. The Wildfire DRO lasted well into August. Even though the main fire was contained in early July, we still had clients to serve and cleanup work to do.

Who would have thought that only six weeks after finishing the Rodeo–Chediski Wildfire, I would be moving to Washington, D.C.? I was appointed as the "Safety & Security, Weapons of Mass Destruction/Terrorism program Function Lead" for the United States and The Territories at the National Headquarters Disaster Operations Center in Washington, D.C. in October 2002.

Yep, I did it, even though I was scared of moving to Washington, D.C. to take on a big job without knowing anyone other than a few Red Crossers. You bet I was nervous and I certainly used all of the techniques in this book to help get myself through all of it!

Fast forward to mid-2005. After working on, supporting and providing leadership on lots of large scale DROs across the US and the Territories, Hurricane Katrina came along! OMG! That would only be the start of some of the largest DROs that the American Red Cross would respond to. Then, there was Hurricane Rita, Hurricane Wilma and lots of other relief operations across the country while we were already working the big ones.

I thought I had seen a lot of destruction and damage in my career. Then, I was deployed on Hurricane Katrina to work directly on the ground with my safety and security teams to look after the life safety of our disaster workers, and the security of the facilities, equipment, vehicles, supplies, and assets that belonged to the American Red Cross.

I had no idea what I was going to see and experience in the weeks from September through November 2005. I spent them on the ground in Mississippi, Louisiana, and Alabama after Hurricane Katrina unleased her fury on the Gulf Coast States!

I was met at the airport in Jackson, Mississippi by a member of one of our safety and security teams, who briefed me about the disaster relief operation as we drove halfway to Gulf Port, Mississippi to meet another safety and security team. They would drive me to the Seabee Base Shelter, which I would call home base for weeks.

Within the first three hours, I heard almost unbelievable accounts of damage over an area that was impossible for me to actually grasp until I saw it for myself.

Scenes of devastation after Hurricane Katrina in Mississippi.

One of the most amazing things about being a disaster relief worker is that, for the most part, even in the most adverse conditions and circumstances, we can just suck it up and do our jobs for quite a while before feeling, or admitting to feeling, affected by the enormity of the situation.

I knew going in that the infrastructure was majorly damaged and that I would be required to stay in staff shelters, and that some of them would probably be very large, hot, and crowded. Oh, I had been in staff shelters before however, I had never stayed for weeks in huge warehouse shelters with 600 to 800 of my new best friends. We did not have any privacy.

At Seabee Base Staff Shelter in MS and SAS Team late briefing

The infrastructure in some areas was literally blown away or flooded out, so we lived and worked in the beginning without air conditioning, flushing toilets, open stores or gas stations and all of the comforts of home that we are used to, rely upon and so often take for granted! It was like that across multiple states and that was a new experience for me.

After my first night, when I got to bed on a portable cot after 2:00 a.m. in what I called the "uber shelter," the lights came on at 6:00 in the morning. Hundreds of people started their day, hustling to get ready and have a hearty breakfast, prepared for us by the U.S. Forest Service contract kitchen teams, then head out to serve our Red Cross clients.

That first day in Mississippi, I was taken to the disaster relief operation headquarters to sign in on the job, get oriented, meet our safety and security team, pick up equipment and a vehicle, and get on the road.

At the headquarters, it was mostly like all of the other disasters that I had been on; some hurry and some wait, and lots of Old Home Week, seeing friends and colleagues from other disaster relief operations. I was met by a friend, Pete Hard, a retired police officer who had been one of my hard-working volunteers when I was a disaster manager in Phoenix, Arizona, at the Grand Canyon Red Cross Chapter.

It was great to reconnect with him, and I found out that he would be the designated driver for my Mississippi Disaster Relief Operation Lead Safety and Security Manager, Pat Munsil, and me. Pete would give us our initial scope of the damage on my orientation to this disaster relief operation.

The Hard Rock Café sign still standing; with Pat and Pete in MS.

We started on the coast at the Hard Rock Cafe guitar sign (which was amazingly still standing). For miles and miles down the Gulf Port, Mississippi coast there was some of the most unimaginable damage and destruction that I had ever personally seen. That first day's experience was only the tip of the iceberg of the destruction that had occurred when Hurricane Katrina made landfall and totally devastated the infrastructure and area.

I do admit that when I first arrive on a disaster relief operation, I do my best to stay focused on what must be done by remaining in what I call my "response mode." For me, that means packing up and putting my feelings aside or on the shelf (to the best of my ability) to get the job done or going. Then, when I am able to address my personal feelings or emotions, I take them off the shelf, unpack them, and address them in a safe and secure environment. However, when I am totally maxed out and they come rushing out and I have to immediately address them in that moment, I stop and look for a private place, such as a port-a-potty, a vehicle, or a storage room. Likewise, during Hurricane Katrina, I made do with whatever little private space was available.

Fortunately for me, we had awesome U.S. Forest Service contract shower trailers that had a big open shower area, good for a quick in-and-out, and four private, locking, single-shower compartments. We were allowed up to 15 minutes in the private shower. The showers were open from about 4:00 or 5:00 a.m. until midnight. I would arrive at about 20 minutes to close and there would be only a few diehard night owls like me there, so I enjoyed 15 minutes of hot shower privacy.

During this time, I would put my fingers on my forehead to clear out the issues, sights, sounds, smells, thoughts, feelings and stress from the day. Then, I would sit in the open canopy area and relax until 1:00 a.m., then go to sleep on my cot in the Seabee Base shelter and start all over again in the morning.

The "Put Your Fingers On Your Forehead" technique is what kept me calm, cool, collected and sane during those weeks. It allowed me to clear out the stress from the day and sleep soundly. Then, I was able to wake up refreshed and ready to take on another day!

Over the days and weeks on the ground in Louisiana, Mississippi, and Alabama, I meet hundreds of dedicated Red Cross workers and clients. The dedication and sense of community after a major disaster is always inspiring to me. It is an honor to serve on national disaster relief operations with people who truly care about fellow human beings who have lived through devastating and life-altering disasters.

The most experienced disaster workers eventually feel the stress of being immersed in the disaster relief operation environment and must have some way to deal with or get past their personal experience of working the situation. Even having some of the best disaster mental health workers in the world on the DROs, there were times when each of us just had to deal with life and emotions ourselves as they came at us. I was privileged to share the "Put Your Fingers On Your Forehead" technique with some of our safety and security team members. Most of them were retired, former or current local, county, state, tribal, federal or international public safety, law-enforcement, fire, military, OSHA, HAZMAT or corporate/industrial security officers and safety engineers who have dealt with very stressful, life-altering situations and incidents in their past lives on the job. Many of these disaster workers have been on both sides of critical incident stress debriefing (CISD) or critical incident stress management (CISM), and some of them have moved forward to become peer counselors in their respective agencies and organizations. Many were able to get positive personal results by simply placing their fingers on their forehead on their own in total privacy, without having to talk to anyone or give any details of the emotional incident that they wanted to clear.

SAS Team MS DRO, Hurricane Katrina.

SAS Team LA DRO, Hurricane Katrina.

Note: Yes, at times it has been necessary to repeat the process over and over multiple times to totally clear out some of the long-time deep-seated events or issues due to prolonged exposure to extreme stress and issues like post-traumatic stress (PTS) however, many of them did clear out and become neutral.

As I said before, I consider this technique as "secret therapy" for me and the multitude of individuals I shared it with.

In our lives, most of us have experienced painful or negative situations or incidents that have made us feel victimized, less than, unworthy, powerless, embarrassed, ashamed, or many other disempowering emotions that we would never want to go public with or even let our colleagues, family, friends or loved ones know about. At times, we may feel like we are the only one who has gone through or experienced this type of situation and we've had worrisome thoughts like: What would everyone else think about me if they knew? How could I deal with the shame of it all?

With the simple "Put Your Fingers On Your Forehead" technique, no one ever has to know. You're in charge! You have the power to positively change your life and you can do it yourself in total privacy! The bottom line and the key to all of this is you! Actually, that statement is very inspiring to me because I believe each and every one of us is a healer, Our Own!

Yes, a healer! Whether you are a Christian or Not, familiar with Christianity or heard about Christianity or Jesus Christ, and if you have studied the Bible, read the Bible, or seen a Bible on TV then you may know that at times Jesus told individuals, "your faith has healed you". It Applies to ALL!

Wow! That is so powerful. Healed by their own faith! Even if you have another faith or no faith, I still believe that we must proactively choose to take charge of our lives and start to clear out the negative emotions that no longer serve us.

Yes, we can start this process wherever we are along on our journey. I have found, after sharing the "Put Your Fingers On Your Forehead" technique with a couple of thousand people, that you do not have to understand it or even believe it in order to have it work for you, it just does if you use it!

Hey, what do you have to lose, except all of those negative thoughts, feelings and emotions? Please spend just a little bit of your precious time to invest in yourself for a few minutes to find out how it may even work for you! And YOU are worth your time, energy and effort!

Now you have been exposed to a simple technique to help you on your way and to aid anyone you choose. Always remember there are a multitude of roads that lead to the same destination and putting your fingers on your forehead is only one of them. However simple it is, for me it has been extremely powerful. Even in the Seabee Base Mega Staff Shelter, working on disaster, I was able to use these techniques to take care of myself, stay calm, focused and get the job done.

Sharing the process at a group in Northern Virginia

In October of 2014, Gary demonstrated the "Put Your Fingers On Your Forehead" technique at a group meeting, which I attended. I had never heard about this novel, quick, convenient method of reducing stress quickly and easily, but became quite intrigued.

Gary explained to us how many of his team, workers and clients of Hurricane Katrina had found remarkable relief from emotional pain while using this simple technique, along with many other clients from all walks of life. Gary asked each of us in attendance to rate an emotionally troubling problem on a scale from one to ten, with ten being the most stressful. Then, he used muscle testing to verify the accuracy (or inaccuracy) of our beliefs regarding the intensity of each issue. I had rated myself as a 7 or 8 before Gary used muscle testing on me, but he determined I was at a 9.5 level.

Next, with our eyes closed, Gary instructed each of us to hold the tips of our eight fingers on our foreheads while we tried our best to immerse ourselves in as much emotional intensity connected with the problem as we possibly could.

When ready and finished, he told us to open our eyes to see if there had been a notable reduction in the extent of our perceived level of discomfort, or, more accurately, in Gary's assessment after doing muscle testing on us. Gary was able to determine through muscle testing me that I had decreased from a 9.5 down to a 2 or 3 after holding my fingers on my forehead for perhaps about five minutes. Then, he told us to repeat the same exercise one more time, after which he would re-evaluate once more with muscle testing. At the second re-evaluation, I was surprised and delighted to discover I had gone down from a 2 or 3 after the first one to a zero! Likewise, every other member in attendance had also reduced down to zero.

Since Gary first demonstrated the "Put Your Fingers On Your Forehead" technique to us a few weeks earlier, I have been learning to use it whenever I feel hurt or wounded by someone, or am upset about anything. The associated reduction in my overall stress level has been quite noteworthy.

I have even been putting my fingers on my forehead for several minutes at night before I fall asleep and have noticed I usually sleep longer and feel more rested after awakening than before I started doing this.

I am now in much closer contact with my true feelings, and some feelings which I had been habitually denying previously, out of fear, are now quite comfortable and usually much easier to acknowledge.

I simply feel much more human now, since I know our feelings truly are the most basic, fundamental part of our human nature. I also know the best way to grow is simply to learn how to feel our true feelings. Using this simple technique suddenly makes this much easier! I will definitely continue to use this powerful aid in reducing my stress level, and I wholeheartedly recommend it to everyone else as well, without reservation.

Thank you so much, Gary, for sharing this with me!

- Bill Y. (Northern Virginia)

Being slammed in the head by a trunk lid likely saved Jennye's life; her story of recovery after emergency brain surgery.

In 2014, I experienced what I fondly call a 'Brain Opportunity', from a hematoma and a brain bleed that covered three of my four brain lobes. I had no symptoms and my body was in the best physical and mental shape of my lifetime. I was working temporarily in California. I had driven across the country from Virginia to get to the job location, and, a few weeks before had flown to Denver, Colorado on solo trips.

The brain opportunity came about three days before, as I was grabbing my gym bag from my trunk to go and work out for an hour, which is something I had been doing three times a week for years. On a clear sunny day, a wind came up out of nowhere and slammed the trunk lid of my car onto my head. I got a massive headache but went into the gym and worked out for an hour.

Three days later, on my way home from my job, I hit two different medians, puncturing two tires. A series of people who I believed were angels in human form helped me to get new tires and I drove myself home. Once home, I was already in a confused state of mind and the evidence of a neurological event escalated rapidly. I called a friend who drove me to a nearby hospital.

My brain surgeon believed I had been walking around with a brain bleed with no symptoms for some time. When the trunk lid slammed into my head, it literally saved my life by popping the blood vessel in my brain where the internal bleed with no symptoms was sitting. When the blood vessel burst and traveled from the left side of my head all the way across to the right side, it resulted in the major brain bleed requiring brain surgery. I had left-sided weakness in my legs and, for the first few hours, slurred speech. I could have just gone to sleep at any point during the previous weeks and not awakened while the slow bleed with no symptoms was bleeding inside my brain.

I have been a Vibrational Shamanic Practitioner since 1985 but still needed to reach out to others for support, in addition to my brain surgeon. Four days after surgery, I was discharged to my condo in California. I did receive home visits with a physical therapist who, amazingly, released me after only three of them, saying I had regained all my balance and no longer required services.

I still could not drive, read for very long or be on my computer while I continued healing because I would get slightly dizzy. Gary Niki was on the East Coast. After my surgery, I called Gary, who reminded me about using the "Put Your Fingers On Your Forehead" technique. I started putting my fingers on my forehead.

I had already had miraculous healing occurring from the inside out, and did not have to go to rehab! I believe the additional Putting My Fingers On My Forehead resulted in calming my anxiety and frustration as I patiently waited on my brain to absorb residual blood and recalibrate itself. I also discovered this natural, simple technique had increased my short term memory of names, ideas and other forgotten bits of information.

As a speech language pathologist of many years, I know the area of my forehead is the location of the frontal lobe, and the area affected by traumatic brain injuries. During my recovery from this brain opportunity, Gary's simple technique was helpful, both emotionally and energetically.

Since that time, by experiencing and observing the success of the "Put Your Fingers On Your Forehead" technique, I have suggested the use of this technique to many of my speech therapy and healing clients experiencing language processing, emotional related challenges and life altering events. Thank you, Gary, for sharing this modality with me and the world!

Jennye Z. Johnson,
Speech Language Pathologist,
Shamanic Priestess and owner of Heart Vibrations Healing (www.heartvibrationshealing.com)

LisaMarie's stories about the loss of beloved Cleo and Gigi

I have volunteered as a rescue worker, and loved and honored animals my entire life, accepting them to be equal family members in my home. My house is "home" to an eclectic assortment of exotic birds, reptiles and pit bulls, as well as adult children. Parrots have a special place in my heart, and Cleo, the Congo African Grey rascal, had a rather large piece. When I came into the room, he always said, "Hello, Sweetheart" with a lisp! He was a heavenly soulmate, complete with attitude and wings, and definitely felt that he owned us and ruled the roost!

Recalling one particular day when Gary came to visit and do energy work, Cleo, the curious little rascal that he was, decided to explore Gary's belongings, which were neatly piled on the couch in the other room, out of sight. Wow, what a surprise we found when Gary went to get something from his bag and saw Cleo chewing a large hole in his beloved Safari hat!

When Gary exclaimed, "Oh no, Cleo, what did you do?" Cleo was as surprised as we were and immediately jumped off the couch and ran across the room to hide under a table. He also chewed up Gary's computer power cord, little brat! Gary called to him, yet he remained under the table, trembling, yelling and squawking at us.

In the spirit of "put your fingers on your forehead", Gary did so and after a few minutes stated, "OK Cleo, I'm not mad at you anymore. I didn't watch my stuff. I forgive you." All of a sudden, as if on cue, Cleo poked his little white beady-eyed head out from his safety zone, and shouted to us, "SOOORRRYYYY!" The little bad boy bird was now in the clear.

Five years later, the unimaginable happened. Cleo left this life and flew over the rainbow bridge. I couldn't even breathe when my son and I found our beloved little rascal silent and lifeless. The terror and pain began to overwhelm me. I fell onto the floor and was paralyzed with grief. My son carried me to the couch and reminded me, "Fingers on your forehead, Ma." Through the trauma of my loss, I could feel my broken heart begin to calm. Thank heavens for Gary and his teaching with loving words of wisdom. Guardian angels come in all forms! Cleo has wings, Gary has fingers.

Several years later, my beloved family and flock guardian Gigi, the kindest Pit Bull ever known, died unexpectedly. It still remains difficult remembering that she's absent when I get into bed each night. My bed-hogging footwarmer is guarding elsewhere forever more. The emptiness was almost unbearable for my entire family. I am forever grateful to Gary for giving us this powerful healing tool "Put Your Fingers On Your Forehead". It has become a part of our everyday life. No matter how minimal or enormous the situation is, IT SIMPLY WORKS. Thank you, Gary.

- LisaMarie, Crazy Bird Lady

Father and Son War Vets on the Ocean a Generation apart in World War II (WWII) and Vietnam, and being there with my Big Bro at the end

It's very hard, if not impossible, to know what's really going on inside someone if they never tell you...

And you may never know how sharing something so simple, that you learned quickly, may help a beloved family member or members in getting through, and possibly clearing, traumatic events in their lives!

My dad and Big Bro served during war time on ships in different eras, during World War II (WWII) and Vietnam, under different circumstances. Neither of them would talk about it.

When I asked my dad what happened and what was it like being on a ship during WWII overseas, he would simply say, "I served my country and did my duty loyally. After being held for six months in the internment camp at the Fresno Assembly Center, I was released and went to serve on a ship, that's it."

At first, I'm sure I said, "OK," and let it drop, being just a little kid. However, as I grew up, from time to time I would ask him, "What did you do? Where were you? What happened? What was your service like on the ship?" He would almost always say the same thing.

"After six months, they let me out of the internment camp to be a Merchant Marine and I served on a ship." That's all he would tell me.

Later, as I grew up, and as I met more people who served during WWII, I would again ask my dad what happened when he was serving. He would always tell me some short version of the above story and then he would drop it and immediately change the subject. Again, that would be that and any inquiring would be over.

Who knows what he experienced during World War II after being interned for being half Japanese?

We didn't know a lot about our dad's side of the family and my Big Bro John did quite a bit of research and digging to find out about our heritage.

My Big Bro, John Carl Gregory Niki, was my half-brother. We were born 20 years apart. We didn't grow up together, however, for a very short time, he stayed with us in Las Vegas, Nevada right after he came back from serving in the Navy in Vietnam. I was most likely around three years old, so I didn't remember a lot about him at that time.

We were both the oldest son and brother in each of our families with the same dad, different moms. John's mom was Mexican and he was three-quarters Mexican and one-quarter Japanese. Both Big Bro John and his mom have died and graduated this life. My mom is Japanese and I am three-quarters Japanese and one-quarter Mexican. My mom is now 88 years old, still living in Arizona.

Even though My Big Bro John and I did not grow up together, we became good friends over the years and kept in touch, especially since we were the main ones who were actually interested in our Japanese heritage. However, just like our dad, when I asked him about his Navy Service in and during Vietnam, what it was like being on a ship and on the ground, being where he was assigned and what did he do, he said, "I served my country, did my job and I'm lucky to be back home. Let's just talk about something else, instead of the war."

In August of 2004, Big Bro John started calling me while I was working in Washington, D.C., saying, "Hey Bro, when are you coming to Paradise? I am in Hawaii on Oahu as the Supervisor of Maintenance Operations in Honolulu for the United States Post Office! Come to Paradise and see me. We can hang out at the beach, we can snorkel, eat musubis (fried Spam, rice, wrapped with a strip of seaweed) and have fun!"

Wow! My Big Bro moved from Long Beach, California to Oahu, Hawaii and there he was living in Paradise!

HA! Not me. In fact, far from it! I was in Washington, D.C. very busy working mega hours for the American Red Cross National Headquarters Disaster Services. I worked in the Disaster Operations Center on multiple large-scale disasters spread across several states, including the Four Florida Hurricanes. I had over 300 of my Safety and Security Team members on the ground working around the clock, so I thought he was crazy asking me when I was going to jump on a plane and fly from Washington, D.C. to hang out with him in paradise on Oahu, Hawaii! I actually told him that he was nuts and to "Pick up the Clue Phone" and realize that there was absolutely no way that I was going to be in Hawaii after these huge disasters!

Oh well, you never know what destiny and life have in mind for us in our lives!

In early January 2005, my boss Ed called me in to his office and said, "Hey, you are maxed out on vacation time. You have almost four weeks, plus use or lose time. You better schedule some time off before March or it is gone!"

I told him that I was way too busy with all of the disasters going on and building up my SAS Team, and there was no way for me to just take time off.

He told me, "Don't be stupid, it is part of your compensation and you have certainly earned it. I won't let you lose your extra time off, so go see your brother in Hawaii. Just book it and go before the end of March!"

I told him again that I had to keep in touch and be there for my growing team and I was way too busy to go!

He said, "You haven't been issued a work Cellular Phone, Alpha Pager, BlackBerry and a laptop with VPN access for nothing. You can still keep in touch with your teams from Hawaii."

I must have been in shock because I just stood there. He looked up and said, "Hey, what are you still standing here for? Get outta here! Go call your brother right now and book your flight. Seriously, get going!"

I left my boss's office, went back to mine and called my Big Bro to leave a message. Amazingly enough, he answered the phone! I asked him what he doing answering the phone at that hour of the morning (there was a six-hour time difference) and he said, "Hey, I'm on the midnight shift right now and I'm going snorkeling after your call. When are you coming to Paradise?!" I told him what happened with my boss and he said, "I'll forget about snorkeling this morning. Let's get on the computers and book your flights right now and we can go snorkeling together!"

Yep, you guessed it! I booked my flights and spent part of February and March on Oahu, Hawaii with my Big Bro! And, bonus! I was able to also travel to Kauai twice to meet Richard Gordon, the Founder of Quantum-Touch and Jennifer Noel Taylor, the CEO, in person. I was able to take advance trainings with them and Alain and Carol Harriot.

OK, back to spending time on Oahu with my Big Bro. We were on Hanauma Bay Beach enjoying the sun and hanging out, eating musubis, snorkeling and just having fun in the warm sun!

Then, we started talking about our dad and our grandfather George Nobuo Niki, whom we never got to meet. We reflected back on the pain of loss when our dad died suddenly in 1983 and how it was still negatively affecting my Big Bro 22 years later, along with many other life events that had affected him long before then. I'm sure some of it was from the war in Vietnam.

I said, "Hey, Big Bro, I know you are not into the same kinda Energy Work Stuff that I am into and I know you don't believe it either however, would you be willing to let me share something that has helped me clear out stuck and painful memories and events ever since I learned it in 1996?" He said, "Sure, why not?"

So, right there lounging on the beach, eating musubis, we started something on the spot that day that I never realized would eventually make a huge positive difference in his life without me even knowing it!

HA! Can you believe it? Right there sitting in the sun, on the sandy beach with the ocean sounds in the background, I demonstrated Muscle Testing with him. I showed him how his sad, negative memories and thoughts could make him weak and how he could quickly and powerfully clear them out by simply using the "Put Your Fingers On Your Forehead" technique.

I'm sure he didn't believe it at first because the Muscle Testing results that showed on his face were priceless! Both before and after the clearing!

My Big Bro was a sharp guy and a quick study, too, so he started asking me lots of questions about the "Put Your Fingers On Your Forehead" technique. He especially wanted to know if he had to tell me what was bothering him and making him weak.

I said to him with emphasis, "ABSOLUTELY NOT!" That certainly made a good impact on him and I could see in his face some sort of relief while his mind was racing away!

I told him, "I call it Secret Therapy. You never have to tell anyone what you are thinking about, sad about, mad about, upset about or what you are clearing out, ever. Period!"

He looked very relieved and asked me to Muscle Test him on something that has been bothering him for quite a while. I did and whatever it was that came up certainly weakened him and his arm went down. Then he said, "OK, take me through the process again. I want to see if it will work for me again on this one."

After he finished the "Put Your Fingers On Your Forehead" technique, he kinda smiled and said, "Yeah, I think it worked again because it was hard to remember how bad it was on the third time through. It felt a lot lighter, like it wasn't a big deal anymore and I feel better. OK, it must have worked, here push on my arm again." Yes, it stayed strong.

We started talking about our dad again and how much we still missed him after two decades. Big Bro said, "I still remember growing up and over the years dad used to sit and put his fingers on his forehead and rub them back and forth when he was bothered by something or someone. I'm sure he did it around you, too, if you think about it."

I'm sure Big Bro was right. Thinking back, our dad never talked about stuff that would bother him and would just say that he was in deep thought while sitting there on his short-wheeled shop stool putting his fingers on his forehead. That was it, end of that conversation.

After that day on the beach in Hanauma Bay, my Big Bro never, ever said anything else to me about Muscle Testing or the "Put Your Fingers On Your Forehead" technique.

That was February 2005, now fast forward to 2009 and my Big Bro traveled for a training class in Baltimore, Maryland. After his class, I drove to Baltimore to pick him up. He stayed with me to sight-see in Washington, D.C. for several days before flying back to Hawaii.

We went all over the place, including to the Air and Space Museum in Chantilly, Virginia. It was amazing and he knew a lot about some of the planes because, like our dad, he was also an A&P Licensed Mechanic and worked for National Airlines in California before working for the United States Postal Service.

Originally, my Big Bro said he wanted me to take him to visit the Vietnam Memorial. On the first full day of sightseeing, I asked if he wanted to go to the Memorial. He simply said, "No, not today, it's not a good day to go."

Every day, it was the same response to me asking him. Then, on his last full day in Washington, D.C., I asked him again if he wanted to visit the Vietnam Memorial. This time, he hesitated then said, "Yes, I have to go there." I drove him straight there and dropped him off. I told him I would park and come and find him in a bit. He didn't say anything and just nodded his head and walked toward the Memorial.

I left him alone for about 45 minutes. When I went to look for him he was sitting with his back against the Memorial wall holding some name rubbings in his hand and he had his fingers on his forehead!

I was totally shocked to see him sitting there with his fingers on his forehead! There were not very many people around the Memorial and when I walked up to him, he looked up at me and said, "Hey." I looked down at him and just said, "Hey" back, then I sat against the wall next to him.

We never said anything else to each other for 30-plus minutes, then he turned to me and said, "Thanks! Good Talk!" We both stood up and walked away, he never looked back at it and he never, ever talked about the Vietnam Memorial again.

Now fast forward to February 2014. Again, I start getting calls from my Big Bro asking, "Hey Bro when are you coming back to Paradise?!" By this time, I was gone from the American Red Cross on my way to retiring, so I told him again that I was not going to Hawaii.

Of course, he was insisting that I get on a plane and fly to Paradise! This time I was just about to graduate my Anger Management Participants on Tuesday night and I still had to do their paperwork and print their graduation certificates.

I finally told my Big Bro that I would fly out on Friday and stay a month with him. He kept insisting that I fly out early Wednesday instead of waiting till Friday. I told him no again and he kept insisting so I finally said "Yes" and was on a plane around 5:00 am flying to Honolulu Airport.

Thankfully, I was able to sleep on the plane and I arrived Wednesday late afternoon. My Big Bro had left me a message that he was having trouble driving after dark, so I was picked up by Kathy and Deirdre, my Ohana (Hawaiian Extended Family). They dropped me off at my Big Bro's house on Palolo, and I realized that something was not going well with his health.

The next morning, we talked and went for breakfast, and I still had no idea that my Big Bro was very ill and going to die just five days after I arrived! My Big Bro never told me he was on the liver transplant list for two years. His son Greg, my nephew, had only found out after a New Year's event when he had to take his dad to the Emergency Hospital and found out from his dad's doctor that he was in very bad shape and was in trouble!

Thursday and Friday night, we all went to the Hawaii State Baseball Games and after the Friday game Greg and I had to take his dad to the Emergency Hospital. The doctor pulled me and Greg outside of his dad's room and asked me if I really knew how sick my Big Bro was. I told her that my Big Bro was a stubborn guy that kept things to himself, like our dad, and he never told me anything about his health issues. I had no idea he was in such bad shape and in trouble. He only retired from the US Post Office three months prior and then he started calling me to come and visit again.

The doctor said, "It's good that you are both here because, right now, you really have no idea how serious he really is!"

Greg and I sat with him for many hours, then he woke up and told all of us that he was hungry and ready to go home. Of course, he argued with the doctor and she finally said "OK." He got dressed and was released. I took him home. He kept saying he was fine and wanted food.

The next day, we hung out at home. He was chatty and talked about life and many other things (except for his war time experiences). He never, ever told me what he saw, what happened, etc. He did finally tell me that he often used the "Put Your Fingers On Your Forehead" technique when stuff bothered or upset him. I was shocked!

He said, "I still like the fact that I don't have to tell anyone anything." Then, one more time he put his fingers on his forehead. When he was done, he said with a smile, "OK, it still works." That was the very last time we ever talked about "Put Your Fingers On Your Forehead".

Greg came over Saturday afternoon and brought lots of our favorite food for us from L&L Hawaiian Barbecue. We all hung out, dug into the awesome food and watched Big Bro John's favorite *Star Wars and Star Trek* movies till late into the night. We had a great time together!

The next day, my Big Bro asked me to go to Walmart and get him some ICY HOT cream for his legs, bottles of water and some other stuff for us. I asked him if he wanted to go with me to get out of the house and go for a ride. He said, "No, I don't want to do anything, you go!"

I left the house and called Greg. I told him what happened and asked if he could go by and check on him after a while. Greg said, "Sure, I'm going surfing and I'll go over when I'm done."

Greg called me about two hours later and said his dad was acting strangely. He fell down and didn't want to get up so Greg called 9-1-1. The Fire and Rescue Squad was there and they said John had to go to the Emergency Hospital, even if he didn't want to go, because he was in bad shape and almost incoherent. So, they loaded him into the ambulance and I met them at the hospital. The doctor met us and told us to sit tight while his condition was assessed. When the doctor finished all of the tests on him she came back and told us that he most likely would not regain consciousness and that he would probably not be leaving the hospital like he did early Saturday morning. The doctor was right and, thankfully, she was preparing Greg and me for his dad's passing. He never regained consciousness.

On Monday March 3, 2014 at 11:01 am on Oahu, Hawaii, in Paradise, my Big Bro, John Carl Gregory Niki completed his Earth Mission, graduated Earth School and crossed over peacefully in his sleep at the hospital. It was an honor for me to be there with him as he transitioned and to be with his son, my nephew Greg and a couple of family friends.

I am grateful to have had the "Put Your Fingers On Your Forehead" technique at that eventful moment in my life. I certainly used it that day!

NOTE: It is July 3, 2017 after starting and stopping the writing of this story many times since December 2015, I was finally able to complete it. Reading it out loud, again I was crying and using the "Put Your Fingers On Your Forehead" technique to help myself while writing this story to put in the book.

Thanks for Serving! Love YOU and miss YOU Big Bro!

Big Bro John at Vietnam Memorial in Washington, D.C. 2009

Big Bro John in Washington, D.C. reminding us:
"Freedom Costs Us Everything!"

Dad (World War II) and Big Bro John (Vietnam) Veterans

Last photo of us: me, Nephew Greg, Big Bro John & Dad

Review: Put Your Fingers On Your Forehead

Once again, the "Put Your Fingers On Your Forehead" technique is a simple, quick, completely natural, and non-invasive process or technique, and it is definitely not new.

Again, you are simply placing the first three or four fingers of each hand on your forehead – above your eyebrows – and keeping them there for a few minutes while you are experiencing the thoughts, feelings and emotions related to a current traumatic situation, or reliving a past event.

The alternative is to put your palms on your forehead in place of your fingers on your forehead. That has proven to work equally as well.

Remember, if you are experiencing a current trauma, keep your fingers on your forehead until you begin to feel better, and throughout the process until you are calm.

If you chose to clear the thoughts, feelings and emotions tied to a painful memory, briefly recall the event to conjure up or remember the thoughts, feelings and emotions associated with it, then "run through" the scenario – complete with thoughts, images, and emotions – while keeping your fingers on your forehead.

I recommend starting with three times. In most cases, people find that by the third time the emotions have subsided greatly, if not completely. If the feeling or emotions come up again, "Put Your Fingers On Your Forehead" and keep doing the same process over again until complete or until it feels lighter.

Experiment and Practice! Keep working on yourself and revise, test your technique or process to make it your own!

REMEMBER: This simple process may be used anytime and anywhere! Whether you are sitting together in a large public group at an event or when you or your loved ones are on your own by yourself in total privacy!

CHAPTER 7

The Energetic Action Process

While the "Put Your Fingers On Your Forehead" technique may clear us out very quickly and bring us back to a balanced or neutral state to be able to immediately function after a traumatic incident or situation, "The Energetic Action Process" provides us a simple technique and tools that empower and allow us to dig down, and get to the roots of our thoughts, feelings and emotions to clear them out.

Essentially, it works like this: Let's say you are experiencing an unpleasant situation at work. You find it hard to get along with your boss, who seems to focus on what went wrong and never acknowledges what you did right.

The first thing that you do, is to identify how this situation is making you feel.

In this example, let's say you feel these things: angry, unappreciated, abused, criticized, and nervous.

Then you also realize that you feel as if you can't do anything right.

It would be good for you to take notes and write those things down.

Now, we will take each of those feelings or experiences individually as a list and put them into the following series of statements.

The Energetic Action Process (The initial statement):

"I deeply love and accept myself even if I feel: _____" (insert one of your words, emotions or phrases in the blank).

In our example, our first word is "angry," so this statement would be:

"I deeply love and accept myself even if I feel angry."

Now, you are going to repeat that sentence three times while drumming or clapping on the side of your hand with the fingers or palm of your other hand. (Or you can just drum the side and palms of your hands against a firm surface, such as a tabletop, your knees or with each hand like clapping.)

Repeat the full statement three times while drumming or clapping the side of your hands.

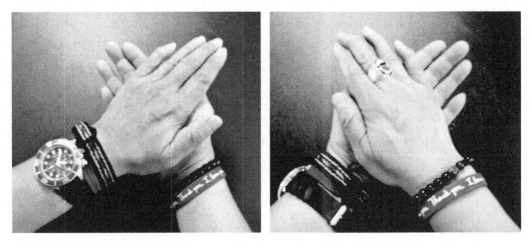

Hand Clapping: Regular style clapping with force and may be loud.

After completing the initial statement three times, you move on to the next statement with the same word of "Angry".

The Energetic Action Process: (The next statement)

"I deeply love and accept myself even if I have hidden or unknown issues with:
_____*" (insert your word or phrase here).*

Since we are working with anger first, you would say:

"I deeply love and accept myself even if I have hidden or unknown issues with anger."

Repeat the full statement three times while drumming or clapping the side of your hands.

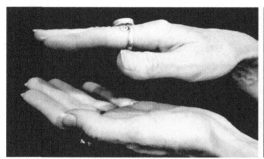 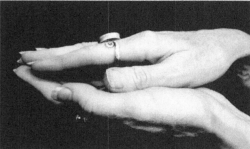

Hand Clapping: Regular style clapping and may be loud.

Hand Clapping: Very slight and light touch very quietly.

After completing the statement three times, on to the next statement for deeper issues with the same word of "Angry".

The Energetic Action Process: (The next statement especially for deeper issues)

Now for the deeper and more powerful issues we will repeat this process with a third and final statement:

> *"I deeply love and accept myself even if I refuse to do the things necessary to be free of _____ " (insert your word or phrase here).*

Again, since we are working with anger first, you would say:

> *"I deeply love and accept myself even if I refuse to do the things necessary to be free of feeling angry."*

Repeat the full statement three times while drumming or clapping the side of your hands.

Hand Clapping: slight and light touch with the right hand fingertips only, completely silent can be used anywhere with no sound.

Next, you would repeat this entire process with each of the words or phrases, using each of the three sets of statements, with each one individually that you used to describe the negative or uncomfortable experience you were having.

The Energetic Action Process: (The entire process)

Now you would repeat this entire process three times each with each of the words or phrases you used to describe the uncomfortable experience you were having:

- ✓ **"I deeply love and accept myself even if I am feeling:** _____" (unappreciated, abused, criticized, nervous, as if I can't do anything right)."
- ✓ **"I deeply love and accept myself even if I have hidden or unknown issues with feeling:** _____" (unappreciated, abused, criticized, nervous, as if I can't do anything right)."
- ✓ **"I deeply love and accept myself even if I refuse to do the things necessary to be free of feeling:** _____" (unappreciated, abused, criticized, nervous, as if I can't do anything right)."

This can also be used on traumas you have experienced many years ago. Time is no barrier to clearing and healing.

Hand Drumming: Sides of hands up and down on table, firm surface, knees.

For some people, naming, identifying or even discovering those feelings may be difficult. And that is perfectly OK!

That's where the "Art of Muscle Testing" can be very helpful. Muscle testing can help you identify or verify what you are or were feeling about a difficult experience. It can also be used after the clearing process to verify that the emotion did become less intense or if it was cleared for the current work session and may be re-tested at a later session.

Once again, before I take you through a technique, of course I have several important stories from individuals that have had positive, life changing experiences, and from me while sharing the techniques. Please keep reading on and moving forward!

Sometimes, I have shared "The Energetic Action Process" technique with an individual who had a powerfully life-changing experience and they took their time to write about their experience of how this technique helped them and how it may help someone else through their story. This example is particularly inspiring.

Devastated after the loss of my husband of 33 years into the transformation of my life and living my full potential

On March 2nd, 2008, I was devastated when my husband passed away! Chuck was an International Lawyer, Marine Corps Colonel, and a Diplomat for the United States Department of State. We were married for 33 years, had three wonderful children, one grandson, we traveled and lived around the world, and suddenly he was gone.

I was still in shock when I received a phone call at 10:00 am from Col. Ed Cercone, USMC, who asked me, "Could I talk to the Colonel?" Crying, I told him, "He just died at 3:00 am and I am unable talk to anyone right now." Ed said, "I have to come see you and talk to you." I said, "We are not receiving any guests right now," and hung up the phone. At about 1:00 pm, there was a knock at the door and Ed was standing there. He said, "I'm sorry that Chuck has died. I want you to know that the Colonel met all of the qualifications to be buried with full Military Honors at Arlington National Cemetery. I want to be able to make all of the funeral arrangements for you and your family."

What a relief that Col. Cercone called at the time he did, would not take no for an answer and showed up like an Angel to help our family with such a great loss! He worked with Chuck for many years and knew that Chuck was to be buried at Arlington National Cemetery with full Military Honors.

For five years, I was in so much pain everyday wondering how I can possibly go on and live without my husband. The pain was so unbearable! Just making the necessary phone calls and dealing with people was more than I could really handle. I did almost nothing during that time except to make it through to survive another day. I just couldn't deal with it. I was telling everyone I was fine but inside my heart was broken. I was even afraid to travel short distances without thinking that I would have to stay in a hotel because of the weather or driving in lots of heavy of traffic.

That's what happened for five years. Then, little by little, I started to take different classes here and there until I met Gary Niki in a training class in Washington, D.C. where he was assisting his teacher LeRoy Malouf, the founder and developer of the Energetic Well Being Process. I was practicing with a fellow student. Gary and LeRoy were walking around the groups, checking in on everyone, when Gary stopped us and asked me, "Is your husband alive or dead?" I was shocked when he asked me that! I said, "He's been dead for five years." Gary said, "That's what I thought you said in the class introductions however, you are talking and acting like he is still alive. Maybe you are stuck attempting to live his life and not your own!"

What a wakeup call! It was shocking to me to realize that yes, I was still wanting to live my past husband's life of being a lawyer and diplomat. I had actually thought about going to Law School. I had no idea that I was wanting to live Chuck's life, not my own!

Gary asked me if, after five years, I was ready to stop wanting to live my past husband's life and to start exploring and living my own life? I said, "Yes, I want to live my own life but, I don't know how or what it would look like and I don't know how to even start!"

At this point in my life, I knew that I could no longer go on the way I was and I was ready to do anything that would help me change! On the last day of LeRoy's class, I was partnered with a Shamanic Practitioner. At the lunch break, she said that I had a lot of stuck energies that were not helping me. She asked if I wanted her to gather them and have Gary get rid of them for me. I had no idea what that meant, however, I said, "Yes, let's get rid of them." She did her work and called Gary over. He asked if it was okay to touch me. I said, "Yes, do what you have to do to get rid of it!" I had never experienced any of this type of work before, I felt a knot in my stomach. Gary knelt down and felt around on my front side, found where the knot was and he made painful toning sounds. Then, with an explosive kind of HUAAAA sound, he pulled it out with his right hand and the knot was gone! I actually felt it tugging on the inside of me while he was making the sounds, then I felt the knot let go and be released. Then he toned in deeper sounds, like chanting monks, blew them in to me, felt my stomach area, stood up and said to me and the others with a smile, "OK, it's done, let's go eat lunch." And that was that. The Shamanic Practitioner and I stayed and talked about what happened and I could feel the big knot was gone. I felt much lighter. What a pleasant surprise!

About a week later, I made an appointment for Gary to come over and work with me. During the week, he called and talked to me about the plethora of modalities that he worked with and we decided to start the first session with him doing Shamanic Work on me with his Vocal Vibrational Toning. He said that if we had time and I was up to it, he would show me what his modality and books were about.

The next week, Gary showed up with a number of bags with drums, flutes, rattles, crystals, sage and a lot of other stuff, and began to set up as we talked. I told him that I was amazed that the knot in my stomach was gone and I still felt lighter. He smiled and said, "Great, now put on your safety belt, we are going to do some heavy work today!

After the Shamanic Work and Vocal Vibrational Toning, Gary started to share the "The Art of Gentle Emotional Transformation" techniques. He said that the real power for me would be to be able to work on myself in between our in-person sessions!

Gary muscle tested me (I actually went to Dr. Goodheart in Detroit, Michigan when I was a child and understood muscle testing very well). I tested strong to continuing on with this modality. Before we started, Gary stopped and said, "The work, techniques and process in this modality are SIMPLE however, it is not easy because you have to actually do the work on yourself, for yourself. It really is d.i.y. and you must take charge for yourself!" He put the emphasis on "simple" just like he wrote in this book. I said, "After experiencing your other work, I'm in for whatever it takes and I will work diligently on myself with these techniques!" He muscle-tested me to find out where to start and to identify the negative feelings and emotions that were holding me back and stopping my life from moving forward, then he wrote them all down.

Next, he said, "We are going to start with the "Put Your Fingers On Your Forehead" technique."

Gary said, "Now here comes the uneasy harder part. You must start thinking about your late husband and make those painful, hurt feelings come up as real and strong as you are able to right now. This is the hard part for you must feel it all!" He emphasized this and said, "Remember it's simple, not easy." He continued, "If something from your childhood comes up, that's good. It's okay to cry. Crying and feeling the pain, suffering and loss is important while you "Put Your Fingers On Your Forehead". Let everything come up and flow out of you and do not take your fingers off of your forehead until you are finished."

I put my fingers on my forehead and started to think about my late husband. The sadness and pain came up, and the tears poured out of me as I played the painful scenario over and over with as much of the original feelings that I had as possible, and I did it! After the initial hard crying, pain and hurting, I kept my fingers on my forehead and played the painful scenario and with every tear came the more release until I was finally calm again.

Gary handed me some tissues after I put my hands down and started to regain composure. Sitting there, I could hardly believe how calm and wonderful I felt!

Next, we cleared out all of the feelings and emotions that were identified with "The Energetic Action Process". Amazingly, by the time we were done, it was hard for me to recall all of the hurt, pain, sad thoughts and feelings that I felt for years!

He had me think about the original situation and I was completely strong to it. At the end of the session, I was strong to every one of the thoughts and feelings, instead of letting them weaken me anymore!

After we were done, all of the heavy sadness felt lifted from my heart and I felt a true awakening, freedom, love, happiness and just pure joy. WOW! Who would have thought that by just putting my fingers on my forehead and using "The Energetic Action Process" techniques, I could start to clear out the pain that I had felt for years and how life changing it could be!

That first session was a powerhouse. I was so ready for it and to be on my path of freedom to live my own life! Over our multiple sessions, besides his own techniques, Gary used other multiple modalities that he worked on me, including Dr. Bradley Nelson's Emotion Code and Body Code, Richard Gordon's Quantum-Touch, Steven Thayer's Integrated Energy Therapy, LeRoy Malouf's Energetic Well Being Process and many others.

Yes, the other work was powerful and life changing for me however, what I love about d.i.y. zen and The Art of Gentle Emotional Transformation is that, with Gary's "Put Your Fingers On Your Forehead" and "The Energetic Action Process" techniques and the tools in this book and workbook, I am able to do them in private for myself with myself and best of all I don't have to tell anyone about what's going on and bothering me to clear them out and get relief!

That was many years ago, fast forward to today and I still use some of Gary's techniques and I have certainly come a long way on my path. I am a Reverend, Angel Messenger and I have my own Radio Show called Everyday Angels. I have worked at healing centers and multiple events throughout Virginia, Maryland and Washington, D.C. providing Angel Messages and teaching classes on a number of subjects. I lost over 30 pounds in weight, Gary calls it "Right Sizing". I still study, take classes and, as Gary would say, "Every day be as happy, healthy, whole and complete as you possibly can be." Looking back, amazingly, the Angels take care of us when we need them the most. Today, I am grateful for all of the positive transformation that I've experienced in my life and I appreciate where I am now.

- Rev. Deborah Oleszycki (Northern Virginia)
Angel Messenger, Host of the Everyday Angels Radio Show

This story is from a Court Ordered Anger Management Participant, who was on probation at the time of his class, sharing his experience using "The Energetic Action Process" with "The Art of Muscle Testing".

Releasing anger while gaining the freedom to feel loved by father and others, then sharing love with the world

Following an anger management class in which I had participated, the instructor, Gary Niki, showed me a technique of drumming or clapping the fingers of the right hand off the leading edge of the left hand while uttering a mantra, something like, "I will allow myself to love myself even though I have made numerous mistakes and hurt many people." I tried it and found it instantly calming. Later, Gary showed me how I could use this same technique to address any number of deep-seated issues that I had been grappling with for years.

I grew up in a privileged family in Richmond, Virginia. I had every advantage and everything one could want, except love. My father, a successful businessman and civic leader, was intelligent and highly educated. He could easily have been a university professor. My mother, active in civic affairs and the arts, was widely admired and loved in the community.

I grew up thinking that I had had the ideal childhood, with parents who complemented each other. But, in fact, I was psychologically numb, as a psychologist pointed out when my world collapsed.

In 2003, my 22-year marriage came to an end, the result of many inappropriate behaviors on my part. Then began a long voyage of exploration in the psychological realm, including psychological testing — which showed I lacked empathy, was paranoid, and was otherwise alienated. I was astounded by this. Since then, I have worked with a half-dozen psychiatrists, psychologists, and counselors, taken several antidepressant medicines, and read extensively about meditation and other topics.

Much of this was useful, such as when one counselor said he thought I was narcissistic as a result of being starved for love. I was not given unconditional love but rather was told, in effect, that my worth was measured in performance.

Why the counselor didn't share this insight two years earlier, when we began our process, I will never know. Some care providers seem to feel that patients should discern these truths for themselves. I think this is very wrong. I was in a deep hole, trying in vain to get out.

Another counselor said I had been psychologically numb all my life. She taught me how to hug my girlfriend and express love physically in other ways.

Does this sound strange to you? It does to me now. But you have to understand that my father and mother never hugged or kissed me. They never put their arms around me or touched me in any other way, nor did they ever say they loved me. A sister, who has a virtual photographic memory, pointed out that neither of our parents spent any time with us. I mentioned that I had a particularly fond memory of my mother tucking me into bed at night.

"Yeah, but that was the only five minutes she spent with you during the day," she said. Incredibly, I did not even realize that there was a problem until my marriage ended.

Since then, try as I might and despite a lot of help and self-reflection, I have still felt hollow inside and unable to connect with others, except in rare flashes — until I met Gary and learned to use several techniques he has found worked for him on his own issues, and for many other people as well.

Along with "The Energetic Action Process", Gary uses the principles of muscle testing, which were discovered in the 1960s and are used in many disciplines to aid in energetic testing for strong or weak. He credits many of the pioneers. However, I believe he has a uniquely practical application of the awesome power that has been demonstrated by many researchers in the past 50 years.

He combines the muscle/energetic testing and "The Energetic Action Process" to help people clear out the negative thoughts that have affected them.

Here is how it worked with me.

I told Gary that I was not loved by my father. He explored the parameters of this feeling using my stretched-out arm and muscle testing (see The Muscle Testing Chapter). We determined that the overarching feeling of loveless-ness actually consisted of a number of components. After having identified these we began to clear them out.

To begin this process, Gary had me drum the fingers of my right hand against the side of my left hand. As I drummed or clapped my fingers against the side of my left hand, I said a mantra that went something like this: "I deeply love and accept myself even though I did not feel loved by my father."

We repeated it three times and did the same drumming/mantra process with each set of new statements based on the negative feelings of not being loved that we had identified connected to my relationship with my father.

After we did this, Gary did another test using the muscle/energy testing.

The results were staggering. He asked me if I believed my father loved me. Incredibly, my arm stayed elevated. My father had loved me. He just couldn't show it. This breakthrough was doubly powerful because, as Gary explained it, one's relationship with one's father informs one's relationship with God. So, the voice in my head was now saying, "My father loved me and God loves me."

I am now able to feel genuine love, affection and closeness for my father and others that I have never been able to feel before!

Edmund Rennolds (Northern Virginia)
Retired Journalist

Overcoming the Fear of Public Speaking

This was one of the first times I actually stepped up in public to share all of the *diy zen and The Art of Gentle Emotional Transformation* modality, with the "Put Your Fingers On Your Forehead", "The Energetic Action Process" and the power of the "Art of Muscle Testing" techniques, at an Instructor Training Certification class held by the Federal Emergency Management Agency (FEMA).

During the late 1990s, I was an adjunct faculty member of the Arizona Division of Emergency Management (ADEM), a national disaster instructor-trainer and a national diversity instructor for the American Red Cross. I found myself in the FEMA instructor school with about 20 other students from a wide variety of backgrounds, meaning they ranged from highly accomplished public speakers and trainers to newer, inexperienced individuals seeking to advance themselves and obtain their first instructor certification.

In our class there was a woman, we will call her Sally (not her real name), who was obviously on the newer end of public speaking and training. She appeared nervous and scared, exhibiting most of the classic fears that all of us have experienced in our speaking and training careers.

On one of the breaks, I talked to Sally and she said that she was worried she might not be able to make it through the class successfully. She explained that her job depended on her being able to speak effectively to groups since she was an executive assistant to the head of an emergency management agency.

I listened to her story, then asked her if she was willing to go through a couple of simple processes that could potentially relieve and clear out her fears of speaking in public to groups of people. She said, "Right now I am willing to try anything that may work."

I briefly explained about muscle testing, then we identified her primary emotions and I wrote them down on a card to clear out with "The Energetic Action Process". Then, I explained about the "Put Your Fingers On Your Forehead" technique and using it while recalling, imagining and experiencing all of the negative thoughts, feelings and emotions in as real a way as possible. (For example, I can't remember what to say; I feel naked in front of them; I'm not good enough to speak to them; I may wet my pants; I feel like throwing up; They will laugh at me, etc.)

Sally smiled and asked, "How did you come up with all of those so quickly?"

I just smiled and said, "It takes one to know one!"

She started laughing and said, "OK, I got it!"

I reminded her that the more she could bring up the original feelings and emotions the faster and more powerfully it clears. Sally nodded, bravely put her fingers on her forehead and she started shaking and crying silently for a few minutes as she played the situation and emotions all the way through three times.

After a couple of minutes, she stopped, smiled, and said, "It feels lighter, and by the end of the third time, it was hard to recall all of the original scary thoughts and feelings."

I re-muscle tested her and she tested strong for being free of the original situation that had make her weak.

Then, we quickly did "The Energetic Action Process" to clear out the list of Stuff that weakened her, and re-muscle tested her. She tested strong for being free of the listed negative emotions and feelings. She was complete and good to go in less than 20 minutes and she was smiling!

Our break was over and we went back to class. The instructor-trainers greeted us with the next assignment of public speaking, and one of them asked who would volunteer to go first.

To all of our surprise, Sally raised her hand and jumped up, saying, "I will." I think our instructor-trainers were shocked, too. One of them said, "That's okay, you don't have to go first." However, Sally insisted that she wanted to go first, even though she was still nervous.

To all of our amazement, she did a 180-degree turn in front of our eyes!

Actually, it was fun for me to watch our instructor-trainers' faces. They looked stunned and kept looking back and forth at each other, almost in disbelief at the change in Sally. After she finished, she got a standing ovation.

She grinned from ear to ear and was kinda bouncing as she went to sit down. One of the instructor-trainers stopped her and said, "Oh, no, it's feedback time before you sit down. Wow! What happened to you? How did you change so quickly from this morning? Did you take some medicine? Or were you just sandbagging us and faking being so scared?" I was sinking down in my seat, attempting to hide, then Sally pointed to me in the back and said, "No way, that was real and Gary cleared me out!"

At that, I waved my hand and said something like, "No, no, it was all her. She did a great job!"

Naturally, the instructor-trainers wouldn't let it go that easily. One of them said, "Okay, what did you do to her? There's no way that she could do a 180 like that without meds or unless it was a good act and she was just sandbagging us!"

I explained that it was a simple modality that I was working with and developing, along with a couple of techniques that I've been using that work for clearing things out. "It's no big deal," I said, attempting to wave it off.

Then the first instructor-trainer said, "No way Mister, you don't get off that easy! She is like a different person. So you have to tell us about it and explain to us what you did to her and how you did it!"

At that point I realized that they would not let it go so, I said, "Okay, I'm willing to show you. However, I will only do it if everyone participates!"

To my surprise, everyone agreed.

It was then I realized that this was my opportunity! It was time to step up and deliver now that it was my dog and pony show for a few minutes! I asked one of our instructor-trainers (Mary) to step forward as a volunteer for the Muscle Testing demonstration.

Everyone was standing in a large circle, and I asked Mary to hold out one of her arms and state her real name. Her arm stayed strong. I then asked her to state that her name was Betty. Her arm went weak and she looked at me with surprise.

"Hey, we are just getting started," I told her. Then I asked her to say, "I am female." When she did, her arm was strong. Then, when I had her say, "I am male," her arm went weak. I next asked her to think of a negative thought, then muscle tested her and her arm was weak. Then I asked her to think of a positive thought and her arm became strong again.

Next, I asked her to step out of the room and close the door. When she was outside, I said to the others left in the room, "When I hold up two fingers behind her, only think negative thoughts about her, using her name, such as, Mary, you are stupid, ugly, I hate you. However, show no expression on your face. Then, when I hold up one finger, only think positive thoughts about her, again using her name, such as Mary, you are wonderful, a beautiful spirit, I love you, GOD bless you."

Now that we were all ready for the experiment, I called Mary back into the room and we proceeded with the muscle testing. When I held up two fingers, I pushed on her arm and it was so weak that it fell hard and fast. Again, she gave me the surprised look. Then I held up one finger behind her and her arm was rock solid. And yep, you guessed it, I got another surprised look. I said to everyone, "Let's do it one more time." I held up one finger and Mary's arm tested strong. I held up two fingers and she tested weak.

After the second time, one of my classmates laughed. I stopped and said, "Hold out your arm." I tested them and they went weak. Then some others laughed and I called them forward. They tested weak as well. They were all stunned and very surprised. Once again, I held up one finger and tested Mary. She was again rock solid. I called the three others forward and, to their amazement, they were all strong, too. I just smiled as I looked at their stunned faces and said, "Don't worry, you are not the only ones and I'm going to go around the circle and get to everyone so they feel it and understand it, too."

As I stepped back into the circle, I said, "How many of you are surprised at how powerful your thoughts are?" Of course, every hand shot up.

Then I asked, "Who was surprised that your negative thoughts not only weakened our test subject however, also weakened you, too?" Again, every hand shot up.

Next, I asked our instructor-trainer Mary what she had felt or noticed. She said that, to her surprise, when I gave the signal for negative thoughts, she had felt her energy was sapped out of her or she felt weakened before I pushed on her arm. She also said she felt more power and strength with the positive thoughts even before I pushed on her arm, and she knew it would stay strong. The three classmates I called out and tested were similarly surprised with the results on themselves.

Once the muscle testing was established and confirmed, I asked everyone to think of a negative situation related to public speaking or training. I then muscle tested everyone and they were all weak.

Next, I told them about putting their fingers on their foreheads and demonstrated on myself while checking everyone's finger positions. I then told them to play all of the negative thoughts that came to mind about their original situation through three times and feel their feelings/emotions as if they were watching the experience as a movie or reliving the situation over again, all while keeping their fingers on their foreheads. I then told them to stop after three times through, put their hands down, and wait for everyone else to complete the process.

Once the last person had put their hands down, I started muscle testing again. I asked them to think about their original situation, and to each person's surprise, their arm stayed strong.

When I asked for feedback and comments, everyone who responded said they were amazed at how something so simple could have that much of an impact on them in a positive manner and that the fact that they were strong when thinking about their situation was amazing.

A number of them reported that by the third time through it was getting hard to even feel the intensity of the emotions.

As a last exercise, I muscle tested each person to determine whether they were strong or weak to these two statements: "I am happy" and "I am miserable". Naturally, before the clearing process everyone was weak for happy and strong for miserable! Of course, like it did to me in 1996 with Virginia Dunstone, it blew their minds!

I walked the whole team through "The Energetic Action Process" with mantra – statement and hand drumming – clapping (three times) then re-muscle tested everyone, and they were all strong for happy and weak for miserable.

Everyone said they felt much stronger since clearing out the negative situation, and most of them were excited to see how it would impact their presentation or speaking ability.

Thanks to the *diy zen and The Art of Gentle Emotional Transformation* modality and techniques, I must say that by the end of our class every one of us did a stellar job on our final presentations, accomplishing our goal with ease. We all successfully passed and became certified instructors for the Federal Emergency Management Agency and our respective State and/or County Emergency Management Agencies.

A huge shift where ordinarily anger would pour out

'Life Transforming' are the best words I can use to describe what Gary has put together.

When I first started reading his book manuscript I thought, Oh, I know this stuff. Just a rehash of what I have learned in the past. The deeper into the book I read, the more amazed I was at the testimonies of the many who were positively changed by these methods. Then came the later chapters. As I started to apply it to my own life, I was not sure I was ready to go there, but I thought oh, well, here goes.

How astounding was the transformative effect of just one simple test of the techniques as I sat under an old poplar tree waiting for my car to be serviced! On the way home, I got to experience the shift when a driver swerved into my lane just feet from my front bumper. I wanted to beep my horn to advise them of my presence but didn't want it to be an irritant to the driver.

That is a huge shift for me where ordinarily anger would pour out generously!

I have been amazed how much our thoughts don't just impact us but everyone around us. How could I have forgotten the fundamental elements of life as stated so clearly by a fellow in the Bible a couple of thousand years ago? 'Whatever you do to anyone, you do to me.' This will be my mantra as I realize the 'me' referenced is indeed me personally as I also am deeply impacted by any stream of thoughts coming out of my mind. This is such an incredible reminder of our oneness and how each minor thought has ripples through all of life, way beyond the perceived privacy of our minds.

The ripples of what Gary taught me through his book manuscript have already had profound effects on what I think, and how I respond to life situations. I deeply thank Gary for following his heart in documenting, teaching, sharing and publishing this material into such an easy to read and ample set of simple methods. It brings major change into any aspect of anyone's life using a very simple set of methods.

Jim Gerlach (North Carolina)

Review: The Energetic Action Process: Entire process

Now, repeat this entire process three times each with each of the words or phrases you used to describe the uncomfortable experience you were having:

- *"I deeply love and accept myself even if I am feeling: _____ (unappreciated, abused, criticized, nervous, as if I can't do anything right)."*
- *"I deeply love and accept myself even if I have hidden or unknown issues with feeling:_____ (unappreciated, abused, criticized, nervous, as if I can't do anything right)."*
- *"I deeply love and accept myself even if I refuse to do the things necessary to be free of feeling: _____ (unappreciated, abused, criticized, nervous, as if I can't do anything right)."*

Remember, this can also be used on traumas you have experienced many years ago. Time is no barrier to healing. If you can identify the feelings your experience created, it is possible for you to clear them with this simple technique.

For some people, identifying or naming those feelings may be difficult. That's where the "Art of Muscle Testing" can be very helpful.

Muscle testing can help you identify or verify what you are or were feeling about a difficult experience. It can also be used after the clearing process to verify that the emotion did become less intense, or if it did get cleared.

CHAPTER 8

The Art of Muscle Testing

Discovering our inner truth through muscle testing

O ver the years, I have found that, due to the seriousness and depth of the incidents, events, and traumas that we have lived through, we have to do some archeological and detective work to get down to the "real" or "core" emotions or feelings that are affecting us.

While the "Put Your Fingers On Your Forehead" and "The Energetic Action Process" techniques are very simple, there may be other work to do to discover the hidden or underlying thoughts, feelings and emotions that are affecting you on a much deeper, energetic level.

"The Art of Muscle Testing" is one way you can do this. Best of all, this very real work may be accomplished by yourself or with a partner!

Partner Muscle Testing: Arm Strong

Partner Muscle Testing: Arm Weak

This work may be done in a number of ways:

✓ You working by yourself
✓ You working with a trusted friend
✓ You working with a coach, counselor, therapist, spiritual leader, colleague, etc.

There are a number of ways to check-in with ourselves and get direct information. However, for me and many others, the quickest and simplest way to identify our feelings, thoughts, and emotions is with muscle testing.

Using this simple yet powerful technique, we can find out for ourselves how a feeling, thought, or emotion either strengthens us or weakens us.

Muscle testing is based on a couple of concepts:

1. **We are energy**. At our most basic level, we are energy and so is everything else. Our energy responds to the energy or vibration of other things, whether foods, medications, animals, or other people. Muscle testing can reveal whether we are strengthened or weakened by these other energies. The energy of a medication we require, for instance, may strengthen our own vibration. On the other hand, the energy of a food we are allergic to may weaken our vibration. The body reveals these reactions through the strength or weakness of the muscles.

2. **We are electrical**. Our bodies have electrical systems. Just as the electrical system in a building can become overloaded, so can our body's. When that happens, the flow of energy can be impeded or cut off. The lack of a clear path for the energy to flow across causes weakness in the body's muscles that can be detected by muscle testing.

Muscle testing is a simple way to get yes/no or strong/weak responses from the body. The "questions" may be statements, substances, thoughts, or feelings. Although many healthcare practitioners use muscle/energetic testing to determine which foods or supplements are most beneficial to their clients, in this book we are using it to simply test how we are either strong or weak to words, thoughts, feelings, emotions and statements.

Why muscle test?

At this point you may be wondering to yourself, Why is muscle testing for myself important? Or you may be thinking, Wow! I get it, what a novel concept. That's what many people have said to me after hearing me say that we can find or identify our own results by asking ourselves or our subconscious mind, then muscle testing for our own truth and answers. I believe muscle testing is very important because it provides us with a simple way to find our truth from deep inside ourselves. We can identify from our very core the feeling, thought, or emotion that makes us either strong or weak, and I consider this a powerful technology and ally immediately available to us 24 hours a day, seven days a week to quickly identify our truth.

Here's why I believe learning to muscle test for ourselves is powerful for us. In step three of the workbook portion of this book, I ask you to question everything, especially everything in this book. In step five, I recommend you become your own detective to personally investigate yourself to identify any issues, thoughts, feelings, and emotions that may affect you in a negative or weakening manner from the inside out.

With these two simple steps we can take back our own power and authority! That's right, your power and authority. Please don't take my word or opinion for your truth (or any other person's, for that matter). Search yourself to find, identify, discover, and determine your own truth. That is where the real power is!

I know you just read about muscle testing in the stories of Chapter Seven, however, I'll share one more with you to give you an idea of the power of simply using "The Art of Muscle Testing" with the "Put Your Fingers On Your Forehead" and "The Energetic Action Process" techniques, along with the "Awful-Distressing-Stuff List" in the back of this book to identify the thoughts, feelings, emotions and statements that negatively affect you and zap your energy and power! And the "Positivity & Empowerment List" is designed to make sure that you are strong to these positives that uplift and empower you!

OK, one more story before we practice Muscle Testing!

For me, this is one of the most profound and inspiring stories about the power of "The Art of Muscle Testing". I'm happy to share this testimonial with you here.

A New Life View - an Inspiring Testimonial story about Muscle Testing from an Anger Management Participant

The moment that changed my life occurred quite by accident. It happened after a session in court-mandated anger management class.

A group of us recovering rage-aholics had stayed after class to talk with the instructor, Gary Niki. During the anger management class, Gary had demonstrated a technique of putting his fingers on his forehead to drain negative emotions. It was a technique that he has taught to hundreds of people going back to his days in public safety and emergency management.

In conversations after the class, he showed some of us a technique of hand drumming or clapping fingers from the right hand off the leading edge of his left hand while uttering a mantra, something like, "I will allow myself to love myself even though I have made numerous mistakes and hurt many people." I tried it and found it instantly calming. But Gary had something much more powerful to show us, which is how we humans affect others with our thoughts, either negatively or positively. It is this that radically changed my life, and in the twinkling of an eye.

Gary asked for a volunteer. It was James, a member of the class. He asked him to stand in the center of the room. James is an executive of a national real estate company, with responsibility for an enormous property portfolio. He has scrabbled his way up from an inner-city background and gives back by coaching athletic teams of kids from similar circumstances. He is a powerful, big man with enormous presence.

Gary instructed James to hold his arm out to his side, parallel with the ground, and hold strong. Gary then began pushing down on it. James's arm remained outstretched and strong. Then Gary asked James to say, "My name is Bob." Remarkably, after doing so, James lost the strength in his arm, despite his best effort to hold it up as Gary pushed downward on it. But when, at Gary's instruction, he said, "My name is James," he was restored to his original Samson-like strength. The true statement strengthened James. The false one — the lie — weakened him. For the next 30 minutes or so, the half-dozen people in the room, including myself, repeated the experiment, always with the same result.

While this was dramatic enough, Gary then demonstrated that our thoughts affect not only ourselves but also others. To demonstrate this, Gary set up a little experiment. He had

James leave the room. James returned to the room and Gary asked him to hold out his arm. Gary instructed him to say his name was James, then Bob to show that the muscle testing was still real and working. Gary then secretly signaled for us to communicate negative thoughts about James. When we did so, James could not hold up his arm even though he was trying to keep his arm strong. We had destroyed his physical strength with our thoughts. The situation was corrected when we thought positively about James. We repeated the demonstration again and again and the results were always the same.

Even more fascinating, Gary showed us that when we thought negatively about someone else, we also weakened ourselves! Thinking positive thoughts about someone else strengthened both the other person and ourselves. So it was either a win-win situation or a lose-lose one. Now it was up to us to choose which we would opt for. I would not have believed this if I had not seen it and felt it, but having seen it and felt it for myself, I was profoundly affected.

I realized in that moment that if we affect others (and ourselves) positively or negatively with our thoughts, it is imperative that we psychologically lift up everyone we meet, without exception — man or woman, black or white, rich or poor, young or old, friend or even foe.

I had grown up in a family where love and affection were not freely expressed. I found out late in life that this had affected me emotionally, leaving me somewhat stunted. Despite a lot of therapeutic help and self-reflection, I had still felt hollow inside and unable to connect with others, except in rare flashes. Until now, when Gary's demonstration changed my social relationships — instantly.

Once I realized the impact I could have on others, I began practicing projecting positive thoughts. Since then, I have felt a kind of peace I have never experienced [before]. Rather than seeing other humans as an impediment or a nuisance, which was all too often my perspective in the past, I now see each person as an opportunity to express and receive love, or at least mutual warmth. There are now six billion opportunities in the world for me.

I am convinced this is possible for others, too. If you learn the habit of lifting up others you will find that you are much more sensitive and aware to their feelings and their circumstances. You can learn empathy, something that was lacking in my life. And anyone who wants to embark on this transformative change can do so by simply saying to themselves that they are required by a sense of decency, if nothing else, to lift up others, in the knowledge that their thoughts have a negative or positive effect on others — and themselves. You can do it right now, without any training or preparation.

I believe if you try to do this it will transform your life in many ways. First, you will see immediate evidence of your lifting up others in their smiles and their responses, some of which will be extraordinary. You will feel calmness instead of irritation or frustration in many daily encounters, where you had previously experienced stress. You will feel much better about yourself. In fact, I think Gary's teaching allows many of us who have not been able to love ourselves appropriately (like me) to finally do so. He has turned the adage of learning to love yourself before loving others on its head. In so doing, he has given humanity a way of becoming one large loving family.

Think about it. Even if you don't love yourself, nothing prevents you from showing love to others right now, even if you feel you are not worthy of receiving their love. By showing love to others you also build yourself up, and in doing so you learn how to love yourself. How perfect.

Edmund Rennolds (Northern Virginia)
Retired Journalist

Tips for muscle testing:

1. As the tester, have confidence along with a positive attitude. Think, I can successfully and accurately muscle test!

    NOTE: Thinking, I can't do this, can and will skew the results. And you will be right.

2. As the tester, remain neutral and nonjudgmental about the answers the testee's body provides.

3. As the tester, apply a consistent amount of pressure when testing the recipient's arm.

4. If the recipient's responses (strong/weak) are difficult to distinguish from one another, ask if he or she has had any water or is thirsty.

    NOTE: If the person is dehydrated, the results will be inconclusive and inaccurate.

    Ask the recipient to drink water and test again.

5. Muscle testing cannot predict the future. Only present-tense statements can be tested. (This is not fortune telling or divining the future!)

6. During testing, it is best not to make direct eye contact. This helps to avoid a situation in which the tester and testee's energies become confused and muddy the responses.
7. Always ask for permission prior to touching or testing any individual.
8. Always test each individual to get a sense of their strong and weak responses. Each person's strength is different.
9. Remember, tell the person being tested, "This is not a strength contest! It is only to determine strong/weak muscle test response."

Working with a Partner to Muscle Test

Ready to get started learning to muscle test? Great! One of the simplest ways to practice and learn how to do muscle testing is to begin by working with a partner.

First, choose who will be the tester and who will be the testee. Be very clear about your role.

The tester must remain totally neutral, focus entirely on the testee and must not mentally project his or her own answers to the questions posed.

Most of the time, it is best not to make direct eye contact. This helps to avoid a situation in which the tester and testee's energies become confused and muddy the responses.

One position many people like to use when doing partner muscle testing is to stand face to face. In this position, the tester may place a hand on one of the testee's shoulders and the other on his/her outstretched arm (place fingers above the wrist bone bump on forearm toward the elbow for best results), which will be used for the testing.

Partner Muscle Testing: Arm Strong

Muscle Testing: Arm Weak

NOTE: If the testee has any shoulder/arm issues, do not use this method. Another would be to have the testee sit in a chair, raise one knee, and hold it up as the tester is pressing lightly on the thigh, just above the knee.

Another position would be for the tester to stand beside the testee, on the side of the outstretched arm. See which you prefer and begin.

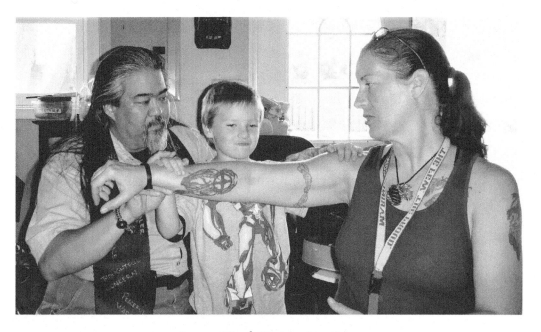

Partner Muscle Testing: Arm Strong

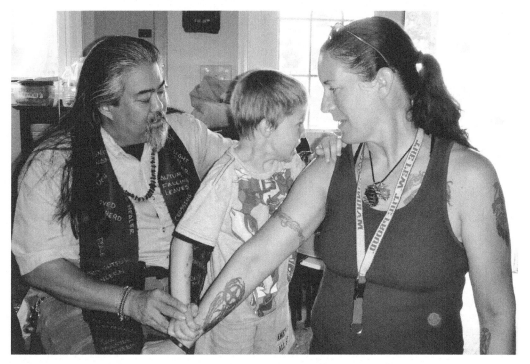

Muscle Testing: Arm Weak

RECIPIENT (TESTEE): Raise one arm to shoulder height straight out in front of your body or to the side. The palm faces down. (Note: Some practitioners find that the arm tires more easily when held out to the side. Experiment with each position and select the one you prefer.) Hold the arm firm when the tester says, "resist." Do not push or lift the arm up. Simply hold it outstretched to the best of your ability.

TESTER: Place two fingers on the testee's outstretched arm, above the wrist (place fingers above the wrist bone bump on forearm toward the elbow for best results). Say, "resist" and push down on the testee's arm with your fingers. Do this several times to get a sense of the strength of this particular testee's arm. This is the "yes" or "strong" response. Do this each time you test a person.

TESTER: ALWAYS, BEFORE TESTING, ask, "Do I/We have permission to muscle test (testee's name) right now?" then say, "Resist." Press gently on the arm.

> If the arm weakens or drops, the answer is no, you must stop!
> - Even if the person says it is alright to continue, do not do so!
> - This could constitute a violation of the person's internal privacy.
> - The body's wisdom must be respected. This is not an appropriate time to muscle test this individual. You may recheck at a later time.

If the arm remains strong, it is OK to proceed.

TESTER: Ask the testee to say, "My name is (their name)." After they have made this statement, instruct them to resist, then press lightly on the testee's outstretched arm. It will remain strong since the statement they have made is true.

RECIPIENT: "My name is (state your name)." Resist.

TESTER: Ask the testee to say, "My name is (a name other than their own)." After they have made this statement, instruct them to resist, then press lightly on the testee's outstretched arm. The arm will become weaker since the statement they have made is false.

RECIPIENT: "My name is (name other than your own)." Resist.

TESTER: Both you and the testee will now have a sense of what strong and weak responses feel like.

You are ready to begin muscle testing for words, thoughts, feelings, statements or emotional states, such as anger, sadness, anxiety, or shame.

TESTER: Say, "Repeat after me. 'I am angry.'"

RECIPIENT: "I am angry."

TESTER: Say, "Resist." Test the arm. If the arm is strong, the statement is considered true. If weak, false. Record the response.

TESTER: Say, "Repeat after me. 'I feel fear.'"

RECIPIENT: "I feel fear."

TESTER: Say, "Resist." Test the arm. Record the response.

TESTER: Say, "Repeat after me. 'I am sad.'"

RECIPIENT: "I am sad."

TESTER: Say, "Resist." Test the arm. Record the response.

TESTER: Say, "Repeat after me. 'I am anxious.'"

RECIPIENT: "I am anxious."

TESTER: Say, "Resist." Test the arm. Record the response.

TESTER: Say, "Repeat after me. 'I feel shame.'"

RECIPIENT: "I feel shame."

TESTER: Say, "Resist." Test the arm. Record the response.

Partner Muscle Testing: Arm Strong

Muscle Testing: Arm Weak

HYBRID: Both (recipient and testee) or either (tester and testee being the same person): Working with a Partner to Muscle Test or Muscle Testing Yourself

Tripod Index Finger and Lobbi Claw Fingers:
These are two of my personal favorites. They are both very simple to use. One kinda reminds me of shooting pool and the other is like my Lobster Buddy's Claw!

Tripod Index Finger: (of the support hand on a surface)
✓ Like the Pool Cue support hand and index finger on a table, desk, knee, log, tree stump, box, step stool, vehicle hood or tail gate, milk crate, 5-gallon paint bucket or other stable surface (requires two hands)

Tripod Index Finger: (of the support hand on a surface)

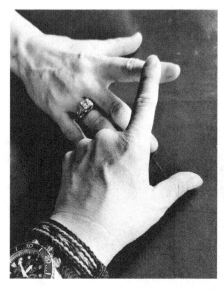 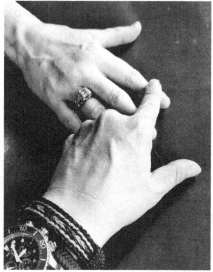

Partner Muscle Testing: Finger Strong   *Muscle Testing: Finger Weak*

Tripod Index Finger: (of the support hand on a surface)
Like the Pool Cue support hand and index finger on a table, desk, knee, log, tree stump, box, step stool, vehicle hood or tail gate, milk crate, 5-gallon paint bucket or other stable surface (requires two hands)

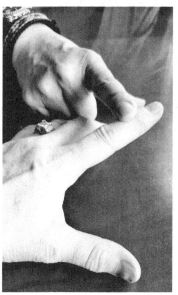 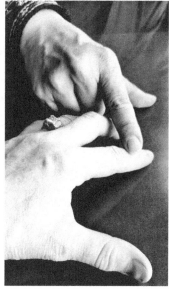

Partner Muscle Testing: Finger Strong, Muscle Testing: Finger Weak

Lobbi Claw Fingers: (in the air without support surface)

   ✓   Like a lobster claw, support hand, and index finger and thumb spread apart in the air without the aid of any type of support surface (requires two hands)

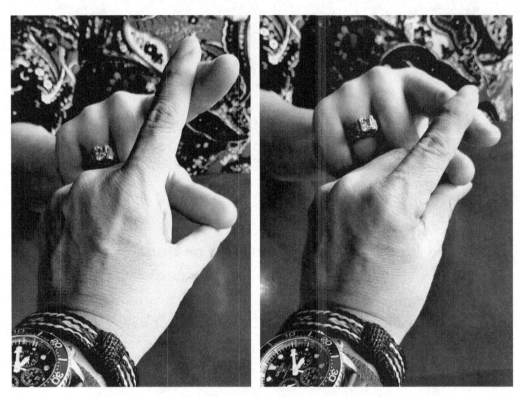

Partner Muscle Testing: Fingers Strong, Muscle Testing: Fingers Weak

Both of these methods use two hands and at least two fingers. They are versatile and can be done alone for yourself. You are able to test with or on another person very simply and quickly.

Tripod Index Finger:

I mostly use this one when working one-on-one with clients in person, sitting at a table or desk as we work together.

Tripod Index Finger: *(of the support hand on a surface)*

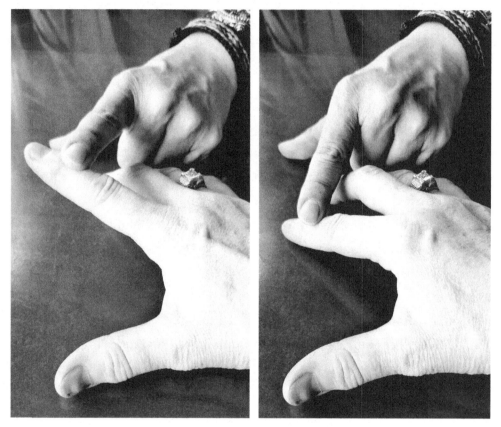

Partner Muscle Testing: Finger Strong, Muscle Testing: Finger Weak

This one is also simple to teach to an individual to use on their own quickly on a hard or stable surface.

I also use this one when working on myself, best case scenario while sitting at a table or desk, and while out in the field on one of my thighs while sitting down.

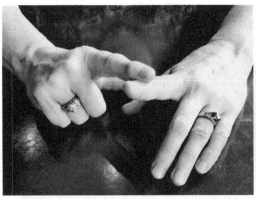 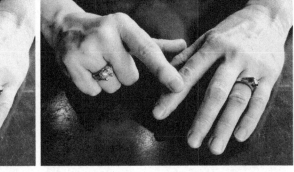

Self-Muscle Testing: Finger Strong　　　　*Self-Muscle Testing: Finger Weak*

Using the Tripod Index Finger method, have the support hand of the recipient on a hard surface or at least a stable surface as described above.

Have the testee hold up their support, or non-dominant, hand index finger for testing with their thumb and other fingers stable on the surface.

Next, the tester uses one of their index fingers (either hand works so use the one that is most comfortable) with the rest of their fingers and thumb supporting on the stable surface to push down on the recipient's index finger to determine either strong or weak.

If you are doing this method on yourself, it is the same as above except you (tester and testee) are using your primary, or dominant, hand index finger for testing on your support, or non-dominant, index finger, to push down and determine either strong or weak.

Lobbi Claw Fingers:

I use this version in the air without a table on stage doing demonstrations, mostly for small to medium groups that can see me clearly without audio visual equipment, or before I ask for a person to come up to be demonstrated on in front of a group.

Self-Muscle Testing: Fingers Strong

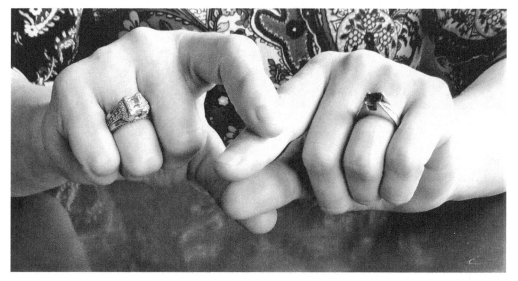

Self-Muscle Testing: Fingers Weak

I also use this one when working one-on-one with clients in person while standing without the use of a table, desk or stable surface as we test together, and I'm unable to use their outstretched arm.

Lobbi Claw Fingers:

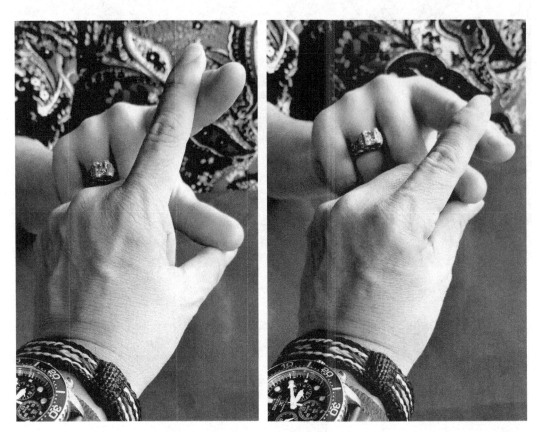

Partner Muscle Testing: Fingers Strong, Muscle Testing: Fingers Weak

The Lobbi Claw Fingers method consists of using the index finger and thumb spread apart on the support or non-dominant hand in the air, while squeezing them together by placing the thumb and index finger of the primary, or dominant hand, over the support, or non-dominant hand, finger and thumb then squeezing together to determine strong or weak.

When testing another person, have the recipient hold up their support or non-dominant hand in the air with their index finger and thumb spread apart for testing. Next, the tester uses the index finger and thumb of either hand over the testee's support or non-dominant hand finger and thumb, then squeeze together to determine strong or weak.

Muscle Testing Yourself
Use the same process as in the Partner process except you are both RECIPIENT (TESTEE) and (TESTER)

There are a variety of ways to muscle test yourself.

Note: I personally believe, after showing people how to muscle test over forty years, that it is best for them to use the process or technique that they are comfortable with as this builds confidence!

Once the favorite technique is chosen, practice, practice, practice and then practice some more until it can be done automatically.

The Lean:

One of the simplest to learn is the "leaning" method.

Leaning forward: Strong; Standing Neutral; Leaning backwards: Weak

1. Stand with your feet a comfortable distance apart (perhaps hip distance) with your arms either by your sides or crossed across your chest.
2. Say, "Show me a yes." Observe how your body moves. In most cases, the body will lean or sway forward. If so, this is your "yes."
3. Say, "Show me a no." Observe how your body moves. In most cases, the body will lean or sway backward. If so, this is your "no."

It may be helpful to close your eyes when doing this test. Do this several times to determine your results. If you have consistent answers that do not match those above, that's fine. Those are your "yes" and your "no." Consistency is what matters.

The Arm:

Self-Muscle Testing: Arm Weak; Self-Muscle Testing: Arm Strong

Another option is to use the outstretched arm technique described in the earlier section about doing muscle testing with a partner. In this case, you are both the tester and the testee. Hold one arm out, make a statement, and test with two fingers of the opposite hand.

The Loop:

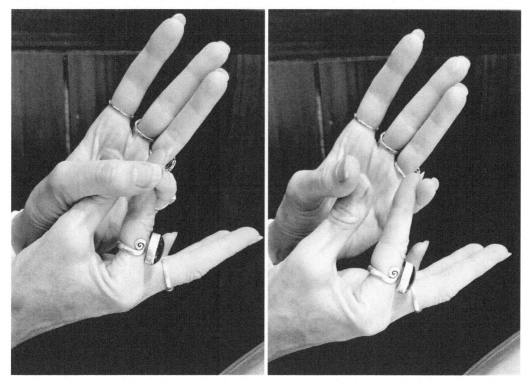

Self-Muscle Testing: Fingers Strong, Muscle Testing: Fingers Weak

Some people prefer the loop method. This involves holding the tips of the thumb and little finger of the non-dominant hand together to form a circle. Next, press the pads of the thumb and forefinger of the other hand together, forming a beak-like shape. Insert those fingers into the loop of the other hand. After asking a question or making a statement, open the fingers of the dominant hand. If the loop holds, the response is strong. If the loop breaks, the response is weak.

The Double Loop:

Self-Muscle Testing: Fingers Strong, Muscle Testing: Fingers Weak

The double-loop method is a variation on the above. In this approach, you would make a circle with the thumb and forefinger of one hand, then do the same with the other hand, interlocking the two loops. After asking a question or making a statement, you would pull the two loops at the point where the fingers come together. If the loop breaks, the response is a weak one. If it holds, the response is a strong one.

Two Fingers:

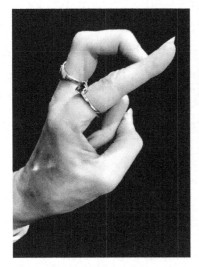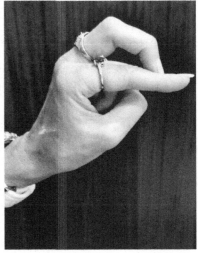

Self-Muscle Testing: Finger Strong, Self-Muscle Testing: Finger Weak

One of my personal favorites is the two-finger approach. This method involves holding the index finger of the primary or dominant hand rigid (pointing). The middle finger is then curved so that its tip is pressing on the first knuckle of the pointer/index finger or on the fingertip. Ask your question or make your statement. Hold the pointer firm, then press with the middle finger.

The positive and negative responses will be subtly different. With practice, you will be able to discern your strong from your weak responses.

Two Fingers:

Self-Muscle Testing: Finger Strong, Self-Muscle Testing: Finger Weak

Big Time CONGRATS!
You have just muscle tested four of the very common emotional, feeling states!

Let's review your experience or process:
- How did you do by yourself?
- How did you and your partner do?

Good either way! Keep practicing!

Experiment with some other emotions, feelings or statements.

With practice, muscle testing will become faster and easier as you get more comfortable, confident and accustomed to the process.

NOTE: Do not worry if you require lots of practice because one of my Great Teachers, Dr. Bradley Nelson, the developer of two amazing healing energy systems *The Emotion Code* and *The Body Code*, told us about what happened when he first learned muscle testing, so don't lose heart if you are not getting the muscle testing down right away! Just keep practicing over and over and over again. Don't ever give up!

Dr. Brad has an excellent sense of humor. He is a Great Guy, a Humble Man and now watching him teach on his videos or in person live you would never know that a Muscle Testing Guru like him ever had to work at muscle testing to get good at it. However, he's hysterical when he tells his story about how he had to practice and practice, over and over again when he was starting out in Chiropractor School, before becoming proficient in muscle testing!

I love Dr. Brad, have met, studied, trained and interacted with him in person at multiple live training events in Utah and Nevada, on videos and internet training classes. He is a fantastic teacher, and one of the best when it comes to encouraging us and being patient when we learn, practice and develop our Muscle Testing stills! So Keep Going!

Another motivational teacher, Tony Little says, *"YOU CAN DO IT!"* Broadcasting on NPR *All Things Considered* Tony said, *"You got to believe in yourself, man. We only have one shot in life and you got to make it a solid one. And, sometimes, it might have to be a hundred shots."* (November 23, 2014)

Keep Positive and Keep Practicing!

YOU Are In Charge and YOU Choose!

Now that I've explained and given examples of the various techniques I've found to be simple ways to transform our lives, please allow me to move into coach mode and be as direct and blunt with you as I possibly can as I relay the following to you:

YOU are charged and empowered by your GOD, Creator, Lord, God, Goddess, Jesus Christ, Jehovah-Jireh, Mighty I AM Presence, Great Spirit, Infinite Spirit, Higher Power, All That Is, Higher Self, Father Sky, or Mother Earth to honor and praise them by positively living your life to the fullest! Happily, successfully, with love and appreciation for all of the above, while you are here on this Earth plane. As written before, "you are a free moral agent."

That means you are in charge of your life to make your own choices and decisions about how you live your life.

Will you be a shining example, a powerful reflection or will you be a poor example?

The choice is yours! It is totally up to you as to how you will live your life and show who you really are!

I'll tell you again why I put all of this down in this book and workbook. Because it works!

d.i.y. zen and *The Art of Gentle Emotional Transformation* became a modality with the "Put Your Fingers On Your Forehead", "The Energetic Action Process" and "The Art of Muscle" Testing techniques.

I have personally used these techniques on myself since the mid-1990s and continually use them regularly on my own and share them with my fellow human beings.

They have worked for me and several thousand individuals: friends, colleagues, clients, students, speakers, trainers, disaster victims, along with the loved ones and others these individuals shared the techniques with.

Every time I share and use them, I still have the fascination and wonderment of a brand-new student who has never experienced them before! They are still so phenomenally exciting and thrilling for me because I realize that any person who chooses to may be able to gently and powerfully take charge of their life by neutralizing, removing, erasing and clearing out the negative thoughts, feelings, emotions or events that have kept us in bondage, chained to the past experiences that have shaped our lives.

The most wonderful and thrilling part of all of this to me is that YOU ARE IN CONTROL!

You are in charge of your life. You are in the driver's seat. You are the captain of your life and the navigator of your destiny.

As my dad and many of my mentors, teachers, coaches, and guides have said to me over and over again, "If it is to be, it is up to me!" Again, it really is "do-it-yourself" (d.i.y.)!

So now, if you choose, it is time for you to take charge of your life. You decide when, where, and how to start reshaping and directing your life and destiny.

The truth is that only YOU can truly change your life and you can start right now!

I totally respect, honor and salute YOU for having the courage to imagine, think and believe that YOU are in charge of your own life.

Always remember, it is YOUR choice to take action and YOU are in charge.

If YOU decide to commit to YOURSELF and start today, I invite you to turn the page to read and, if YOU agree, to sign a Personal Contract with YOURSELF.

Then, I invite YOU to GO FOR IT Right Now and start to live YOUR life as Healthy, Whole and Complete as is possible!

As of this moment,

    I, _____

(your name), choose to commit to myself and take charge of my life and destiny by clearing out any and all negative thoughts, issues, actions, and situations that no longer serve me and my highest good.

    From this moment forward, I freely release them and live my life to the fullest in positive ways that bring happiness and joy into my life and serve me well.

_____

(sign your name)

_____

(Today's Date)

Wow! Congratulations. You have taken charge of your life! Now fasten your safety belt and get ready for a wild ride in a positive direction.

PART V

The Energetic Action Process
33-Day Workbook

FOREWORD

by Dr. Patricia Carrington

In the workbook portion of this book, Gary gives us the precious gift of being so down to earth and real that we can't help but feel him as a friend. At the same time, he teaches us profound truths.

The personal transformation in this 33-Day Workbook is a must for anyone wanting to put into effect Gary Niki's system of on-the-spot stress reduction and clearing. What I find particularly compelling about it are these features:

1. It is relentlessly thorough. The reader doesn't get away with neglecting a single thing that must be done to allow the method Gary Niki teaches to truly change their life.

2. Gary cheers you on at every step with deep enthusiasm. You know you have a friend in your corner when you apply this method and you don't want to let him or yourself down as you are pushing through to your own transformation through this process.

3. Is the *d.i.y. zen and The Art of Gentle Emotional Transformation* modality or "The Energetic Action Process" technique like EFT and the other energy psychology therapies? Because EFT is one of my areas of

expertise I can answer that with a strong YES. However, it is clearly different in that it brings the inimitable energy of Gary Niki into the mix and voilà! You are changing and shifting before you know it.

4. Gary takes you carefully and deliberately through a predetermined series of steps, which can bring you directly to the goal of transforming not only yourself but your entire life. The process is deceptively simple and easy to follow, and profound.

5. Like all expert teachers, Gary eventually leaves you on your own to continue your journey of personal growth as he ends his workbook by asking you to insert your own daily entries.

6. The two lists, one negative the "Awful-Distressing-Stuff List" and one positive the "Positivity and Empowerment List" included at the end of the book will stimulate you and help you to locate many a hidden negative emotional roadblock and gives you carte blanche to clear them by using "The Energetic Action Process" and to make sure you are strong to the positive ones. If regularly used for clearings, these lists alone will alter your life.

In short, author Gary Niki has managed to convey within a small space, an entirely new way of life. This is an impressive accomplishment and is aided by the book's frequent levity, its constant readability and its simplicity.

The book and this workbook actually do what they set out to do, they constitute a true contribution to human happiness.

Patricia Carrington, PhD.
Associate Clinical Professor of Psychiatry Rutgers School of Biomedical and Health Sciences Piscataway, New Jersey
Originator of the EFT Choices Method

WHY A WORKBOOK?

The truth is, right here and right now IS where and when YOU get to be in charge and take the action to make a positive difference in YOUR life, starting Right Now!

Remember, I said, "You are the Captain of your life and the navigator of your destiny."

With that said, what do I want you to do? I want YOU to Carry On, of course!

"Aye, Aye, Captain! I acknowledge YOUR Authority and Captain-ness!
After all, YOU are in charge!"

Here we go... This workbook may serve as a guide for you so make it your own, make it personal and mark it up.

Hey, why not? YOU bought it, or got it for a gift, and now it is in your possession, so please mark it up, make it personal and make it your own!

Here are some suggestions and guidance

1. Be real!

I mean get serious and stop any namby-pamby, wimpy excuses that let you off the hook or remove the responsibility from yourself.

You made the personal commitment and now it is time to take action on your decision right now.

2. Give 100%

You deserve 100 percent of your effort and ability along with your full energy to get the job done right.

Whatever it takes, you only lose if you quit and give up!

I know that will not happen to you because you have decided, and you are in charge of your life and destiny, and that is a very important and powerful position to be in.

Now you may ask, why 100 percent?

Why not 110 percent or 115 percent or 200 percent? Oh, I hear ya! I was always considered a 115 percenter (by others and myself) and always wondered why I am wiped out, tired, frustrated or a failure.

don Miguel Ruiz (one of my teachers and heroes) says in his book *The Four Agreements*, *"Always do your best,"*(Agreement number four). *"Your best is going to change from moment to moment. It will be different when you are healthy as opposed to sick, under any circumstance simply do your best and you will avoid self-judgment, self-abuse, and regret."* — *don Miguel Ruiz.*

From my experience, in the past I have certainly pushed myself hard as a work-a-holic into a downward spiraling frenzy, trying to be all things to all people telling myself, "I'm a 115 percenter and I can handle it."

HA! That didn't work out so well. However, I had to learn that the hard way, time and time again!

Please Stop Right Now and Honor Yourself by Deciding to do 100 percent! Certainly No More or No Less.

"Always do your best." -don Miguel Ruiz

3. **Question everything and muscle test everything and check it out for yourself!**

    Hey, don't just take my word for it! You take it step by step and question everything, including this workbook and process. Then, when you have your questions down, stop again, review the wording of your questions or statements and muscle test (either yourself or have another person assist you with your muscle testing).

    If you are not sure you have it down for yourself or if you are like me and tell yourself there is no way that's true, ask someone else to come and push on your arm and help you with muscle testing.

4. **Give yourself time**

    Become slow and methodical. Take it step by step, ask lots of personal questions while you are working your way through this workbook.

    Please take it slow! Seriously, it does not do you any good to overdo it and feel wiped out. Remember to breathe! Take time to ponder your questions, statements, and thoughts.

    Write them down in the workbook and then muscle test each one. Write down or check the result on the following pages and jot down a few notes for yourself.

5. **Become your own detective and archeologist**

    Now that you have given yourself time to slow down, continue to dig like an archeologist who is fascinated by the dig site, and investigate yourself just like a great detective would.

    Start by asking yourself who, what, where, why, when, how questions.

    How, why and when am I affected negatively by my family of origin, my family now, my close personal inner circle of friends, fellow workers, teachers, coaches, religious/spiritual leaders, any influential persons that may have affected me at any time in my life?

    By acting as your very own detective, you will be able to identify the above and acquire the details and information to complete the pages of this workbook. All the while, you will be able to clear out any and all of the negative issues that have haunted, followed, and chained you energetically to your past.

Freedom from the bondage of that past is now yours to enjoy.

6. Now that you know, do something about it right now

Okay, okay. Hey, I'm guilty of it, too. Many, many times the insights and information have come to me and made themselves known in a myriad of ways.

I have let doubt, fear, and disbelief take hold of me when procrastination sets in and weeks, months, or at times, years go by without any action on my part.

Then all of a sudden, wham! A 2x4 or a big stick whacks me square in the forehead! Only then do I start to answer the wake-up call and get coherent again.

Looking back, I realize I was totally warned, alerted, and given the insight to address the situation and I did not get the clue or, if I did, I did not take the time and opportunity to address it, deal with it, or clear it before it got to be the big wake-up call!

7. Be the master of your life

What a novel concept you may say, however, I can tell you that it has not been easy for me!

I was certainly dragged kicking and screaming, pulled backwards through knotholes over broken glass and cactus just to be right where I am right now, sharing this information, insights, and myself with you! Hey, just remember, we are all the same human beings.

Now I ask you to go from a human being to becoming a human of action who is starting to master their life as a human, who is doing whatever it takes to be strong to the positivity to become as Happy, Healthy, Whole and Complete as is possible!

I am certainly not here to tell you or even imply that this journey you are about to embark on is fun, happy, smooth, or easy. I assure you that it certainly is not!

Quite the contrary, in order for you to be the master of your life you will have to become stronger than you can imagine, more tenacious than you believe you can be and downright stubborn to not turn back or run back scared and screaming to the old easy, familiar, comfortable, and miserable inner world that got you here today!

The truth is that I have done exactly that too many times to count!

I can assure you that it is totally worth it once you are through it and on the other side of it all!

Now that I am working on being a human of action, I am able to guide you to suggestion number eight.

Are you ready? Okay, here it is.

8. **First day of my new life: "My New Beginning"**

Now that is a powerful concept in any endeavor, adventure, or journey. We have to start somewhere. As has been said to me in many fortune cookies, *"The journey of a thousand miles starts with the first step."*

Actually, that is a very profound insight, great advice, and guidance for all of us, and it sounds kinda zen!

Let us all state out loud:

"This is the first day of my new life and now, as I turn the page of my workbook, I enthusiastically take charge of my new beginning."

OK, let's Take Charge. GO FOR IT! Turn the page to Make a Positive Difference in Your Life Starting Right Now!

Let's start at the very beginning with the basics:
1. Remember KISS—Keep It Simple Superstar!
2. Go slowly and take your time.
3. Please honor yourself and do not overdo it by attempting to clear everything today!
4. Check in with yourself often, keep an open mind!
5. Be patient with yourself.
6. Follow the workbook pages and systematically muscle test and clear.

Breathing is extremely important!

"Breathe In, Breathe Out" (Repeat over and over)

Balance is also one of the important parts of a zen life.

Before starting each workbook day/session with clearing using the:

"Put Your Fingers On Your Forehead" technique

"The Energetic Action Process" technique

"Awful-Distressing-Stuff List" tool

"Positivity and Empowerment List" tool

I recommend that you take a moment to balance your physical, energetic, neurological and spirit self.

Simply say or think this statement three times before starting each day/session:

"God, be a part of everything
I think, say, feel, and do."

"God, be a part of everything
I think, say, feel, and do."

"God, be a part of everything
I think, say, feel, and do."

I recommend that you use this statement at least three times as above and three times a day, every day whether you are working and clearing or not.

Day One (01)--
Welcome to the FIRST of 33 days of transformation!

- Breathe in, breathe out (take several deep, cleansing breaths).
- Think or state three times: "God, be a part of everything I think, say, feel, and do."

What do you notice and how do you feel right now?

_____

_____

_____

_____

Great! (Remember, wherever you are is right for your life's journey.)
Today we will check in via muscle testing on the first of six feelings/emotions (listed below).

Muscle test yourself – STRONG or WEAK – one at a time.

Example: "I feel _____." Insert the feeling/emotion in the blank. Muscle test yourself for each statement. After each one, place a check mark to indicate your response using the blank on the left side of the slash (/). The blank to the right side of the slash is to indicate your response after you have done the clearing work.

Strong / Weak		FEELING or EMOTION
__/__	__/__	Fear
__/__	__/__	Guilt
__/__	__/__	Anger/Angry
__/__	__/__	Hate
__/__	__/__	Shame
__/__	__/__	Betrayed

Were you surprised by your actual responses via muscle testing?
Either way, good!

It is time to clear using the Energetic Action Process. Simply drum or clap the fingers of either hand on the side of your other hand below your pinky finger and above your wrist, or clap both hands together while saying:

"**I deeply love and accept myself even if I feel** _____." (Insert the FEELING or EMOTION.) Repeat the statement three (3) times. Continue the drumming/clapping motion.

"**I deeply love and accept myself even if I have hidden or unknown issues with** _____." (Insert the FEELING or EMOTION.) Repeat the statement three (3) times. Continue the drumming/clapping motion.

"**I deeply love and accept myself even if I refuse to do the things necessary to free myself from feeling** _____." (Insert the FEELING or EMOTION.) Repeat the statement three (3) times. Continue the drumming/clapping motion.

What do you notice and how do you feel right now?

_____

_____

_____

_____

Excellent! Now go back and re-muscle test each FEELING or EMOTION for STRONG or WEAK and mark your results in the blanks to the right of the slash mark.

Please remember, you are always able to repeat the above steps anytime you choose or feel it necessary as YOU are in charge of your life!

Please end your day with a few minutes of using the technique of "Put Your Fingers on Your Forehead" while replaying any of the thoughts, feelings, emotions, or statements that may have felt negative, painful, or oppressive and did not feel good, uplifting, or positive.

Wow! Big-time congratulations! You made it through the FIRST DAY!

Day Two (02)---
Great! You came back for more! Welcome to DAY TWO!

- Breathe in, breathe out (take several deep, cleansing breaths).
- Think or state three times: "God, be a part of everything I think, say, feel, and do."

What do you notice and how do you feel right now?

_____

_____

_____

_____

Great! (Remember, wherever you are is right for your life's journey.)

Today we will check in via muscle testing on six more feelings/emotions (listed below).

Muscle test yourself – STRONG or WEAK – one at a time.

Example: "I feel _____." Insert the feeling/emotion in the blank. Muscle test yourself for each statement. After each one, place a check mark to indicate your response using the blank on the left side of the slash (/). The blank to the right side of the slash is to indicate your response after you have done the clearing work.

Strong / Weak		FEELING or EMOTION
__/__	__/__	Worry
__/__	__/__	Hopeless/Hopelessness
__/__	__/__	Unworthy
__/__	__/__	Unlovable
__/__	__/__	Powerless
__/__	__/__	Disbelief

Were you surprised by your actual responses via muscle testing?
Either way, good!

It is time to clear using the Energetic Action Process. Simply drum or clap the fingers of either hand on the side of your other hand below your pinky finger and above your wrist, or clap both hands together while saying:

"I deeply love and accept myself even if I feel _____." (Insert the FEELING or EMOTION.) Repeat the statement three (3) times. Continue the drumming/clapping motion.

"I deeply love and accept myself even if I have hidden or unknown issues with _____." (Insert the FEELING or EMOTION.) Repeat the statement three (3) times. Continue the drumming/clapping motion.

"I deeply love and accept myself even if I refuse to do the things necessary to free myself from feeling _____." (Insert the FEELING or EMOTION.) Repeat the statement three (3) times. Continue the drumming/clapping motion.

What do you notice and how do you feel right now?

_____

_____

_____

_____

Excellent! Now go back and re-muscle test each FEELING or EMOTION for STRONG or WEAK and mark your results in the blanks to the right of the slash mark.

Please remember, you are always able to repeat the above steps anytime you choose or feel it necessary as YOU are in charge of your life!

Please end your day with a few minutes of using the technique of Put Your Fingers on Your Forehead while replaying any of the thoughts, feelings, emotions, or statements that may have felt negative, painful, or oppressive and did not feel good, uplifting, or positive.

You made it through DAY TWO! Terrific! See you tomorrow!

Day Three (03)---
The third time's the charm! Welcome to DAY THREE!

- Breathe in, breathe out (take several deep, cleansing breaths).
- Think or state three times: "God, be a part of everything I think, say, feel, and do."

What do you notice and how do you feel right now?

_____
_____
_____
_____

Great! (Remember, wherever you are is right for your life's journey.)
Today we will check in via muscle testing on six new feelings/emotions (listed below).
 Muscle test yourself – STRONG or WEAK – one at a time.

 Example: "I feel _____." Insert the feeling/emotion in the blank. Muscle test yourself for each statement. After each one, place a check mark to indicate your response using the blank on the left side of the slash (/). The blank to the right side of the slash is to indicate your response after you have done the clearing work.

Strong / Weak		FEELING or EMOTION
__/__	__/__	Anxiety
__/__	__/__	Upset
__/__	__/__	Helpless
__/__	__/__	Panic
__/__	__/__	Resentment/Resentful
__/__	__/__	Doubt

Were you surprised by your actual responses via muscle testing?
Either way, good!

It is time to clear using the Energetic Action Process. Simply drum or clap the fingers of either hand on the side of your other hand below your pinky finger and above your wrist, or clap both hands together while saying:

"**I deeply love and accept myself even if I feel** _____." (Insert the FEELING or EMOTION.) Repeat the statement three (3) times. Continue the drumming/clapping motion.

"**I deeply love and accept myself even if I have hidden or unknown issues with** _____." (Insert the FEELING or EMOTION.) Repeat the statement three (3) times. Continue the drumming/clapping motion.

"**I deeply love and accept myself even if I refuse to do the things necessary to free myself from feeling** _____." (Insert the FEELING or EMOTION.) Repeat the statement three (3) times. Continue the drumming/clapping motion.

What do you notice and how do you feel right now?

_____

_____

_____

_____

Excellent! Now go back and re-muscle test each FEELING or EMOTION for STRONG or WEAK and mark your results in the blanks to the right of the slash mark.

Please remember, you are always able to repeat the above steps anytime you choose or feel it necessary as YOU are in charge of your life!

Please end your day with a few minutes of using the technique of Put Your Fingers on Your Forehead while replaying any of the thoughts, feelings, emotions, or statements that may have felt negative, painful, or oppressive and did not feel good, uplifting, or positive.

Wow! Wee! You made it through DAY THREE! Keep coming back! It works!

Day Four (04)--
Kick negativity out the door! Welcome to DAY FOUR!

- Breathe in, breathe out (take several deep, cleansing breaths).
- Think or state three times: "God, be a part of everything I think, say, feel, and do."

What do you notice and how do you feel right now?

_____
_____
_____
_____

Great! (Remember, wherever you are is right for your life's journey.)
Today we will check in via muscle testing on six new feelings/emotions (listed below).
    Muscle test yourself – STRONG or WEAK – one at a time.

    Example: "I feel _____." Insert the feeling/emotion in the blank. Muscle test yourself for each statement. After each one, place a check mark to indicate your response using the blank on the left side of the slash (/). The blank to the right side of the slash is to indicate your response after you have done the clearing work.

Strong / Weak		FEELING or EMOTION
__/__	__/__	Self-conscious
__/__	__/__	Discomfort
__/__	__/__	Shy/Shyness
__/__	__/__	Judged
__/__	__/__	Uncertain
__/__	__/__	Distress

Were you surprised by your actual responses via muscle testing?
Either way, good!

It is time to clear using the Energetic Action Process. Simply drum or clap the fingers of either hand on the side of your other hand below your pinky finger and above your wrist, or clap both hands together while saying:

"**I deeply love and accept myself even if I feel** _____." (Insert the FEELING or EMOTION.) Repeat the statement three (3) times. Continue the drumming/clapping motion.

"**I deeply love and accept myself even if I have hidden or unknown issues with** _____." (Insert the FEELING or EMOTION.) Repeat the statement three (3) times. Continue the drumming/clapping motion.

"**I deeply love and accept myself even if I refuse to do the things necessary to free myself from feeling** _____." (Insert the FEELING or EMOTION.) Repeat the statement three (3) times. Continue the drumming/clapping motion.

What do you notice and how do you feel right now?

_____

_____

_____

_____

Excellent! Now go back and re-muscle test each FEELING or EMOTION for STRONG or WEAK and mark your results in the blanks to the right of the slash mark.

Please remember, you are always able to repeat the above steps anytime you choose or feel it necessary as YOU are in charge of your life!

Please end your day with a few minutes of using the technique of Put Your Fingers on Your Forehead while replaying any of the thoughts, feelings, emotions, or statements that may have felt negative, painful, or oppressive and did not feel good, uplifting, or positive.

You made it through DAY FOUR! And kicked negativity out the door!

Day Five (05)--

Hey, you are STILL ALIVE! Welcome to DAY FIVE!

- Breathe in, breathe out (take several deep, cleansing breaths).
- Think or state three times: "God, be a part of everything I think, say, feel, and do."

What do you notice and how do you feel right now?

_____

_____

_____

_____

Great! (Remember, wherever you are is right for your life's journey.)

Today we will check in via muscle testing on six new feelings/emotions (listed below).

Muscle test yourself – STRONG or WEAK – one at a time.

Example: "I feel _____." Insert the feeling/emotion in the blank. Muscle test yourself for each statement. After each one, place a check mark to indicate your response using the blank on the left side of the slash (/). The blank to the right side of the slash is to indicate your response after you have done the clearing work.

Strong / Weak		FEELING or EMOTION
__/__	__/__	Miserable
__/__	__/__	Desperate
__/__	__/__	Frustrated
__/__	__/__	Vulnerable
__/__	__/__	Judgmental
__/__	__/__	Dissatisfied

Were you surprised by your actual responses via muscle testing?
Either way, good!

It is time to clear using the Energetic Action Process. Simply drum or clap the fingers of either hand on the side of your other hand below your pinky finger and above your wrist, or clap both hands together while saying:

"**I deeply love and accept myself even if I feel** _____." (Insert the FEELING or EMOTION.) Repeat the statement three (3) times. Continue the drumming/clapping motion.

"**I deeply love and accept myself even if I have hidden or unknown issues with** _____." (Insert the FEELING or EMOTION.) Repeat the statement three (3) times. Continue the drumming/clapping motion.

"**I deeply love and accept myself even if I refuse to do the things necessary to free myself from feeling** _____." (Insert the FEELING or EMOTION.) Repeat the statement three (3) times. Continue the drumming/ clapping motion.

What do you notice and how do you feel right now?

_____

_____

_____

_____

Excellent! Now go back and re-muscle test each FEELING or EMOTION for STRONG or WEAK and mark your results in the blanks to the right of the slash mark.

Please remember, you are always able to repeat the above steps anytime you choose or feel it necessary as YOU are in charge of your life!

Please end your day with a few minutes of using the technique of Put Your Fingers on Your Forehead while replaying any of the thoughts, feelings, emotions, or statements that may have felt negative, painful, or oppressive and did not feel good, uplifting, or positive.

You made it through DAY FIVE! You're ALIVE and ready for more!

Day Six (06)--
Time to nix out old tricks! Welcome to DAY SIX!

- Breathe in, breathe out (take several deep, cleansing breaths).
- Think or state three times: "God, be a part of everything I think, say, feel, and do."

What do you notice and how do you feel right now?

_____

_____

_____

_____

Great! (Remember, wherever you are is right for your life's journey.)
Today we will check in via muscle testing on six new feelings/emotions (listed below).
Muscle test yourself – STRONG or WEAK – one at a time.

Example: "I feel _____." Insert the feeling/emotion in the blank.
Muscle test yourself for each statement. After each one, place a check mark to indicate your response using the blank on the left side of the slash (/). The blank to the right side of the slash is to indicate your response after you have done the clearing work.

Strong / Weak		FEELING or EMOTION
__/__	__/__	Depression/Depressed
__/__	__/__	Aggravated/Aggravation
__/__	__/__	Criticized
__/__	__/__	Impeded
__/__	__/__	Undeserving
__/__	__/__	Frustrated/Frustration

Were you surprised by your actual responses via muscle testing?
Either way, good!

It is time to clear using the Energetic Action Process. Simply drum or clap the fingers of either hand on the side of your other hand below your pinky finger and above your wrist, or clap both hands together while saying:

"I deeply love and accept myself even if I feel _____." (Insert the FEELING or EMOTION.) Repeat the statement three (3) times. Continue the drumming/clapping motion.

"I deeply love and accept myself even if I have hidden or unknown issues with _____." (Insert the FEELING or EMOTION.) Repeat the statement three (3) times. Continue the drumming/clapping motion.

"I deeply love and accept myself even if I refuse to do the things necessary to free myself from feeling _____." (Insert the FEELING or EMOTION.) Repeat the statement three (3) times. Continue the drumming/clapping motion.

What do you notice and how do you feel right now?

_____

_____

_____

_____

Excellent! Now go back and re-muscle test each FEELING or EMOTION for STRONG or WEAK and mark your results in the blanks to the right of the slash mark.

Please remember, you are always able to repeat the above steps anytime you choose or feel it necessary as YOU are in charge of your life!

Please end your day with a few minutes of using the technique of Put Your Fingers on Your Forehead while replaying any of the thoughts, feelings, emotions, or statements that may have felt negative, painful, or oppressive and did not feel good, uplifting, or positive.

You made it through DAY SIX! Woo hoo! You nixed out old tricks!

Day Seven (07)---

Wow! You've been at it for a week! Welcome to DAY SEVEN!

- Breathe in, breathe out (take several deep, cleansing breaths).
- Think or state three times: "God, be a part of everything I think, say, feel, and do."

What do you notice and how do you feel right now?

_____

_____

_____

_____

Great! (Remember, wherever you are is right for your life's journey.)
Today we will check in via muscle testing on six new feelings/emotions (listed below).
Muscle test yourself – STRONG or WEAK – one at a time.

Example: "I feel _____." Insert the feeling/emotion in the blank. Muscle test yourself for each statement. After each one, place a check mark to indicate your response using the blank on the left side of the slash (/). The blank to the right side of the slash is to indicate your response after you have done the clearing work.

Strong / Weak		FEELING or EMOTION
__/__	__/__	No Self-Confidence
__/__	__/__	Incapable
__/__	__/__	Hindered
__/__	__/__	Inferior/Inferiority
__/__	__/__	Cowardly
__/__	__/__	Dismissed

Were you surprised by your actual responses via muscle testing?
Either way, good!

It is time to clear using the Energetic Action Process. Simply drum or clap the fingers of either hand on the side of your other hand below your pinky finger and above your wrist, or clap both hands together while saying:

"**I deeply love and accept myself even if I feel** _____." (Insert the FEELING or EMOTION.) Repeat the statement three (3) times. Continue the drumming/clapping motion.

"**I deeply love and accept myself even if I have hidden or unknown issues with** _____." (Insert the FEELING or EMOTION.) Repeat the statement three (3) times. Continue the drumming/clapping motion.

"**I deeply love and accept myself even if I refuse to do the things necessary to free myself from feeling** _____." (Insert the FEELING or EMOTION.) Repeat the statement three (3) times. Continue the drumming/clapping motion.

What do you notice and how do you feel right now?

_____

_____

_____

_____

Excellent! Now go back and re-muscle test each FEELING or EMOTION for STRONG or WEAK and mark your results in the blanks to the right of the slash mark.

Please remember, you are always able to repeat the above steps anytime you choose or feel it necessary as YOU are in charge of your life!

Please end your day with a few minutes of using the technique of Put Your Fingers on Your Forehead while replaying any of the thoughts, feelings, emotions, or statements that may have felt negative, painful, or oppressive and did not feel good, uplifting, or positive.

I made it through DAY SEVEN! In one week, I AM no longer weak!

Day Eight (08)--
Here comes freedom from hate! Welcome to DAY EIGHT!

- Breathe in, breathe out (take several deep, cleansing breaths).
- Think or state three times: "God, be a part of everything I think, say, feel, and do."

What do you notice and how do you feel right now?

_____

_____

_____

_____

Great! (Remember, wherever you are is right for your life's journey.)
Today we will check in via muscle testing on six new feelings/emotions (listed below).
Muscle test yourself – STRONG or WEAK – one at a time.

Example: "I feel _____." Insert the feeling/emotion in the blank. Muscle test yourself for each statement. After each one, place a check mark to indicate your response using the blank on the left side of the slash (/). The blank to the right side of the slash is to indicate your response after you have done the clearing work.

Strong / Weak		FEELING or EMOTION
__/__	__/__	Loathing
__/__	__/__	Hatred
__/__	__/__	Malevolence
__/__	__/__	Despised
__/__	__/__	Scorned
__/__	__/__	Contempt

Were you surprised by your actual responses via muscle testing?
Either way, good!

It is time to clear using the Energetic Action Process. Simply drum or clap the fingers of either hand on the side of your other hand below your pinky finger and above your wrist, or clap both hands together while saying:

"I deeply love and accept myself even if I feel _____." (Insert the FEELING or EMOTION.) Repeat the statement three (3) times. Continue the drumming/clapping motion.

"I deeply love and accept myself even if I have hidden or unknown issues with _____." (Insert the FEELING or EMOTION.) Repeat the statement three (3) times. Continue the drumming/clapping motion.

"I deeply love and accept myself even if I refuse to do the things necessary to free myself from feeling _____." (Insert the FEELING or EMOTION.) Repeat the statement three (3) times. Continue the drumming/clapping motion.

What do you notice and how do you feel right now?

_____

_____

_____

_____

Excellent! Now go back and re-muscle test each FEELING or EMOTION for STRONG or WEAK and mark your results in the blanks to the right of the slash mark.

Please remember, you are always able to repeat the above steps anytime you choose or feel it necessary as YOU are in charge of your life!

Please end your day with a few minutes of using the technique of Put Your Fingers on Your Forehead while replaying any of the thoughts, feelings, emotions, or statements that may have felt negative, painful, or oppressive and did not feel good, uplifting, or positive.

I made it through DAY EIGHT! I AM free of hate! Oooeee, can I love ME!

Day Nine (09)--
Time to connect to YOUR DIVINE! Welcome to DAY NINE!

- Breathe in, breathe out (take several deep, cleansing breaths).
- Think or state three times: "God, be a part of everything I think, say, feel, and do."

What do you notice and how do you feel right now?

_____

_____

_____

_____

Great! (Remember, wherever you are is right for your life's journey.)

Today we will check in via muscle testing on six new feelings/emotions (listed below).
Muscle test yourself – STRONG or WEAK – one at a time.

Example: "I feel _____." Insert the feeling/emotion in the blank. Muscle test yourself for each statement. After each one, place a check mark to indicate your response using the blank on the left side of the slash (/). The blank to the right side of the slash is to indicate your response after you have done the clearing work.

Strong / Weak		FEELING or EMOTION
__/__	__/__	Cut off from God/My Divine/My Highest Power
__/__	__/__	Defiled
__/__	__/__	Unforgiven
__/__	__/__	Shunned
__/__	__/__	Persecuted
__/__	__/__	Forgotten

Were you surprised by your actual responses via muscle testing?
Either way, good!

It is time to clear using the Energetic Action Process. Simply drum or clap the fingers of either hand on the side of your other hand below your pinky finger and above your wrist, or clap both hands together while saying:

"**I deeply love and accept myself even if I feel** _____." (Insert the FEELING or EMOTION.) Repeat the statement three (3) times. Continue the drumming/clapping motion.

"**I deeply love and accept myself even if I have hidden or unknown issues with** _____." (Insert the FEELING or EMOTION.) Repeat the statement three (3) times. Continue the drumming/clapping motion.

"**I deeply love and accept myself even if I refuse to do the things necessary to free myself from feeling** _____." (Insert the FEELING or EMOTION.) Repeat the statement three (3) times. Continue the drumming/clapping motion.

What do you notice and how do you feel right now?

_____

_____

_____

_____

Excellent! Now go back and re-muscle test each FEELING or EMOTION for STRONG or WEAK and mark your results in the blanks to the right of the slash mark.

Please remember, you are always able to repeat the above steps anytime you choose or feel it necessary as YOU are in charge of your life!

Please end your day with a few minutes of using the technique of Put Your Fingers on Your Forehead while replaying any of the thoughts, feelings, emotions, or statements that may have felt negative, painful, or oppressive and did not feel good, uplifting, or positive.

I made it through DAY NINE! I AM connected to MY DIVINE!

Day Ten (10)--
What? When? Yep, you're already at DAY TEN!
- Breathe in, breathe out (take several deep, cleansing breaths).
- Think or state three times: "God, be a part of everything I think, say, feel, and do."

What do you notice and how do you feel right now?

_____

_____

_____

_____

Great! (Remember, wherever you are is right for your life's journey.)
Today we will check in via muscle testing on six new feelings/emotions (listed below).
Muscle test yourself – STRONG or WEAK – one at a time.

Example: "I feel _____." Insert the feeling/emotion in the blank. Muscle test yourself for each statement. After each one, place a check mark to indicate your response using the blank on the left side of the slash (/). The blank to the right side of the slash is to indicate your response after you have done the clearing work.

Strong / Weak		FEELING or EMOTION
__/__	__/__	Disoriented
__/__	__/__	Fragmented
__/__	__/__	Confused/Confusion
__/__	__/__	Jittery
__/__	__/__	Agitated/Agitation
__/__	__/__	Impaired

Were you surprised by your actual responses via muscle testing?
Either way, good!

It is time to clear using the Energetic Action Process. Simply drum or clap the fingers of either hand on the side of your other hand below your pinky finger and above your wrist, or clap both hands together while saying:

"**I deeply love and accept myself even if I feel** _____." (Insert the FEELING or EMOTION.) Repeat the statement three (3) times. Continue the drumming/clapping motion.

"**I deeply love and accept myself even if I have hidden or unknown issues with** _____." (Insert the FEELING or EMOTION.) Repeat the statement three (3) times. Continue the drumming/clapping motion.

"**I deeply love and accept myself even if I refuse to do the things necessary to free myself from feeling** _____." (Insert the FEELING or EMOTION.) Repeat the statement three (3) times. Continue the drumming/clapping motion.

What do you notice and how do you feel right now?

_____

_____

_____

_____

Excellent! Now go back and re-muscle test each FEELING or EMOTION for STRONG or WEAK and mark your results in the blanks to the right of the slash mark.

Please remember, you are always able to repeat the above steps anytime you choose or feel it necessary as YOU are in charge of your life!

Please end your day with a few minutes of using the technique of Put Your Fingers on Your Forehead while replaying any of the thoughts, feelings, emotions, or statements that may have felt negative, painful, or oppressive and did not feel good, uplifting, or positive.

I made it through DAY TEN! AM I now ZEN?

Day Eleven (11)---
You are four days past seven! Welcome to DAY ELEVEN!

- Breathe in, breathe out (take several deep, cleansing breaths).
- Think or state three times: "God, be a part of everything I think, say, feel, and do."

What do you notice and how do you feel right now?

_____

_____

_____

_____

Great! (Remember, wherever you are is right for your life's journey.)

Today we will check in via muscle testing on six new feelings/emotions (listed below).

Muscle test yourself – STRONG or WEAK – one at a time.

Example: "I feel _____." Insert the feeling/emotion in the blank. Muscle test yourself for each statement. After each one, place a check mark to indicate your response using the blank on the left side of the slash (/). The blank to the right side of the slash is to indicate your response after you have done the clearing work.

Strong / Weak		FEELING or EMOTION
__/__	__/__	Egotistical
__/__	__/__	Arrogant
__/__	__/__	Lacking
__/__	__/__	Devalued
__/__	__/__	Unhappy
__/__	__/__	Joyless

Were you surprised by your actual responses via muscle testing?
Either way, good!

It is time to clear using the Energetic Action Process. Simply drum or clap the fingers of either hand on the side of your other hand below your pinky finger and above your wrist, or clap both hands together while saying:

"**I deeply love and accept myself even if I feel** _____." (Insert the FEELING or EMOTION.) Repeat the statement three (3) times. Continue the drumming/clapping motion.

"**I deeply love and accept myself even if I have hidden or unknown issues with** _____." (Insert the FEELING or EMOTION.) Repeat the statement three (3) times. Continue the drumming/clapping motion.

"**I deeply love and accept myself even if I refuse to do the things necessary to free myself from feeling** _____." (Insert the FEELING or EMOTION.) Repeat the statement three (3) times. Continue the drumming/clapping motion.

What do you notice and how do you feel right now?

_____

_____

_____

_____

Excellent! Now go back and re-muscle test each FEELING or EMOTION for STRONG or WEAK and mark your results in the blanks to the right of the slash mark.

Please remember, you are always able to repeat the above steps anytime you choose or feel it necessary as YOU are in charge of your life!

Please end your day with a few minutes of using the technique of Put Your Fingers on Your Forehead while replaying any of the thoughts, feelings, emotions, or statements that may have felt negative, painful, or oppressive and did not feel good, uplifting, or positive.

I made it through DAY ELEVEN! Soon my life will be a heaven!

Day Twelve (12)--

Wow! Congratulate yourself! Welcome to DAY TWELVE!

- Breathe in, breathe out (take several deep, cleansing breaths).
- Think or state three times: "God, be a part of everything I think, say, feel, and do."

What do you notice and how do you feel right now?

_____

_____

_____

_____

Great! (Remember, wherever you are is right for your life's journey.)

Today we will check in via muscle testing on six new feelings/emotions (listed below).

Muscle test yourself – STRONG or WEAK – one at a time.

Example: "I feel _____." Insert the feeling/emotion in the blank. Muscle test yourself for each statement. After each one, place a check mark to indicate your response using the blank on the left side of the slash (/). The blank to the right side of the slash is to indicate your response after you have done the clearing work.

Strong / Weak		FEELING or EMOTION
__/__	__/__	Annoyed
__/__	__/__	Bitter
__/__	__/__	Blaming
__/__	__/__	Enraged
__/__	__/__	Disgusted
__/__	__/__	Holding a grudge

Were you surprised by your actual responses via muscle testing? Either way, good!

It is time to clear using the Energetic Action Process. Simply drum or clap the fingers of either hand on the side of your other hand below your pinky finger and above your wrist, or clap both hands together while saying:

"**I deeply love and accept myself even if I feel** _____." (Insert the FEELING or EMOTION.) Repeat the statement three (3) times. Continue the drumming/clapping motion.

"**I deeply love and accept myself even if I have hidden or unknown issues with** _____." (Insert the FEELING or EMOTION.) Repeat the statement three (3) times. Continue the drumming/clapping motion.

"**I deeply love and accept myself even if I refuse to do the things necessary to free myself from feeling** _____." (Insert the FEELING or EMOTION.) Repeat the statement three (3) times. Continue the drumming/clapping motion.

What do you notice and how do you feel right now?

_____

_____

_____

_____

Excellent! Now go back and re-muscle test each FEELING or EMOTION for STRONG or WEAK and mark your results in the blanks to the right of the slash mark.

Please remember, you are always able to repeat the above steps anytime you choose or feel it necessary as YOU are in charge of your life!

Please end your day with a few minutes of using the technique of Put Your Fingers on Your Forehead while replaying any of the thoughts, feelings, emotions, or statements that may have felt negative, painful, or oppressive and did not feel good, uplifting, or positive.

Hey, I am really buzzin'! Made it through an even dozen!

Day Thirteen (13)---
Become a joy-making machine! Welcome to DAY THIRTEEN!
- Breathe in, breathe out (take several deep, cleansing breaths).
- Think or state three times: "God, be a part of everything I think, say, feel, and do."

What do you notice and how do you feel right now?

_____

_____

_____

_____

Great! (Remember, wherever you are is right for your life's journey.)
Today we will check in via muscle testing on six new feelings/emotions (listed below).
Muscle test yourself – STRONG or WEAK – one at a time.

Example: "I feel _____." Insert the feeling/emotion in the blank. Muscle test yourself for each statement. After each one, place a check mark to indicate your response using the blank on the left side of the slash (/). The blank to the right side of the slash is to indicate your response after you have done the clearing work.

Strong / Weak		FEELING or EMOTION
__/__	__/__	Troubled
__/__	__/__	Lacking compassion
__/__	__/__	Inconsiderate
__/__	__/__	Indecisive
__/__	__/__	Unfocused
__/__	__/__	Tactless

Were you surprised by your actual responses via muscle testing?
Either way, good!

It is time to clear using the Energetic Action Process. Simply drum or clap the fingers of either hand on the side of your other hand below your pinky finger and above your wrist, or clap both hands together while saying:

"**I deeply love and accept myself even if I feel** _____." (Insert the FEELING or EMOTION.) Repeat the statement three (3) times. Continue the drumming/clapping motion.

"**I deeply love and accept myself even if I have hidden or unknown issues with** _____." (Insert the FEELING or EMOTION.) Repeat the statement three (3) times. Continue the drumming/clapping motion.

"**I deeply love and accept myself even if I refuse to do the things necessary to free myself from feeling** _____." (Insert the FEELING or EMOTION.) Repeat the statement three (3) times. Continue the drumming/clapping motion.

What do you notice and how do you feel right now?

_____

_____

_____

_____

Excellent! Now go back and re-muscle test each FEELING or EMOTION for STRONG or WEAK and mark your results in the blanks to the right of the slash mark.

Please remember, you are always able to repeat the above steps anytime you choose or feel it necessary as YOU are in charge of your life!

Please end your day with a few minutes of using the technique of Put Your Fingers on Your Forehead while replaying any of the thoughts, feelings, emotions, or statements that may have felt negative, painful, or oppressive and did not feel good, uplifting, or positive.

I'm a joy-making machine! Made it through DAY THIRTEEN!

Day Fourteen (14)---
You've been transforming yourself for two whole weeks! Welcome to DAY FOURTEEN!

- Breathe in, breathe out (take several deep, cleansing breaths).
- Think or state three times: "God, be a part of everything I think, say, feel, and do."

What do you notice and how do you feel right now?

_____

_____

_____

_____

Great! Remember, wherever you are is right for your life's journey.)
Today we will check in via muscle testing on six new feelings/emotions (listed below).
   Muscle test yourself – STRONG or WEAK – one at a time.

   Example: "I feel _____." Insert the feeling/emotion in the blank. Muscle test yourself for each statement. After each one, place a check mark to indicate your response using the blank on the left side of the slash (/). The blank to the right side of the slash is to indicate your response after you have done the clearing work.

Strong / Weak		FEELING or EMOTION
__/__	__/__	Unforgiving
__/__	__/__	Offended
__/__	__/__	Vengeful
__/__	__/__	Not safe
__/__	__/__	Restless
__/__	__/__	Tense

Were you surprised by your actual responses via muscle testing?
Either way, good!

It is time to clear using the Energetic Action Process. Simply drum or clap the fingers of either hand on the side of your other hand below your pinky finger and above your wrist, or clap both hands together while saying:

"I deeply love and accept myself even if I feel _____." (Insert the FEELING or EMOTION.) Repeat the statement three (3) times. Continue the drumming/clapping motion.

"I deeply love and accept myself even if I have hidden or unknown issues with _____." (Insert the FEELING or EMOTION.) Repeat the statement three (3) times. Continue the drumming/clapping motion.

"I deeply love and accept myself even if I refuse to do the things necessary to free myself from feeling _____." (Insert the FEELING or EMOTION.) Repeat the statement three (3) times. Continue the drumming/clapping motion.

What do you notice and how do you feel right now?

_____

_____

_____

_____

Excellent! Now go back and re-muscle test each FEELING or EMOTION for STRONG or WEAK and mark your results in the blanks to the right of the slash mark.

Please remember, you are always able to repeat the above steps anytime you choose or feel it necessary as YOU are in charge of your life!

Please end your day with a few minutes of using the technique of Put Your Fingers on Your Forehead while replaying any of the thoughts, feelings, emotions, or statements that may have felt negative, painful, or oppressive and did not feel good, uplifting, or positive.

I AM feeling at my peak! Made it through my SECOND WEEK!

Day Fifteen (15)---

Hooray, hooray! It's your FIFTEENTH DAY!

- Breathe in, breathe out (take several deep, cleansing breaths).
- Think or state three times: "God, be a part of everything I think, say, feel, and do."

What do you notice and how do you feel right now?

_____

_____

_____

_____

Great! (Remember, wherever you are is right for your life's journey.)
Today we will check in via muscle testing on six new feelings/emotions (listed below).
Muscle test yourself – STRONG or WEAK – one at a time.

Example: "I feel _____." Insert the feeling/emotion in the blank. Muscle test yourself for each statement. After each one, place a check mark to indicate your response using the blank on the left side of the slash (/). The blank to the right side of the slash is to indicate your response after you have done the clearing work.

Strong / Weak		FEELING or EMOTION
__/__	__/__	Restricted
__/__	__/__	Passionless
__/__	__/__	Mean
__/__	__/__	Overbearing
__/__	__/__	Hardened
__/__	__/__	Ignored

Were you surprised by your actual responses via muscle testing?
Either way, good!

It is time to clear using the Energetic Action Process. Simply drum or clap the fingers of either hand on the side of your other hand below your pinky finger and above your wrist, or clap both hands together while saying:

"**I deeply love and accept myself even if I feel** _____." (Insert the FEELING or EMOTION.) Repeat the statement three (3) times. Continue the drumming/clapping motion.

"**I deeply love and accept myself even if I have hidden or unknown issues with** _____." (Insert the FEELING or EMOTION.) Repeat the statement three (3) times. Continue the drumming/clapping motion.

"**I deeply love and accept myself even if I refuse to do the things necessary to free myself from feeling** _____." (Insert the FEELING or EMOTION.) Repeat the statement three (3) times. Continue the drumming/clapping motion.

What do you notice and how do you feel right now?

_____

_____

_____

_____

Excellent! Now go back and re-muscle test each FEELING or EMOTION for STRONG or WEAK and mark your results in the blanks to the right of the slash mark.

Please remember, you are always able to repeat the above steps anytime you choose or feel it necessary as YOU are in charge of your life!

Please end your day with a few minutes of using the technique of Put Your Fingers on Your Forehead while replaying any of the thoughts, feelings, emotions, or statements that may have felt negative, painful, or oppressive and did not feel good, uplifting, or positive.

Oh, the changes I've seen! Just completed DAY FIFTEEN!

Day Sixteen (16)--

Sweet sixteen, here you come! Your second week, plus one and one!

- Breathe in, breathe out (take several deep, cleansing breaths).
- Think or state three times: "God, be a part of everything I think, say, feel, and do."

What do you notice and how do you feel right now?

_____

_____

_____

_____

Great! (Remember, wherever you are is right for your life's journey.)

Today we will check in via muscle testing on six new feelings/emotions (listed below).

Muscle test yourself – STRONG or WEAK – one at a time.

Example: "I feel _____." Insert the feeling/emotion in the blank. Muscle test yourself for each statement. After each one, place a check mark to indicate your response using the blank on the left side of the slash (/). The blank to the right side of the slash is to indicate your response after you have done the clearing work.

Strong / Weak		FEELING or EMOTION
__/__	__/__	Untrusting
__/__	__/__	Lonely
__/__	__/__	Isolated
__/__	__/__	Unloved
__/__	__/__	Grief
__/__	__/__	Despair

Were you surprised by your actual responses via muscle testing?
Either way, good!

It is time to clear using the Energetic Action Process. Simply drum or clap the fingers of either hand on the side of your other hand below your pinky finger and above your wrist, or clap both hands together while saying:

"I deeply love and accept myself even if I feel _____." (Insert the FEELING or EMOTION.) Repeat the statement three (3) times. Continue the drumming/clapping motion.

"I deeply love and accept myself even if I have hidden or unknown issues with _____." (Insert the FEELING or EMOTION.) Repeat the statement three (3) times. Continue the drumming/clapping motion.

"I deeply love and accept myself even if I refuse to do the things necessary to free myself from feeling _____." (Insert the FEELING or EMOTION.) Repeat the statement three (3) times. Continue the drumming/clapping motion.

What do you notice and how do you feel right now?

_____

_____

_____

_____

Excellent! Now go back and re-muscle test each FEELING or EMOTION for STRONG or WEAK and mark your results in the blanks to the right of the slash mark.

Please remember, you are always able to repeat the above steps anytime you choose or feel it necessary as YOU are in charge of your life!

Please end your day with a few minutes of using the technique of Put Your Fingers on Your Forehead while replaying any of the thoughts, feelings, emotions, or statements that may have felt negative, painful, or oppressive and did not feel good, uplifting, or positive.

SWEET! SIXTEEN DAYS complete!

Day Seventeen (17)---
You're on a roll and more than halfway to your goal! Welcome to
DAY SEVENTEEN!
- Breathe in, breathe out (take several deep, cleansing breaths).
- Think or state three times: "God, be a part of everything I think, say, feel, and do."

What do you notice and how do you feel right now?

_____

_____

_____

_____

Great! (Remember, wherever you are is right for your life's journey.)
Today we will check in via muscle testing on six new feelings/emotions (listed below).
Muscle test yourself – STRONG or WEAK – one at a time.

Example: "I feel _____." Insert the feeling/emotion in the blank.
Muscle test yourself for each statement. After each one, place a check mark to indicate
your response using the blank on the left side of the slash (/). The blank to the right
side of the slash is to indicate your response after you have done the clearing work.

Strong / Weak		FEELING or EMOTION
__/__	__/__	Disappointed
__/__	__/__	Desperate
__/__	__/__	Wounded
__/__	__/__	Apathetic
__/__	__/__	Ashamed
__/__	__/__	Regretful

Were you surprised by your actual responses via muscle testing?
Either way, good!

It is time to clear using the Energetic Action Process. Simply drum or clap the fingers of either hand on the side of your other hand below your pinky finger and above your wrist, or clap both hands together while saying:

"**I deeply love and accept myself even if I feel** _____." (Insert the FEELING or EMOTION.) Repeat the statement three (3) times. Continue the drumming/clapping motion.

"**I deeply love and accept myself even if I have hidden or unknown issues with** _____." (Insert the FEELING or EMOTION.) Repeat the statement three (3) times. Continue the drumming/clapping motion.

"**I deeply love and accept myself even if I refuse to do the things necessary to free myself from feeling** _____." (Insert the FEELING or EMOTION.) Repeat the statement three (3) times. Continue the drumming/clapping motion.

What do you notice and how do you feel right now?

_____

_____

_____

_____

Excellent! Now go back and re-muscle test each FEELING or EMOTION for STRONG or WEAK and mark your results in the blanks to the right of the slash mark.

Please remember, you are always able to repeat the above steps anytime you choose or feel it necessary as YOU are in charge of your life!

Please end your day with a few minutes of using the technique of Put Your Fingers on Your Forehead while replaying any of the thoughts, feelings, emotions, or statements that may have felt negative, painful, or oppressive and did not feel good, uplifting, or positive.

Over the hump and well on my way! I made it through my SEVENTEENTH DAY!

Day Eighteen (18)--
Celebrate! You've arrived at DAY ONE-EIGHT!

- Breathe in, breathe out (take several deep, cleansing breaths).
- Think or state three times: "God, be a part of everything I think, say, feel, and do."

What do you notice and how do you feel right now?

_____

_____

_____

_____

Great! (Remember, wherever you are is right for your life's journey.)
Today we will check in via muscle testing on six new feelings/emotions (listed below).
Muscle test yourself – STRONG or WEAK – one at a time.

Example: "I feel _____." Insert the feeling/emotion in the blank. Muscle test yourself for each statement. After each one, place a check mark to indicate your response using the blank on the left side of the slash (/). The blank to the right side of the slash is to indicate your response after you have done the clearing work.

Strong / Weak		FEELING or EMOTION
__/__	__/__	Dissatisfied
__/__	__/__	Used
__/__	__/__	Hurt
__/__	__/__	Traumatized
__/__	__/__	Unable to express myself
__/__	__/__	Overly sensitive

Were you surprised by your actual responses via muscle testing?
Either way, good!

It is time to clear using the Energetic Action Process. Simply drum or clap the fingers of either hand on the side of your other hand below your pinky finger and above your wrist, or clap both hands together while saying:

"**I deeply love and accept myself even if I feel** _____." (Insert the FEELING or EMOTION.) Repeat the statement three (3) times. Continue the drumming/clapping motion.

"**I deeply love and accept myself even if I have hidden or unknown issues with** _____." (Insert the FEELING or EMOTION.) Repeat the statement three (3) times. Continue the drumming/clapping motion.

"**I deeply love and accept myself even if I refuse to do the things necessary to free myself from feeling** _____." (Insert the FEELING or EMOTION.) Repeat the statement three (3) times. Continue the drumming/clapping motion.

What do you notice and how do you feel right now?

_____

_____

_____

_____

Excellent! Now go back and re-muscle test each FEELING or EMOTION for STRONG or WEAK and mark your results in the blanks to the right of the slash mark.

Please remember, you are always able to repeat the above steps anytime you choose or feel it necessary as YOU are in charge of your life!

Please end your day with a few minutes of using the technique of Put Your Fingers on Your Forehead while replaying any of the thoughts, feelings, emotions, or statements that may have felt negative, painful, or oppressive and did not feel good, uplifting, or positive.

EIGHTEEN DAYS under my belt! Good for me!

Day Nineteen (19)---
You're going strong! Welcome to DAY NINETEEN!
- Breathe in, breathe out (take several deep, cleansing breaths).
- Think or state three times: "God, be a part of everything I think, say, feel, and do."

What do you notice and how do you feel right now?

_____

_____

_____

_____

Great! (Remember, wherever you are is right for your life's journey.)
Today we will check in via muscle testing on six new feelings/emotions (listed below).
Muscle test yourself – STRONG or WEAK – one at a time.

Example: "I feel _____." Insert the feeling/emotion in the blank. Muscle test yourself for each statement. After each one, place a check mark to indicate your response using the blank on the left side of the slash (/). The blank to the right side of the slash is to indicate your response after you have done the clearing work.

Strong / Weak		FEELING or EMOTION
__/__	__/__	Self-doubting
__/__	__/__	Unfeeling
__/__	__/__	Self-loathing
__/__	__/__	Inferior
__/__	__/__	Insignificant
__/__	__/__	Out of control

Were you surprised by your actual responses via muscle testing?
Either way, good!

It is time to clear using the Energetic Action Process. Simply drum or clap the fingers of either hand on the side of your other hand below your pinky finger and above your wrist, or clap both hands together while saying:

"**I deeply love and accept myself even if I feel** _____." (Insert the FEELING or EMOTION.) Repeat the statement three (3) times. Continue the drumming/clapping motion.

"**I deeply love and accept myself even if I have hidden or unknown issues with** _____." (Insert the FEELING or EMOTION.) Repeat the statement three (3) times. Continue the drumming/clapping motion.

"**I deeply love and accept myself even if I refuse to do the things necessary to free myself from feeling** _____." (Insert the FEELING or EMOTION.) Repeat the statement three (3) times. Continue the drumming/clapping motion.

What do you notice and how do you feel right now?

_____

_____

_____

_____

Excellent! Now go back and re-muscle test each FEELING or EMOTION for STRONG or WEAK and mark your results in the blanks to the right of the slash mark.

Please remember, you are always able to repeat the above steps anytime you choose or feel it necessary as YOU are in charge of your life!

Please end your day with a few minutes of using the technique of Put Your Fingers on Your Forehead while replaying any of the thoughts, feelings, emotions, or statements that may have felt negative, painful, or oppressive and did not feel good, uplifting, or positive.

I honor myself on DAY NINETEEN! Hooray for me!

Day Twenty (20)---
It's your time of INNER PLENTY! Welcome, welcome to DAY TWENTY!
- Breathe in, breathe out (take several deep, cleansing breaths).
- Think or state three times: "God, be a part of everything I think, say, feel, and do."

What do you notice and how do you feel right now?

_____

_____

_____

_____

Great! (Remember, wherever you are is right for your life's journey.)
Today we will check in via muscle testing on six new feelings/emotions (listed below).
Muscle test yourself – STRONG or WEAK – one at a time.

Example: "I feel _____." Insert the feeling/emotion in the blank. Muscle test yourself for each statement. After each one, place a check mark to indicate your response using the blank on the left side of the slash (/). The blank to the right side of the slash is to indicate your response after you have done the clearing work.

Strong / Weak		FEELING or EMOTION
__/__	__/__	Irritated
__/__	__/__	Bored
__/__	__/__	Not good enough
__/__	__/__	Poor
__/__	__/__	Stupid
__/__	__/__	Suppressed

Were you surprised by your actual responses via muscle testing?
Either way, good!

It is time to clear using the Energetic Action Process. Simply drum or clap the fingers of either hand on the side of your other hand below your pinky finger and above your wrist, or clap both hands together while saying:

"I deeply love and accept myself even if I feel _____." (Insert the FEELING or EMOTION.) Repeat the statement three (3) times. Continue the drumming/clapping motion.

"I deeply love and accept myself even if I have hidden or unknown issues with _____." (Insert the FEELING or EMOTION.) Repeat the statement three (3) times. Continue the drumming/clapping motion.

"I deeply love and accept myself even if I refuse to do the things necessary to free myself from feeling _____." (Insert the FEELING or EMOTION.) Repeat the statement three (3) times. Continue the drumming/clapping motion.

What do you notice and how do you feel right now?

_____

_____

_____

_____

Excellent! Now go back and re-muscle test each FEELING or EMOTION for STRONG or WEAK and mark your results in the blanks to the right of the slash mark.

Please remember, you are always able to repeat the above steps anytime you choose or feel it necessary as YOU are in charge of your life!

Please end your day with a few minutes of using the technique of Put Your Fingers on Your Forehead while replaying any of the thoughts, feelings, emotions, or statements that may have felt negative, painful, or oppressive and did not feel good, uplifting, or positive.

I AM feeling in the know! Just made it through the big TWO-O!

Day Twenty-One (21)---
You are in for bigtime FUN! Welcome to DAY TWENTY-ONE!
- Breathe in, breathe out (take several deep, cleansing breaths).
- Think or state three times: "God, be a part of everything I think, say, feel, and do."

What do you notice and how do you feel right now?

_____

_____

_____

_____

Great! (Remember, wherever you are is right for your life's journey.)
Today we will check in via muscle testing on six new feelings/emotions (listed below).
Muscle test yourself – STRONG or WEAK – one at a time.

Example: "I feel _____." Insert the feeling/emotion in the blank. Muscle test yourself for each statement. After each one, place a check mark to indicate your response using the blank on the left side of the slash (/). The blank to the right side of the slash is to indicate your response after you have done the clearing work.

Strong / Weak		FEELING or EMOTION
__/__	__/__	Vain
__/__	__/__	Weak
__/__	__/__	Belittled
__/__	__/__	Abandoned
__/__	__/__	Deceived
__/__	__/__	Disgraced

Were you surprised by your actual responses via muscle testing?
Either way, good!

It is time to clear using the Energetic Action Process. Simply drum or clap the fingers of either hand on the side of your other hand below your pinky finger and above your wrist, or clap both hands together while saying:

"**I deeply love and accept myself even if I feel** _____." (Insert the FEELING or EMOTION.) Repeat the statement three (3) times. Continue the drumming/clapping motion.

"**I deeply love and accept myself even if I have hidden or unknown issues with** _____." (Insert the FEELING or EMOTION.) Repeat the statement three (3) times. Continue the drumming/clapping motion.

"**I deeply love and accept myself even if I refuse to do the things necessary to free myself from feeling** _____." (Insert the FEELING or EMOTION.) Repeat the statement three (3) times. Continue the drumming/clapping motion.

What do you notice and how do you feel right now?

_____

_____

_____

_____

Excellent! Now go back and re-muscle test each FEELING or EMOTION for STRONG or WEAK and mark your results in the blanks to the right of the slash mark.

Please remember, you are always able to repeat the above steps anytime you choose or feel it necessary as YOU are in charge of your life!

Please end your day with a few minutes of using the technique of Put Your Fingers on Your Forehead while replaying any of the thoughts, feelings, emotions, or statements that may have felt negative, painful, or oppressive and did not feel good, uplifting, or positive.

Away, old baggage! I'm done, done, done. I just completed DAY TWENTY-ONE!

Day Twenty-Two (22)--
Woo Hoo for YOU! You've arrived at DAY TWENTY-TWO!

- Breathe in, breathe out (take several deep, cleansing breaths).
- Think or state three times: "God, be a part of everything I think, say, feel, and do."

What do you notice and how do you feel right now?

_____
_____
_____
_____

Great! (Remember, wherever you are is right for your life's journey.)
Today we will check in via muscle testing on six new feelings/emotions (listed below).
    Muscle test yourself – STRONG or WEAK – one at a time.

    Example: "I feel _____." Insert the feeling/emotion in the blank. Muscle test yourself for each statement. After each one, place a check mark to indicate your response using the blank on the left side of the slash (/). The blank to the right side of the slash is to indicate your response after you have done the clearing work.

Strong / Weak		FEELING or EMOTION
__/__	__/__	Left out
__/__	__/__	Neglected
__/__	__/__	Not heard
__/__	__/__	Shamed
__/__	__/__	Unappreciated
__/__	__/__	Unforgiven

Were you surprised by your actual responses via muscle testing?
Either way, good!

It is time to clear using the Energetic Action Process. Simply drum or clap the fingers of either hand on the side of your other hand below your pinky finger and above your wrist, or clap both hands together while saying:

"I deeply love and accept myself even if I feel _____." (Insert the FEELING or EMOTION.) Repeat the statement three (3) times. Continue the drumming/clapping motion.

"I deeply love and accept myself even if I have hidden or unknown issues with _____." (Insert the FEELING or EMOTION.) Repeat the statement three (3) times. Continue the drumming/clapping motion.

"I deeply love and accept myself even if I refuse to do the things necessary to free myself from feeling _____." (Insert the FEELING or EMOTION.) Repeat the statement three (3) times. Continue the drumming/clapping motion.

What do you notice and how do you feel right now?

_____

_____

_____

_____

Excellent! Now go back and re-muscle test each FEELING or EMOTION for STRONG or WEAK and mark your results in the blanks to the right of the slash mark.

Please remember, you are always able to repeat the above steps anytime you choose or feel it necessary as YOU are in charge of your life!

Please end your day with a few minutes of using the technique of Put Your Fingers on Your Forehead while replaying any of the thoughts, feelings, emotions, or statements that may have felt negative, painful, or oppressive and did not feel good, uplifting, or positive.

I AM on fire! TWENTY-TWO days and still committed!

Day Twenty-Three (23)--
We're off to the races. Wheee! Welcome to DAY TWENTY-THREE!
- Breathe in, breathe out (take several deep, cleansing breaths).
- Think or state three times: "God, be a part of everything I think, say, feel, and do."

What do you notice and how do you feel right now?

_____

_____

_____

_____

Great! (Remember, wherever you are is right for your life's journey.)
Today we will check in via muscle testing on six new feelings/emotions (listed below).
  Muscle test yourself – STRONG or WEAK – one at a time.

  Example: "I feel _____." Insert the feeling/emotion in the blank. Muscle test yourself for each statement. After each one, place a check mark to indicate your response using the blank on the left side of the slash (/). The blank to the right side of the slash is to indicate your response after you have done the clearing work.

Strong / Weak		FEELING or EMOTION
__/__	__/__	Inadequate
__/__	__/__	Unforgiving
__/__	__/__	Violated
__/__	__/__	Victimized
__/__	__/__	Dirty
__/__	__/__	Lost

Were you surprised by your actual responses via muscle testing?
Either way, good!

It is time to clear using the Energetic Action Process. Simply drum or clap the fingers of either hand on the side of your other hand below your pinky finger and above your wrist, or clap both hands together while saying:

"I deeply love and accept myself even if I feel _____." (Insert the FEELING or EMOTION.) Repeat the statement three (3) times. Continue the drumming/clapping motion.

"I deeply love and accept myself even if I have hidden or unknown issues with _____." (Insert the FEELING or EMOTION.) Repeat the statement three (3) times. Continue the drumming/clapping motion.

"I deeply love and accept myself even if I refuse to do the things necessary to free myself from feeling _____." (Insert the FEELING or EMOTION.) Repeat the statement three (3) times. Continue the drumming/clapping motion.

What do you notice and how do you feel right now?

_____

_____

_____

_____

Excellent! Now go back and re-muscle test each FEELING or EMOTION for STRONG or WEAK and mark your results in the blanks to the right of the slash mark.

Please remember, you are always able to repeat the above steps anytime you choose or feel it necessary as YOU are in charge of your life!

Please end your day with a few minutes of using the technique of Put Your Fingers on Your Forehead while replaying any of the thoughts, feelings, emotions, or statements that may have felt negative, painful, or oppressive and did not feel good, uplifting, or positive.

Wowza! Good for me, it's a biggie! I made it through DAY TWENTY-THREE!

Day Twenty-Four (24)--
Ready for more? Welcome to DAY TWENTY-FOUR!

- Breathe in, breathe out (take several deep, cleansing breaths).
- Think or state three times: "God, be a part of everything I think, say, feel, and do."

What do you notice and how do you feel right now?

_____
_____
_____
_____

Great! (Remember, wherever you are is right for your life's journey.)
Today we will check in via muscle testing on six new feelings/emotions (listed below).
Muscle test yourself – STRONG or WEAK – one at a time.

Example: "I feel _____." Insert the feeling/emotion in the blank. Muscle test yourself for each statement. After each one, place a check mark to indicate your response using the blank on the left side of the slash (/). The blank to the right side of the slash is to indicate your response after you have done the clearing work.

Strong / Weak		FEELING or EMOTION
__/__	__/__	Indiscreet
__/__	__/__	Unattractive
__/__	__/__	Blocked
__/__	__/__	Cynical
__/__	__/__	Greedy
__/__	__/__	Jealous

Were you surprised by your actual responses via muscle testing?
Either way, good!

It is time to clear using the Energetic Action Process. Simply drum or clap the fingers of either hand on the side of your other hand below your pinky finger and above your wrist, or clap both hands together while saying:

"**I deeply love and accept myself even if I feel** _____." (Insert the FEELING or EMOTION.) Repeat the statement three (3) times. Continue the drumming/clapping motion.

"**I deeply love and accept myself even if I have hidden or unknown issues with** _____." (Insert the FEELING or EMOTION.) Repeat the statement three (3) times. Continue the drumming/clapping motion.

"**I deeply love and accept myself even if I refuse to do the things necessary to free myself from feeling** _____." (Insert the FEELING or EMOTION.) Repeat the statement three (3) times. Continue the drumming/clapping motion.

What do you notice and how do you feel right now?

_____

_____

_____

_____

Excellent! Now go back and re-muscle test each FEELING or EMOTION for STRONG or WEAK and mark your results in the blanks to the right of the slash mark.

Please remember, you are always able to repeat the above steps anytime you choose or feel it necessary as YOU are in charge of your life!

Please end your day with a few minutes of using the technique of Put Your Fingers on Your Forehead while replaying any of the thoughts, feelings, emotions, or statements that may have felt negative, painful, or oppressive and did not feel good, uplifting, or positive.

This is GREAT! I want more! I just cleared for DAY TWENTY-FOUR!

Day Twenty-Five (25)--

Are you ready to thrive? Welcome to DAY TWENTY-FIVE!

- Breathe in, breathe out (take several deep, cleansing breaths).
- Think or state three times: "God, be a part of everything I think, say, feel, and do."

What do you notice and how do you feel right now?

_____

_____

_____

_____

Great! (Remember, wherever you are is right for your life's journey.)

Today we will check in via muscle testing on six new feelings/emotions (listed below).

Muscle test yourself – STRONG or WEAK – one at a time.

Example: "I feel _____." Insert the feeling/emotion in the blank. Muscle test yourself for each statement. After each one, place a check mark to indicate your response using the blank on the left side of the slash (/). The blank to the right side of the slash is to indicate your response after you have done the clearing work.

Strong / Weak		FEELING or EMOTION
__/__	__/__	Rude
__/__	__/__	Bullying
__/__	__/__	Obnoxious
__/__	__/__	Loud
__/__	__/__	Blunt
__/__	__/__	Cruel

Were you surprised by your actual responses via muscle testing? Either way, good!

It is time to clear using the Energetic Action Process. Simply drum or clap the fingers of either hand on the side of your other hand below your pinky finger and above your wrist, or clap both hands together while saying:

"**I deeply love and accept myself even if I feel** _____." (Insert the FEELING or EMOTION.) Repeat the statement three (3) times. Continue the drumming/clapping motion.

"**I deeply love and accept myself even if I have hidden or unknown issues with** _____." (Insert the FEELING or EMOTION.) Repeat the statement three (3) times. Continue the drumming/clapping motion.

"**I deeply love and accept myself even if I refuse to do the things necessary to free myself from feeling** _____." (Insert the FEELING or EMOTION.) Repeat the statement three (3) times. Continue the drumming/clapping motion.

What do you notice and how do you feel right now?

_____

_____

_____

_____

Excellent! Now go back and re-muscle test each FEELING or EMOTION for STRONG or WEAK and mark your results in the blanks to the right of the slash mark.

Please remember, you are always able to repeat the above steps anytime you choose or feel it necessary as YOU are in charge of your life!

Please end your day with a few minutes of using the technique of Put Your Fingers on Your Forehead while replaying any of the thoughts, feelings, emotions, or statements that may have felt negative, painful, or oppressive and did not feel good, uplifting, or positive.

Wow! I think I've hit my STRIDE! Made it through DAY TWENTY-FIVE!

Day Twenty-Six (26)--
You're hooked, huh? Well, get your fix. Welcome to DAY TWENTY-SIX!
- Breathe in, breathe out (take several deep, cleansing breaths).
- Think or state three times: "God, be a part of everything I think, say, feel, and do."

What do you notice and how do you feel right now?

_____

_____

_____

_____

Great! (Remember, wherever you are is right for your life's journey.)
Today we will check in via muscle testing on six new feelings/emotions (listed below).
Muscle test yourself – STRONG or WEAK – one at a time.

Example: "I feel _____." Insert the feeling/emotion in the blank. Muscle test yourself for each statement. After each one, place a check mark to indicate your response using the blank on the left side of the slash (/). The blank to the right side of the slash is to indicate your response after you have done the clearing work.

Strong / Weak		FEELING or EMOTION
__/__	__/__	Unscrupulous
__/__	__/__	Dishonest
__/__	__/__	Embarrassed
__/__	__/__	Like a failure
__/__	__/__	Unimportant
__/__	__/__	Exposed

Were you surprised by your actual responses via muscle testing?
Either way, good!

It is time to clear using the Energetic Action Process. Simply drum or clap the fingers of either hand on the side of your other hand below your pinky finger and above your wrist, or clap both hands together while saying:

"I deeply love and accept myself even if I feel _____." (Insert the FEELING or EMOTION.) Repeat the statement three (3) times. Continue the drumming/clapping motion.

"I deeply love and accept myself even if I have hidden or unknown issues with _____." (Insert the FEELING or EMOTION.) Repeat the statement three (3) times. Continue the drumming/clapping motion.

"I deeply love and accept myself even if I refuse to do the things necessary to free myself from feeling _____." (Insert the FEELING or EMOTION.) Repeat the statement three (3) times. Continue the drumming/clapping motion.

What do you notice and how do you feel right now?

_____

_____

_____

_____

Excellent! Now go back and re-muscle test each FEELING or EMOTION for STRONG or WEAK and mark your results in the blanks to the right of the slash mark.

Please remember, you are always able to repeat the above steps anytime you choose or feel it necessary as YOU are in charge of your life!

Please end your day with a few minutes of using the technique of Put Your Fingers on Your Forehead while replaying any of the thoughts, feelings, emotions, or statements that may have felt negative, painful, or oppressive and did not feel good, uplifting, or positive.

TWENTY-SIX DAYS on my way to a new me!

Day Twenty-Seven (27)--
You're smokin'! What dedication! Welcome to DAY TWENTY-SEVEN!
- Breathe in, breathe out (take several deep, cleansing breaths).
- Think or state three times: "God, be a part of everything I think, say, feel, and do."

What do you notice and how do you feel right now?

_____

_____

_____

_____

Great! (Remember, wherever you are is right for your life's journey.)
Today we will check in via muscle testing on six new feelings/emotions (listed below).
Muscle test yourself – STRONG or WEAK – one at a time.

Example: "I feel _____." Insert the feeling/emotion in the blank. Muscle test yourself for each statement. After each one, place a check mark to indicate your response using the blank on the left side of the slash (/). The blank to the right side of the slash is to indicate your response after you have done the clearing work.

Strong / Weak		FEELING or EMOTION
__/__	__/__	Foolish
__/__	__/__	Humiliated
__/__	__/__	Burnt out
__/__	__/__	Exhausted
__/__	__/__	Stressed
__/__	__/__	Cursed

Were you surprised by your actual responses via muscle testing?
Either way, good!

It is time to clear using the Energetic Action Process. Simply drum or clap the fingers of either hand on the side of your other hand below your pinky finger and above your wrist, or clap both hands together while saying:

"**I deeply love and accept myself even if I feel** _____." (Insert the FEELING or EMOTION.) Repeat the statement three (3) times. Continue the drumming/clapping motion.

"**I deeply love and accept myself even if I have hidden or unknown issues with** _____." (Insert the FEELING or EMOTION.) Repeat the statement three (3) times. Continue the drumming/clapping motion.

"**I deeply love and accept myself even if I refuse to do the things necessary to free myself from feeling** _____." (Insert the FEELING or EMOTION.) Repeat the statement three (3) times. Continue the drumming/clapping motion.

What do you notice and how do you feel right now?

_____

_____

_____

_____

Excellent! Now go back and re-muscle test each FEELING or EMOTION for STRONG or WEAK and mark your results in the blanks to the right of the slash mark.

Please remember, you are always able to repeat the above steps anytime you choose or feel it necessary as YOU are in charge of your life!

Please end your day with a few minutes of using the technique of Put Your Fingers on Your Forehead while replaying any of the thoughts, feelings, emotions, or statements that may have felt negative, painful, or oppressive and did not feel good, uplifting, or positive.

I AM doing this! Made it through DAY TWENTY-SEVEN!

Day Twenty-Eight (28)---

Have I mentioned that I think you're great? Welcome to DAY TWENTY-EIGHT!

- Breathe in, breathe out (take several deep, cleansing breaths).
- Think or state three times: "God, be a part of everything I think, say, feel, and do."

What do you notice and how do you feel right now?

_____

_____

_____

_____

Great! (Remember, wherever you are is right for your life's journey.)

Today we will check in via muscle testing on six new feelings/emotions (listed below).

Muscle test yourself – STRONG or WEAK – one at a time.

Example: "I feel _____." Insert the feeling/emotion in the blank. Muscle test yourself for each statement. After each one, place a check mark to indicate your response using the blank on the left side of the slash (/). The blank to the right side of the slash is to indicate your response after you have done the clearing work.

Strong / Weak		FEELING or EMOTION
__/__	__/__	Uneasy
__/__	__/__	Trapped
__/__	__/__	Stubborn
__/__	__/__	Entitled
__/__	__/__	Defensive
__/__	__/__	Tied down

Were you surprised by your actual responses via muscle testing?
Either way, good!

It is time to clear using the Energetic Action Process. Simply drum or clap the fingers of either hand on the side of your other hand below your pinky finger and above your wrist, or clap both hands together while saying:

"I deeply love and accept myself even if I feel _____." (Insert the FEELING or EMOTION.) Repeat the statement three (3) times. Continue the drumming/clapping motion.

"I deeply love and accept myself even if I have hidden or unknown issues with _____." (Insert the FEELING or EMOTION.) Repeat the statement three (3) times. Continue the drumming/clapping motion.

"I deeply love and accept myself even if I refuse to do the things necessary to free myself from feeling _____." (Insert the FEELING or EMOTION.) Repeat the statement three (3) times. Continue the drumming/clapping motion.

What do you notice and how do you feel right now?

_____

_____

_____

_____

Excellent! Now go back and re-muscle test each FEELING or EMOTION for STRONG or WEAK and mark your results in the blanks to the right of the slash mark.

Please remember, you are always able to repeat the above steps anytime you choose or feel it necessary as YOU are in charge of your life!

Please end your day with a few minutes of using the technique of Put Your Fingers on Your Forehead while replaying any of the thoughts, feelings, emotions, or statements that may have felt negative, painful, or oppressive and did not feel good, uplifting, or positive.

HELLO, ME, I kept our date! Made it through DAY TWENTY-EIGHT!

Day Twenty-Nine (29)--
You're still at it and doing FINE! Welcome to DAY TWENTY-NINE!
- Breathe in, breathe out (take several deep, cleansing breaths).
- Think or state three times: "God, be a part of everything I think, say, feel, and do."

What do you notice and how do you feel right now?

_____

_____

_____

_____

Great! (Remember, wherever you are is right for your life's journey.)
Today we will check in via muscle testing on six new feelings/emotions (listed below).
Muscle test yourself — STRONG or WEAK — one at a time.

Example: "I feel _____." Insert the feeling/emotion in the blank. Muscle test yourself for each statement. After each one, place a check mark to indicate your response using the blank on the left side of the slash (/). The blank to the right side of the slash is to indicate your response after you have done the clearing work.

Strong / Weak		FEELING or EMOTION
__/__	__/__	Possessive
__/__	__/__	Naive
__/__	__/__	Raw
__/__	__/__	Pitiful
__/__	__/__	Suffocated
__/__	__/__	Shocked

Were you surprised by your actual responses via muscle testing?
Either way, good!

It is time to clear using the Energetic Action Process. Simply drum or clap the fingers of either hand on the side of your other hand below your pinky finger and above your wrist, or clap both hands together while saying:

"**I deeply love and accept myself even if I feel** _____." (Insert the FEELING or EMOTION.) Repeat the statement three (3) times. Continue the drumming/clapping motion.

"**I deeply love and accept myself even if I have hidden or unknown issues with** _____." (Insert the FEELING or EMOTION.) Repeat the statement three (3) times. Continue the drumming/clapping motion.

"**I deeply love and accept myself even if I refuse to do the things necessary to free myself from feeling** _____." (Insert the FEELING or EMOTION.) Repeat the statement three (3) times. Continue the drumming/clapping motion.

What do you notice and how do you feel right now?

_____

_____

_____

_____

Excellent! Now go back and re-muscle test each FEELING or EMOTION for STRONG or WEAK and mark your results in the blanks to the right of the slash mark.

Please remember, you are always able to repeat the above steps anytime you choose or feel it necessary as YOU are in charge of your life!

Please end your day with a few minutes of using the technique of Put Your Fingers on Your Forehead while replaying any of the thoughts, feelings, emotions, or statements that may have felt negative, painful, or oppressive and did not feel good, uplifting, or positive.

Transformation is MINE! Made it through DAY TWENTY-NINE!

Day Thirty (30)--

It's your one-month healing anniversary! Welcome to DAY THIRTY!

- Breathe in, breathe out (take several deep, cleansing breaths).
- Think or state three times: "God, be a part of everything I think, say, feel, and do."

What do you notice and how do you feel right now?

_____

_____

_____

_____

Great! (Remember, wherever you are is right for your life's journey.)

Today we will check in via muscle testing on six new feelings/emotions (listed below).

Muscle test yourself – STRONG or WEAK – one at a time.

Example: "I feel _____." Insert the feeling/emotion in the blank. Muscle test yourself for each statement. After each one, place a check mark to indicate your response using the blank on the left side of the slash (/). The blank to the right side of the slash is to indicate your response after you have done the clearing work.

Strong / Weak		FEELING or EMOTION
__/__	__/__	Chained
__/__	__/__	Reproachful
__/__	__/__	Not at peace
__/__	__/__	Envious
__/__	__/__	Loud
__/__	__/__	[Choose feeling or emotion]

Were you surprised by your actual responses via muscle testing? Either way, good!

It is time to clear using the Energetic Action Process. Simply drum or clap the fingers of either hand on the side of your other hand below your pinky finger and above your wrist, or clap both hands together while saying:

"I deeply love and accept myself even if I feel _____." (Insert the FEELING or EMOTION.) Repeat the statement three (3) times. Continue the drumming/clapping motion.

"I deeply love and accept myself even if I have hidden or unknown issues with _____." (Insert the FEELING or EMOTION.) Repeat the statement three (3) times. Continue the drumming/clapping motion.

"I deeply love and accept myself even if I refuse to do the things necessary to free myself from feeling _____." (Insert the FEELING or EMOTION.) Repeat the statement three (3) times. Continue the drumming/clapping motion.

What do you notice and how do you feel right now?

_____

_____

_____

_____

Excellent! Now go back and re-muscle test each FEELING or EMOTION for STRONG or WEAK and mark your results in the blanks to the right of the slash mark.

Please remember, you are always able to repeat the above steps anytime you choose or feel it necessary as YOU are in charge of your life!

Please end your day with a few minutes of using the technique of Put Your Fingers on Your Forehead while replaying any of the thoughts, feelings, emotions, or statements that may have felt negative, painful, or oppressive and did not feel good, uplifting, or positive.

I ROCK, look at ME! Made it through DAY THIRTY!

Day Thirty-One (31)--
We've only started having FUN! Welcome to DAY THIRTY-ONE!
- Breathe in, breathe out (take several deep, cleansing breaths).
- Think or state three times: "God, be a part of everything I think, say, feel, and do."

What do you notice and how do you feel right now?

_____

_____

_____

_____

Great! (Remember, wherever you are is right for your life's journey.)
Today we will check in via muscle testing on six new feelings/emotions (listed below).
Muscle test yourself – STRONG or WEAK – one at a time.

Example: "I feel _____." Insert the feeling/emotion in the blank. Muscle test yourself for each statement. After each one, place a check mark to indicate your response using the blank on the left side of the slash (/). The blank to the right side of the slash is to indicate your response after you have done the clearing work.

Strong / Weak		FEELING or EMOTION
__/__	__/__	Lacking spontaneity
__/__	__/__	Neglectful
__/__	__/__	Overly responsible
__/__	__/__	Overwhelmed
__/__	__/__	[Choose feeling or emotion]
__/__	__/__	[Choose feeling or emotion]

Were you surprised by your actual responses via muscle testing?
Either way, good!

It is time to clear using the Energetic Action Process. Simply drum or clap the fingers of either hand on the side of your other hand below your pinky finger and above your wrist, or clap both hands together while saying:

"**I deeply love and accept myself even if I feel** _____." (Insert the FEELING or EMOTION.) Repeat the statement three (3) times. Continue the drumming/clapping motion.

"**I deeply love and accept myself even if I have hidden or unknown issues with** _____." (Insert the FEELING or EMOTION.) Repeat the statement three (3) times. Continue the drumming/clapping motion.

"**I deeply love and accept myself even if I refuse to do the things necessary to free myself from feeling** _____." (Insert the FEELING or EMOTION.) Repeat the statement three (3) times. Continue the drumming/clapping motion.

What do you notice and how do you feel right now?

_____

_____

_____

_____

Excellent! Now go back and re-muscle test each FEELING or EMOTION for STRONG or WEAK and mark your results in the blanks to the right of the slash mark.

Please remember, you are always able to repeat the above steps anytime you choose or feel it necessary as YOU are in charge of your life!

Please end your day with a few minutes of using the technique of Put Your Fingers on Your Forehead while replaying any of the thoughts, feelings, emotions, or statements that may have felt negative, painful, or oppressive and did not feel good, uplifting, or positive.

Wow! A month is done! I made it through DAY THIRTY-ONE!

Day Thirty-Two (32)--

You're doing GREAT, too! Woo Hoo! Welcome to DAY THIRTY-TWO!

- Breathe in, breathe out (take several deep, cleansing breaths).
- Think or state three times: "God, be a part of everything I think, say, feel, and do."

What do you notice and how do you feel right now?

_____

_____

_____

_____

Great! (Remember, wherever you are is right for your life's journey.)

Today we will check in via muscle testing on six new feelings/emotions (listed below).

Muscle test yourself – STRONG or WEAK – one at a time.

Example: "I feel _____." Insert the feeling/emotion in the blank. Muscle test yourself for each statement. After each one, place a check mark to indicate your response using the blank on the left side of the slash (/). The blank to the right side of the slash is to indicate your response after you have done the clearing work.

Strong / Weak		FEELING or EMOTION
__/__	__/__	Irresponsible
__/__	__/__	Lazy
__/__	__/__	Driven
__/__	__/__	[Choose feeling or emotion]
__/__	__/__	[Choose feeling or emotion]
__/__	__/__	[Choose feeling or emotion]

Were you surprised by your actual responses via muscle testing?
Either way, good!

It is time to clear using the Energetic Action Process. Simply drum or clap the fingers of either hand on the side of your other hand below your pinky finger and above your wrist, or clap both hands together while saying:

"**I deeply love and accept myself even if I feel** _____." (Insert the FEELING or EMOTION.) Repeat the statement three (3) times. Continue the drumming/clapping motion.

"**I deeply love and accept myself even if I have hidden or unknown issues with** _____." (Insert the FEELING or EMOTION.) Repeat the statement three (3) times. Continue the drumming/clapping motion.

"**I deeply love and accept myself even if I refuse to do the things necessary to free myself from feeling** _____." (Insert the FEELING or EMOTION.) Repeat the statement three (3) times. Continue the drumming/clapping motion.

What do you notice and how do you feel right now?

_____

_____

_____

_____

Excellent! Now go back and re-muscle test each FEELING or EMOTION for STRONG or WEAK and mark your results in the blanks to the right of the slash mark.

Please remember, you are always able to repeat the above steps anytime you choose or feel it necessary as YOU are in charge of your life!

Please end your day with a few minutes of using the technique of Put Your Fingers on Your Forehead while replaying any of the thoughts, feelings, emotions, or statements that may have felt negative, painful, or oppressive and did not feel good, uplifting, or positive.

My goal is in VIEW! Made it through DAY THIRTY-TWO!

Day Thirty-Three (33)--
How does it feel to be so FREE? Welcome to DAY THIRTY-THREE!
- Breathe in, breathe out (take several deep, cleansing breaths).
- Think or state three times: "God, be a part of everything I think, say, feel, and do."

What do you notice and how do you feel right now?

_____

_____

_____

_____

Great! (Remember, wherever you are is right for your life's journey.)
Today we will check in via muscle testing on six new feelings/emotions (listed below).
Muscle test yourself – STRONG or WEAK – one at a time.

Example: "I feel _____." Insert the feeling/emotion in the blank. Muscle test yourself for each statement. After each one, place a check mark to indicate your response using the blank on the left side of the slash (/). The blank to the right side of the slash is to indicate your response after you have done the clearing work.

Strong / Weak		FEELING or EMOTION
__/__	__/__	Lacking direction
__/__	__/__	Like an oddball
__/__	__/__	Unsupported
__/__	__/__	[Choose feeling or emotion]
__/__	__/__	[Choose feeling or emotion]
__/__	__/__	[Choose feeling or emotion]

Were you surprised by your actual responses via muscle testing?
Either way, good!

It is time to clear using the Energetic Action Process. Simply drum or clap the fingers of either hand on the side of your other hand below your pinky finger and above your wrist, or clap both hands together while saying:

"I deeply love and accept myself even if I feel _____." (Insert the FEELING or EMOTION.) Repeat the statement three (3) times. Continue the drumming/clapping motion.

"I deeply love and accept myself even if I have hidden or unknown issues with _____." (Insert the FEELING or EMOTION.) Repeat the statement three (3) times. Continue the drumming/clapping motion.

"I deeply love and accept myself even if I refuse to do the things necessary to free myself from feeling _____." (Insert the FEELING or EMOTION.) Repeat the statement three (3) times. Continue the drumming/clapping motion.

What do you notice and how do you feel right now?

_____

_____

_____

_____

Excellent! Now go back and re-muscle test each FEELING or EMOTION for STRONG or WEAK and mark your results in the blanks to the right of the slash mark.

Please remember, you are always able to repeat the above steps anytime you choose or feel it necessary as YOU are in charge of your life!

Please end your day with a few minutes of using the technique of Put Your Fingers on Your Forehead while replaying any of the thoughts, feelings, emotions, or statements that may have felt negative, painful, or oppressive and did not feel good, uplifting, or positive.

**Hooray, Hooray, Hooray for ME! I'm FEELING FREE!
And I Made it through DAY THIRTY-THREE!**

Big Time CONGRATS!!!

YOU made it through the 33-day workbook and now it's a part of YOU!

It's great that you made it through and completed the *Energetic Action Process 33-Day Workbook!*

YES! Keep up the good work!

Please keep working with yourself on a regular basis…

To assist you on your Journey and Adventure, I have included seven blank forms with the following printed on it:

(Please feel free to copy this Blank Document to use for yourself!)

These blank forms are for you to use in the book and to freely duplicate for yourself as you continue on your Journey moving forward to becoming fully Happy, Healthy, Whole and Complete as is possible!

Again, Great Job and Big Time CONGRATS to YOU and I AM Sending YOU lots of love, blessings and good energy!

Best Wishes!

Mahalo! (Thank You!)

THX GARY…

Date: _____

Keep going! Use this blank worksheet to track your progress as you continue to clear feelings and emotions that arise in your life!

(Please feel free to copy this Blank Document to use for yourself!)

- Breathe in, breathe out (take several deep, cleansing breaths).
- Think or state three times: "God, be a part of everything I think, say, feel, and do."

What do you notice and how do you feel right now?

_____

_____

_____

_____

Great! (Remember, wherever you are is right for your life's journey.)

Today we will check in via muscle testing on six new feelings/emotions (listed below).

Muscle test yourself – STRONG or WEAK – one at a time.

Example: "I feel _____." Insert the feeling/emotion in the blank. Muscle test yourself for each statement. After each one, place a check mark to indicate your response using the blank on the left side of the slash (/). The blank to the right side of the slash is to indicate your response after you have done the clearing work.

Strong / Weak   FEELING or EMOTION

__/__   __/__   _____

__/__   __/__   _____

__/__   __/__   _____

__/__   __/__   _____

__/__   __/__   _____

__/__   __/__   _____

Were you surprised by your actual responses via muscle testing?
Either way, good!

It is time to clear using the Energetic Action Process. Simply drum or clap the fingers of either hand on the side of your other hand below your pinky finger and above your wrist, or clap both hands together while saying:

"**I deeply love and accept myself even if I feel** _____." (Insert the FEELING or EMOTION.) Repeat the statement three (3) times. Continue the drumming/clapping motion.

"**I deeply love and accept myself even if I have hidden or unknown issues with** _____." (Insert the FEELING or EMOTION.) Repeat the statement three (3) times. Continue the drumming/clapping motion.

"**I deeply love and accept myself even if I refuse to do the things necessary to free myself from feeling** _____." (Insert the FEELING or EMOTION.) Repeat the statement three (3) times Continue the drumming/clapping motion.

What do you notice and how do you feel right now?

_____

_____

_____

_____

Excellent! Now go back and re-muscle test each FEELING or EMOTION for STRONG or WEAK and mark your results in the blanks to the right of the slash mark.

Please remember, you are always able to repeat the above steps anytime you choose or feel it necessary as YOU are in charge of your life!

Please end your day with a few minutes of using the technique of Put Your Fingers on Your Forehead while replaying any of the thoughts, feelings, emotions, or statements that may have felt negative, painful, or oppressive and did not feel good, uplifting, or positive.

Good for you! You've cleared some more emotions! You are healing yourself and making space for wonderful new energies to enter your experience. Keep up the good work!

Date: _____

Keep going! Use this blank worksheet to track your progress as you continue to clear feelings and emotions that arise in your life!

(Please feel free to copy this Blank Document to use for yourself!)

- Breathe in, breathe out (take several deep, cleansing breaths).
- Think or state three times: "God, be a part of everything I think, say, feel, and do."

What do you notice and how do you feel right now?

_____

_____

_____

_____

Great! (Remember, wherever you are is right for your life's journey.)

Today we will check in via muscle testing on six new feelings/emotions (listed below).

Muscle test yourself – STRONG or WEAK – one at a time.

Example: "I feel _____." Insert the feeling/emotion in the blank. Muscle test yourself for each statement. After each one, place a check mark to indicate your response using the blank on the left side of the slash (/). The blank to the right side of the slash is to indicate your response after you have done the clearing work.

Strong / Weak		FEELING or EMOTION
__/__	__/__	_____
__/__	__/__	_____
__/__	__/__	_____
__/__	__/__	_____
__/__	__/__	_____
__/__	__/__	_____

Were you surprised by your actual responses via muscle testing?

Either way, good!

It is time to clear using the Energetic Action Process. Simply drum or clap the fingers of either hand on the side of your other hand below your pinky finger and above your wrist, or clap both hands together while saying:

"**I deeply love and accept myself even if I feel** _____." (Insert the FEELING or EMOTION.) Repeat the statement three (3) times. Continue the drumming/clapping motion.

"**I deeply love and accept myself even if I have hidden or unknown issues with** _____." (Insert the FEELING or EMOTION.) Repeat the statement three (3) times. Continue the drumming/clapping motion.

"**I deeply love and accept myself even if I refuse to do the things necessary to free myself from feeling** _____." (Insert the FEELING or EMOTION.) Repeat the statement three (3) times. Continue the drumming/clapping motion.

What do you notice and how do you feel right now?

_____

_____

_____

_____

Excellent! Now go back and re-muscle test each FEELING or EMOTION for STRONG or WEAK and mark your results in the blanks to the right of the slash mark.

Please remember, you are always able to repeat the above steps anytime you choose or feel it necessary as YOU are in charge of your life!

Please end your day with a few minutes of using the technique of Put Your Fingers on Your Forehead while replaying any of the thoughts, feelings, emotions, or statements that may have felt negative, painful, or oppressive and did not feel good, uplifting, or positive.

Good for you! You've cleared some more emotions! You are healing yourself and making space for wonderful new energies to enter your experience. Keep up the good work!

Date: _____

Keep going! Use this blank worksheet to track your progress as you continue to clear feelings and emotions that arise in your life!

(Please feel free to copy this Blank Document to use for yourself!)

- Breathe in, breathe out (take several deep, cleansing breaths).
- Think or state three times: "God, be a part of everything I think, say, feel, and do."

What do you notice and how do you feel right now?

_____

_____

_____

_____

Great! (Remember, wherever you are is right for your life's journey.)

Today we will check in via muscle testing on six new feelings/emotions (listed below).

Muscle test yourself – STRONG or WEAK – one at a time.

Example: "I feel _____." Insert the feeling/emotion in the blank. Muscle test yourself for each statement. After each one, place a check mark to indicate your response using the blank on the left side of the slash (/). The blank to the right side of the slash is to indicate your response after you have done the clearing work.

Strong / Weak   **FEELING or EMOTION**

__/__   __/__   _____

__/__   __/__   _____

__/__   __/__   _____

__/__   __/__   _____

__/__   __/__   _____

__/__   __/__   _____

Were you surprised by your actual responses via muscle testing?

Either way, good!

It is time to clear using the Energetic Action Process. Simply drum or clap the fingers of either hand on the side of your other hand below your pinky finger and above your wrist, or clap both hands together while saying:

"I deeply love and accept myself even if I feel _____." (Insert the FEELING or EMOTION.) Repeat the statement three (3) times. Continue the drumming/clapping motion.

"I deeply love and accept myself even if I have hidden or unknown issues with _____." (Insert the FEELING or EMOTION.) Repeat the statement three (3) times. Continue the drumming/clapping motion.

"I deeply love and accept myself even if I refuse to do the things necessary to free myself from feeling _____." (Insert the FEELING or EMOTION.) Repeat the statement three (3) times. Continue the drumming/clapping motion.

What do you notice and how do you feel right now?

_____

_____

_____

_____

Excellent! Now go back and re-muscle test each FEELING or EMOTION for STRONG or WEAK and mark your results in the blanks to the right of the slash mark.

Please remember, you are always able to repeat the above steps anytime you choose or feel it necessary as YOU are in charge of your life!

Please end your day with a few minutes of using the technique of Put Your Fingers on Your Forehead while replaying any of the thoughts, feelings, emotions, or statements that may have felt negative, painful, or oppressive and did not feel good, uplifting, or positive.

Good for you! You've cleared some more emotions! You are healing yourself and making space for wonderful new energies to enter your experience. Keep up the good work!

Date: _____

Keep going! Use this blank worksheet to track your progress as you continue to clear feelings and emotions that arise in your life!

(Please feel free to copy this Blank Document to use for yourself!)

• Breathe in, breathe out (take several deep, cleansing breaths).

• Think or state three times: "God, be a part of everything I think, say, feel, and do."

What do you notice and how do you feel right now?

_____

_____

_____

_____

Great! (Remember, wherever you are is right for your life's journey.)

Today we will check in via muscle testing on six new feelings/emotions (listed below).

Muscle test yourself – STRONG or WEAK – one at a time.

Example: "I feel _____." Insert the feeling/emotion in the blank. Muscle test yourself for each statement. After each one, place a check mark to indicate your response using the blank on the left side of the slash (/). The blank to the right side of the slash is to indicate your response after you have done the clearing work.

Strong / Weak   **FEELING or EMOTION**

__/__   __/__   _____

__/__   __/__   _____

__/__   __/__   _____

__/__   __/__   _____

__/__   __/__   _____

__/__   __/__   _____

Were you surprised by your actual responses via muscle testing?

Either way, good!

It is time to clear using the Energetic Action Process. Simply drum or clap the fingers of either hand on the side of your other hand below your pinky finger and above your wrist, or clap both hands together while saying:

"I deeply love and accept myself even if I feel _____." (Insert the FEELING or EMOTION.) Repeat the statement three (3) times. Continue the drumming/clapping motion.

"I deeply love and accept myself even if I have hidden or unknown issues with _____." (Insert the FEELING or EMOTION.) Repeat the statement three (3) times. Continue the drumming/clapping motion.

"I deeply love and accept myself even if I refuse to do the things necessary to free myself from feeling _____." (Insert the FEELING or EMOTION.) Repeat the statement three (3) times. Continue the drumming/clapping motion.

What do you notice and how do you feel right now?

_____

_____

_____

_____

Excellent! Now go back and re-muscle test each FEELING or EMOTION for STRONG or WEAK and mark your results in the blanks to the right of the slash mark.

Please remember, you are always able to repeat the above steps anytime you choose or feel it necessary as YOU are in charge of your life!

Please end your day with a few minutes of using the technique of Put Your Fingers on Your Forehead while replaying any of the thoughts, feelings, emotions, or statements that may have felt negative, painful, or oppressive and did not feel good, uplifting, or positive.

Good for you! You've cleared some more emotions! You are healing yourself and making space for wonderful new energies to enter your experience. Keep up the good work!

Date: _____

Keep going! Use this blank worksheet to track your progress as you continue to clear feelings and emotions that arise in your life!

    (Please feel free to copy this Blank Document to use for yourself!)

- Breathe in, breathe out (take several deep, cleansing breaths).
- Think or state three times: "God, be a part of everything I think, say, feel, and do."

What do you notice and how do you feel right now?

_____

_____

_____

_____

Great! (Remember, wherever you are is right for your life's journey.)

Today we will check in via muscle testing on six new feelings/emotions (listed below).

    Muscle test yourself – STRONG or WEAK – one at a time.

    Example: "I feel _____." Insert the feeling/emotion in the blank. Muscle test yourself for each statement. After each one, place a check mark to indicate your response using the blank on the left side of the slash (/). The blank to the right side of the slash is to indicate your response after you have done the clearing work.

Strong / Weak		FEELING or EMOTION
__/__	__/__	_____
__/__	__/__	_____
__/__	__/__	_____
__/__	__/__	_____
__/__	__/__	_____
__/__	__/__	_____

Were you surprised by your actual responses via muscle testing?

Either way, good!

It is time to clear using the Energetic Action Process. Simply drum or clap the fingers of either hand on the side of your other hand below your pinky finger and above your wrist, or clap both hands together while saying:

"**I deeply love and accept myself even if I feel** _____." (Insert the FEELING or EMOTION.) Repeat the statement three (3) times. Continue the drumming/clapping motion.

"**I deeply love and accept myself even if I have hidden or unknown issues with** _____." (Insert the FEELING or EMOTION.) Repeat the statement three (3) times. Continue the drumming/clapping motion.

"**I deeply love and accept myself even if I refuse to do the things necessary to free myself from feeling** _____." (Insert the FEELING or EMOTION.) Repeat the statement three (3) times. Continue the drumming/clapping motion.

What do you notice and how do you feel right now?

_____

_____

_____

_____

Excellent! Now go back and re-muscle test each FEELING or EMOTION for STRONG or WEAK and mark your results in the blanks to the right of the slash mark.

Please remember, you are always able to repeat the above steps anytime you choose or feel it necessary as YOU are in charge of your life!

Please end your day with a few minutes of using the technique of Put Your Fingers on Your Forehead while replaying any of the thoughts, feelings, emotions, or statements that may have felt negative, painful, or oppressive and did not feel good, uplifting, or positive.

Good for you! You've cleared some more emotions! You are healing yourself and making space for wonderful new energies to enter your experience. Keep up the good work!

Date: _____

Keep going! Use this blank worksheet to track your progress as you continue to clear feelings and emotions that arise in your life!

(Please feel free to copy this Blank Document to use for yourself!)

- Breathe in, breathe out (take several deep, cleansing breaths).
- Think or state three times: "God, be a part of everything I think, say, feel, and do."

What do you notice and how do you feel right now?

_____

_____

_____

_____

Great! (Remember, wherever you are is right for your life's journey.)

Today we will check in via muscle testing on six new feelings/emotions (listed below).

Muscle test yourself – STRONG or WEAK – one at a time.

Example: "I feel _____." Insert the feeling/emotion in the blank. Muscle test yourself for each statement. After each one, place a check mark to indicate your response using the blank on the left side of the slash (/). The blank to the right side of the slash is to indicate your response after you have done the clearing work.

Strong / Weak   FEELING or EMOTION

__/__   __/__   _____

__/__   __/__   _____

__/__   __/__   _____

__/__   __/__   _____

__/__   __/__   _____

__/__   __/__   _____

Were you surprised by your actual responses via muscle testing?

Either way, good!

It is time to clear using the Energetic Action Process. Simply drum or clap the fingers of either hand on the side of your other hand below your pinky finger and above your wrist, or clap both hands together while saying:

"I deeply love and accept myself even if I feel _____." (Insert the FEELING or EMOTION.) Repeat the statement three (3) times. Continue the drumming/clapping motion.

"I deeply love and accept myself even if I have hidden or unknown issues with _____." (Insert the FEELING or EMOTION.) Repeat the statement three (3) times. Continue the drumming/clapping motion.

"I deeply love and accept myself even if I refuse to do the things necessary to free myself from feeling _____." (Insert the FEELING or EMOTION.) Repeat the statement three (3) times. Continue the drumming/clapping motion.

What do you notice and how do you feel right now?

_____

_____

_____

_____

Excellent! Now go back and re-muscle test each FEELING or EMOTION for STRONG or WEAK and mark your results in the blanks to the right of the slash mark.

Please remember, you are always able to repeat the above steps anytime you choose or feel it necessary as YOU are in charge of your life!

Please end your day with a few minutes of using the technique of Put Your Fingers on Your Forehead while replaying any of the thoughts, feelings, emotions, or statements that may have felt negative, painful, or oppressive and did not feel good, uplifting, or positive.

Good for you! You've cleared some more emotions! You are healing yourself and making space for wonderful new energies to enter your experience. Keep up the good work!

Date: _____

Keep going! Use this blank worksheet to track your progress as you continue to clear feelings and emotions that arise in your life!

(Please feel free to copy this Blank Document to use for yourself!)

- Breathe in, breathe out (take several deep, cleansing breaths).
- Think or state three times: "God, be a part of everything I think, say, feel, and do."

What do you notice and how do you feel right now?

_____

_____

_____

_____

Great! (Remember, wherever you are is right for your life's journey.)

Today we will check in via muscle testing on six new feelings/emotions (listed below).

Muscle test yourself – STRONG or WEAK – one at a time.

Example: "I feel _____." Insert the feeling/emotion in the blank. Muscle test yourself for each statement. After each one, place a check mark to indicate your response using the blank on the left side of the slash (/). The blank to the right side of the slash is to indicate your response after you have done the clearing work.

Strong / Weak   FEELING or EMOTION

__/__   __/__   _____

__/__   __/__   _____

__/__   __/__   _____

__/__   __/__   _____

__/__   __/__   _____

__/__   __/__   _____

Were you surprised by your actual responses via muscle testing?

Either way, good!

It is time to clear using the Energetic Action Process. Simply drum or clap the fingers of either hand on the side of your other hand below your pinky finger and above your wrist, or clap both hands together while saying:

"I deeply love and accept myself even if I feel _____." (Insert the FEELING or EMOTION.) Repeat the statement three (3) times. Continue the drumming/clapping motion.

"I deeply love and accept myself even if I have hidden or unknown issues with _____." (Insert the FEELING or EMOTION.) Repeat the statement three (3) times. Continue the drumming/clapping motion.

"I deeply love and accept myself even if I refuse to do the things necessary to free myself from feeling _____." (Insert the FEELING or EMOTION.) Repeat the statement three (3) times. Continue the drumming/clapping motion.

What do you notice and how do you feel right now?

_____

_____

_____

_____

Excellent! Now go back and re-muscle test each FEELING or EMOTION for STRONG or WEAK and mark your results in the blanks to the right of the slash mark.

Please remember, you are always able to repeat the above steps anytime you choose or feel it necessary as YOU are in charge of your life!

Please end your day with a few minutes of using the technique of Put Your Fingers on Your Forehead while replaying any of the thoughts, feelings, emotions, or statements that may have felt negative, painful, or oppressive and did not feel good, uplifting, or positive.

Good for you! You've cleared some more emotions! You are healing yourself and making space for wonderful new energies to enter your experience. Keep up the good work!

PART VI

Awful-Distressing-Stuff List

Words, Thoughts, Feelings, Emotions, Events, Situations and Statements for Clearing

IMPORTANT NOTE before you get into working with and using the "Awful-Distressing-Stuff List" as a 'Tool':

As with any new 'Tool' that you are starting to use and operate, PLEASE GO SLOWLY while you work with the "Awful-Distressing-Stuff List". Use it like any power tool and get used to it. Go through the workbook just like an operations manual. Take your time being your own detective and archaeologist while you investigate and dig through your life to identify what is coming up and is ready to be released and cleared.

Now that you are here at the "Awful-Distressing-Stuff List" you will see there is a lot of content right here alone! Please take your time, take it slowly, especially while going through it the first time, and please follow the *Energetic Action Processing 33-Day Workbook*.

This is a long list of words, feelings, thoughts, emotions, events and statements that I have collected over the last decade, and that I have identified, worked on and cleared with friends, family, colleagues, clients, and, many times, with individuals that I just met by happenstance or, as some have said, "It must have been by the grace of God or divine intervention that we met and cleared these things out!"

While reading and exploring the lists, I would not be surprised if you find some of them to be shocking or feel very uncomfortable the first time you read them. I will certainly agree with you that that may be true. However, after going back and forth with myself, along with talking to numerous individuals about listing the majority of the feelings, thoughts, emotions, and statements that were identified and cleared by myself and by very brave, real individuals, I made the choice to list every single one in this book because they have directly helped individuals to identify hurtful things that happened to them. They were shocked and surprised to see them in print and felt they were validated and able to clear them out.

AND Still this is certainly NOT the entire list of hurtful "Awful-Distressing-Stuff" that I have worked on to clear out with them! There are way too many hurtful words and statements that have been worked on to put in this volume!

Why am I telling you this? Because some of these brave individuals have been through extremely painful, shameful, embarrassing situations and events that have caused them post-traumatic-stress. These had huge negative and life-changing consequences before being worked on!

Over the years, as I and others collected these feelings, thoughts, emotions, and statements on napkins from Starbucks, Jack-in-the-Box, Sonic, McDonald's, and Silver Diner, on pizza boxes and in a pink "Hello Kitty" notebook that my dear friends Deirdre and Kathy gave me as a gag gift (yes, it is definitely pink and I really did use it for the list).

This "Awful-Distressing-Stuff" List started to grow on its own. I was working with individuals who would seem to be stuck or hit a wall, and could not identify or guess anymore to find their specific feeling or thought. I would hand them the stack of napkins that I carried around (until they were transcribed into notepads) and, many times to their surprise, they would look at me with a stunned expression and say, "Oh, my God, I am not the only one!" or, "You've got to be kidding me. I thought I was the only one!" as they pointed to one or more of the items on the list.

Just like me, some of them were actually crying tears of relief realizing that they were not the only one — a freak, a kook, a crackpot, or some pathetic weirdo or outcast (yes, those were the actual words they used, and many others that I cannot put in the book). YES, truth IS stranger than fiction!

Looking back over my lifetime, I certainly would love to have had this book and list when I was a youth, teenager, young adult or, okay, mid-thirty-something adult too, while I was struggling to make it through life, or, at times, just to the next sunrise. All the while, sadly believing or thinking that I was the only one and that no one would ever be able to understand, relate to, accept, or forgive me!

Alrighty then, AGAIN with all of that said about the list, I will say, in the spirit of U.S. President Harry S. Truman, "the buck stops here". I made the final choice to include all of the feelings, thoughts, emotions, events and statements in the Awful-Distressing-Stuff List in this book.

Also NOTE: The Awful-Distressing-Stuff List is NOT in a strict alphabetical order, or logically organized. It has been typed and re-organized by multiple dedicated individuals and by me, so blame ME and only me for any criticisms about the format, order or content in this list, book and workbook!

Okay, 'nuff said, Let's Get Down To Business and Go For It!

Reality Warning: If you are sensitive proceed slowly, this is Very Real!

NOTE: The Awful-Distressing-Stuff List contains, The REAL, the Actual Negative, the Horrific, the Hateful, the Dark, the Racist, the Abuse, the events, sayings and STUFF, etc. that were endured by many, many individuals!

And YES, ALL of these are REAL and have all been identified, written down (by me) then worked on and cleared by the brave individuals that have used the techniques in this book!

Use The Art of Muscle Testing to check yourself
(Do the test on yourself - are you strong or weak for items on The List?)

Again Reality Warning:

If you are sensitive proceed slowly, this is Very Real!

Hey, it's an "Awful-Distressing-Stuff List".

And YES, ALL of these are REAL and have been identified, worked on and cleared by the brave individuals that have used the techniques in this book!

OK! Now that You are still here, Let's Go For It, Find It and Clear it Out!

Anger/Angry

Aggravation

Anger

Angry

Angry at my inner god

Angry at myself

Angry at the universe

Angry thoughts

Annoyance

Annoyed

Bitter

Bitterness

Blame

Burning rage

Critical

Disgust

Enraged

Frustrated

Frustration

Furious

Grudge

Hate

Hidden anger

Incensed

Irate

Irritated

Livid

Loathing

Not forgiving

Offended

Outrage

Protracted hostility

Rage

Resentful

Resentment

Resentment of you

Resentment to my own detriment

Resistance to forgiving

Revenge

Sarcastic

Sharpness

Suppressed anger

Unfair/lack of fairness

Unjust/injustice

With/at Women

With/at Men

With/at GOD

With/at _____ (ADD YOUR OWN STUFF HERE!)

Fear/Anxiety

Afraid

Afraid of bad news

Agitation

Anticipating/anticipation

Anxiety

Anxious

Anxious over _____

Apprehensive

Concerned

Doubt

Fear

Fear and anxiety

Fear of being authentic

Fear of exposure

Fear of future

Fear of stepping forward in life

Fear of the future _____

Fearing the future

Feel a need for protection

Frantic

Fretful

Frightened

I am afraid I will be way too powerful

I am afraid of other people's envy of my power and abilities

I am afraid that people will discover the true me and reject me

I am afraid to believe

I have fear handling any situation

I have fear on my mind

I'm afraid of what other people think of me

I'm afraid that I won't be protected if I tap into my own extrasensory perception (ESP)

Inner pressure

It is not safe to open up

It's not safe for me to receive love

Jitters

Mistrust

Nervous

Not safe

Panic

Panicky

Rattled

Restless

Scared

Tense

Terror

Uber fear

Uneasy

Unsure

Untrusting

Vulnerable

Worried

Worry

Lonely

Alone

Isolated

Lonely

Unlovable

Unloved

I'm all alone

I don't have anyone

Sadness/Grief/Upset

Deep-seated grief

Depression

Despair

Desperate

Disappointed

Disheartened

Distressed

Gloomy

Grief

Heartbroken

Miserable

Sad

The missing piece of my heart

Unable to express inner grief

Unhappy

Upset

Wounded

Depression

Apathetic

Apathy

Depressed

Depression

I am a failure

I have nothing to contribute to the world, why bother

I have nothing to live for

Joyless

Not enjoying my place in life

Not wanting to get up in the morning

Resigned

Resisting life

Shame

Suicidal

Troubled

Why bother?

Boredom

Apathy

Bored

Feeling bored

Fretful

Restless

Hurt/Pain/Discomfort

Agony

Betrayed

Criticized

Discomfort

Dissatisfied

Distraught

Distress

Frustrated

Hurt feelings unexpressed

Hurt pride

Powerful

Trauma

Uncomfortable

Used

Wounded

Negative Self-Perceptions/ Self-Talk

Can't express myself effectively

Can't face issues

Can't make it on my own

Can't take care of self

Can't trust self

Can't trust senses

Cannot resolve emotional upsets

Cannot see my own self-worth

Doubt myself

Egotistical

Greedy

Helpless

I am afraid to believe

I am caught off guard

I am complicated

I am concerned about what other people think

I am embarrassed by parts of myself

I am no good or effective working as a team

I am not a powerful healer or channel

I am not allowed to own or acknowledge my own feelings

I am not free to believe what I believe

I am not ready

I am oversensitive

I am sharp-tongued

I am surprised

I am unloved by myself

I am unprepared

I am upset that my life did not turn out the way I expected

I can't believe it

I can't love myself

I cannot accept

I cannot believe in

I cannot get past this

I cannot honor my feelings or desires

I cannot relate to

I cannot understand

I do not have access to my psychic abilities

I don't acknowledge my psychic abilities

I don't believe it

I don't have enough energy to be

successful

I don't love a lot of myself

I doubt my ability to heal

I doubt the power in my healing

I feel unloved by myself

I feel unsafe

I feel used

I have attachments

I have doubt and disbelief

I have no resolution

I must take care of everyone's feelings

I am not worthy to channel divine love

I refuse to see it

I will never win

I'm afraid of living

I'm afraid of my psychic abilities

I'm blocking my psychic abilities

I'm not strong enough to be vulnerable

Impaired

Incapable

Indecisive

Inferior

Inferiority

Insignificant

Lack of control

Lack of understanding

Lacking

Lacking self-confidence

No good

Not forgiving

Not good enough

Not receiving love

Poor

Powerless

Self-conscious

Stupid

Suppressed

Uncertain

Undeserving

Unlovable

Unworthy

Vain

Weak

Not Appreciated/Loved/
Included/Cared For

Abandoned

Belittled

Betrayal

Betrayed

Deceived

Devalued

Disgraced

Dismissed

Disrespected

Downtrodden

Forgotten

I am discriminated against

I am dishonored

I am dismissed

Insulted

Left out

Neglected

Not accepted, dishonored

Not believed

Not heard

Not included

Not valued

Offended

Outcast

Persecuted

Shamed

Shunned

Unaccepted

Unappreciated

Unforgiven

Victimized

Abused

Being a victim

Betrayed

Can't stand up for myself

Conned

Deceived

Defiled

Duped

Helpless

Not able to defend myself

Taken advantage of

Used

Victim

Victimized

Violated

Guilt

Abandoned siblings
Abandoned family
Abandoned children
Beating up myself over my past
Blamed
Guilt for sex outside of marriage
Guilt for playing with myself
Guilt of masturbating
I couldn't save my brother
I couldn't save my dad
I couldn't save my wife
I couldn't save my children
I couldn't save my kid
I couldn't save my child
I couldn't save my dog
I couldn't save my bird
I couldn't save my horse
I couldn't save my cat
I shouldn't have driven drunk
I shouldn't have been stoned
I shouldn't have lost control
I shouldn't have done what I did
I robbed someone
I held up a store
I'm a felon
I'm an ex-con
I was in prison
I was in jail
I was arrested
I'm a thief
I'm a robber

I'm damaged goods
I'm no good
I can't be good to anyone
I'm afraid I will be found out
I'm afraid my secret will get out
I'm afraid my family will find out
I'm afraid my boss will find out
I'm afraid my wife will find out
I'm afraid my husband will find out
I'm afraid I will get caught
I'm afraid my mom will find out
I'm afraid my dad will find out
I'm afraid my minister will find out
I had an abortion
I had abortions
I aborted my pregnancy

War Veterans & Public Safety

Guilt of _____'s death
Guilty of _____
I shouldn't be here
I should have died
I couldn't save my buddies
I couldn't save my team
I couldn't save my squad
I couldn't save my men or women
I couldn't save my brothers or sisters
I couldn't save my partner
I stabbed someone
I shot someone
I beat someone
I defended my life

I defended others
I'm still here and they are not
I couldn't save my friend

Weakness

Can't stand up for myself
Cowardly
Helpless
Not able to defend myself
Powerless
Vulnerable
Weak
I'm a sissy
I'm just not tough enough
I just can't defend myself
I can't tell them _____
I can't do _____
I'm afraid

Relationship with God

Don't believe God will provide for me
Fear of eternal hell
Fear of hell
Fear of hell fire
I don't believe God anoints me
I don't believe God cares about me
I don't believe God gives me faith and
strength
I don't believe God gives me financial
abundance
I don't believe God gives me health

I don't believe God is my conduit for
healing and power
I don't believe God loves me
I don't believe God provided for me
God doesn't love me
God doesn't care about me
God has forgotten me
In hell forever
No love from God

Relationship with Father (can reflect relationship with God)

I don't feel loved by my father or by
god
I am afraid of my father
I believe I am not whole because my
father did not love me
I don't admire my father
I don't feel compassion for my father
I don't respect my father
I feel my father was pathetic
I feel sorry for my father
I must compete with my father
I must win over my father
Looking for Dad

Relationship with Mother

Abandoned by mother
Alienated by my mother
Believe I was disowned by my mother
Betrayed by mother

Don't respect mother
Feel contempt for mother
Feel sorry for mother
Feel unwanted by my mother
I'm not a priority to my mother
I'm not important enough to
my mother
Missing Mom so much and let
her down
My mother was irresponsible
Neglected by my mother
Never seeing Mom again
Taken from Mom

Sex/Sexuality
I believe sex without marriage means I
will be a dirty bad boy
I believe sex without marriage means I
will be a dirty bad girl
I believe sex without marriage means I
will be disrespected
I believe sex without marriage means I
will be thought of badly
Frigid
Guilt for sex outside of marriage
Having a child would ruin my life
I am a dirty bad girl
I am afraid of getting pregnant
I am damaged goods because I was
molested
I am damaged goods because I
was raped

I cannot be a pretty girl because of
my mom
I cannot have vaginal orgasms
I choose unavailable men
I choose unavailable women
I don't enjoy sex
I don't like people looking at me
sexually
I don't love sex
I don't want sex
I hate my sexuality
I have negative issues with sex
I have never been sexually committed
I use sex for power and control
I'm afraid of my sexuality
If I am sexy, I have no control
If I am sexy, men will take advantage
of me
If I'm sexy, I will be raped
My sexuality gives me control over
a man
Unavailable men are emotionally safe
for me
With a man I am stingy with
my organisms
With a woman I am stingy about
pleasuring her
I like women restraining me
I like men restraining me
I feel guilty about the kind of sex I
want done to me
I want kinky sex

I am afraid to tell someone I want to have sex with them
I don't want to have sex just for you
I want lots of sex
I love sex
I just want to be loved when I am having sex
I don't deserve to be loved when I am having sex
I don't want to be forced to have sex anymore
I just want to feel good having sex

Sexual Abuse
I did not fight back
I just gave in
Abandoning siblings
Afraid of being blamed
Bad
Defiled
Did not feel right
Dirty

Relationships with Women
Do not feel ready with women
Fear with women
Hurt pride
Inadequate with women
Unpleasant relationships
Unsafe with girls
Unsafe with women
Unworthy with women

Vulnerable with women

Relationships with Men
Do not feel ready to be with
Fear with men
Hurt pride
Inadequate with men
Unpleasant male relationships
Unsafe with males
Unsafe with men
Unworthy of men
Vulnerable with men

Attitudes about Relationships
Don't want to be free
I want to be free
I don't want to be in this anymore
I hate this and I cannot leave
She wants me too much
He wants me too much
She doesn't want me enough
He doesn't want me enough
I hate myself for being in this
I am stupid for getting involved
I believe a committed relationship ties me down
I believe a monogamous relationship ties me down
I believe marriage ties me down
I cannot be happy until I get married
I will never be happy alone
I will never be happy as an old spinster

I will never be happy without someone
I cannot be old and alone
I cannot live with him
I cannot live with her
I like my freedom living alone

Relationship with Body

Afraid to let out the girly girl
I cannot be a manly man
I am wimpy
I cannot gain weight
I am way too skinny
I cannot lose weight
I am too heavy
I am too fat
I am chubby
I am a fatty
Fat thoughts
Skinny thoughts
I am disappointed with my body
I am embarrassed by my body
I am embarrassed, fat, and shy
I am embarrassed, skinny and quiet
I am vulnerable because of my breasts
I don't appreciate my body
I hate my body
My body hates me
I don't believe my body serves me well
I don't care about my body
I hate my body
I'm not pretty
My weight is my protection
Thin thoughts

Physical Sensations

Feel like a knot in stomach
Feel like burning in stomach
Feel like ulcer in stomach
Feel like _____
Feel _____

Blocked/Held Back

Blocked
Constrained
Hindered
Impeded
Restricted
Unable to move forward
My family is holding me back
My mom is holding me back
My dad is holding me back
My grandma is holding me back
My grandfather is holding me back
My cat is holding me back
My dog is holding me back
My fish are holding me back
My birds are holding me back
My animals are holding me back
My children are holding me back
Taking care of my mother is blocking
my life
Taking care of my father is holding me
back
Taking care of my grandparents is
holding me back
Taking care of my parents blocks
my life

Not Seeing/ Lack of Clarity

Cannot see clearly

Confused

Confusion

Cynical

Do not feel ready

Fragmented

I am afraid to believe

I cannot accept

I cannot relate to

I don't want to see the world clearly

I refuse to see it

I'm afraid to see the world clearly

If I see clearly, I must take action

Indecision

It's not safe to see the world clearly

Life is weak and out of focus

Not seeing life as it is

Not seeing the truth

Not wanting to understand what I am seeing

Scattered

Seeing the world clearly is painful

Uncertain/uncertainty

Disbelief

I am afraid to believe

I believe I cannot have a fresh start

I can't believe it

I cannot believe in

I don't believe it

Conflict

Disharmony

Feel a need for protection

Grudge

I must defend myself

I must fight back

Not seeing eye to eye with others

Abundance/Lack/Financial/ Property/Career

Blocking the flow of prosperity

Financial abundance

Financial wealth

Greedy

I am not allowed to make money doing healing

I believe owning property or a home ties me down

I believe in the creative process: ask, believe, receive

I believe whatever you are thinking and feeling today is creating your future

I cannot sell the house as it is

I don't believe enough people will come to me as a teacher to be successful

I don't govern money

I feel conflict being rich

I hate the color of my appliances

I honor what I am giving and doing

It is not safe for others to know more than me

Judge people with money

Lack of control

Lack of understanding

Lacking

Limitations related to money

Money is the answer to all problems

Negative prosperity consciousness

Self-worth related to money

Taken advantage of monetarily

Uber lack

Undervalued

Unlimited resources

Unscrupulous with money

Unwilling to alter my current lifestyle

Failure

Embarrassed

Failure

I am a failure

I am a loser

I cannot be a catalyst for change

I cannot do it

I cannot help anyone

I cannot help myself

I cannot engage people

I cannot genuinely connect to people

I cannot inspire people

I cannot motivate people

I cannot tell a winning story

I cannot please GOD

I don't believe my convictions

I don't believe myself or my convictions

I feel disconnected from divine inspiration

I feel disconnected from the power of the universe

I have nothing left to give

I have nothing to contribute to the world

I have nothing to contribute to the world, why bother

I have nothing to live for

Let myself down

My life is a failure

Not wanting to get up in the morning

Shame

Unsuccessful

Children

Having a child would ruin my life

I am at peace about not having children

I hate myself because I cannot have children

I am no good since I cannot have kids

I am broken since I cannot have kids

Having children would make my life complete

I am not a real woman because I cannot have children

I am a broken / defective man since I can't get my wife pregnant

I am a defective woman because I cannot get pregnant

I believe I would be a bad mother

I believe I would be a bad father

I believe I would be a bad stepfather

I believe I would be a bad stepmother

I feel loss about not having children

I am cursed by GOD because I cannot have children

I am no good because I cannot adopt children

I am no good because I cannot take care of my own children

I am a bad man because I cannot take care of my wife's children

I am a bad woman because I cannot take care of my husband's children

Shame

Ashamed
Belittled
Embarrassed
Exposed
Foolish
Humiliated
Hurt pride
Let myself down
Shame
Should have known

Tired

Burnt out with work and relationships
Emotional drain
Energy drain
Exhaustion
Depressed

Stress

Burnt out
Emotionally drained
Energy drain
Exhaustion
Stress
Tension

Trapped

Blocked
Chained

Controlled
Cursed
Trapped

Stubbornness/Control

Being right
Defensive
Defiant
Entitlement
Stubborn

Jealousy

Envious
Jealous
Possessive

Other

Naïve
Neglect
No peace
Not free
Pity
Raw
Remorse
Reproach
Shocked
Shyness
Still have feelings
Suffocating

Gay, Lesbian, Bisexual, Transgender, Questioning, Non-Binary, Homosexual, Heterosexual, Hermaphrodite, Gender Identity, Cross Dressing:

ADD in: I've been called a, I was harassed for being, I, I'm a, You are a, We are, They are, And You Too, (insert any other before or after wording for your situation if necessary):

Fagot

Queer

Queen

Bastard

Prude

Lesbo

Damaged goods

Useless fag

Damn lesbian

Fucking queer

I hate you, fagot.

How did I spawn a queer like you?

You are not my son anymore.

You are not my daughter.

We disown you.

I can't believe you are from our family.

You are not family.

Get out, you're not my family anymore.

You selfish bastard, you're out of our family.

You selfish bitch, you're out of our family.

You're not my brother anymore; I can't believe you are doing this to our family.

You selfish fagot, you are breaking Dad's heart.

You greedy queer, Mother is devastated because of you.

You can change if you want to – you're not really a lesbian, go find a nice guy.

If you stay a homo you are out of our family for good and out of our will; you will get nothing.

I can't believe you wanna be a girl. What's wrong with you?

No way you want to be a woman. What's wrong with you?

If you go through with this sex change, then my son is dead to me.

What's the matter with you, if you become a girl you will break your mother's heart?

How can you even think about doing this to your Father? You are so selfish.

Your mother always wanted a boy, not a girl. This will kill her.

You will kill your father if you switch to a girl. How can you do this to him?

If you go through with this sex change, your family will be devastated and embarrassed.

If you switch to a man, your mother will lose her little girl.

Your Dad will be devastated to lose his little girl.

You are going to be a joke if you switch to being a guy.

If you switch, your family will lose their only boy and who will carry on the family name?

How can you be so selfish and destroy your family like this?

What are you thinking? This will destroy your family if they lose their daughter.

Hey, what are you doing wearing your mother's clothes? What's the matter with you?

You should be ashamed of yourself; take off that dress and be a man.

If you wear women's clothes, you will grow up a queer.

Take off that make up! Do you want to be a girl? What's wrong with you?

Take off your brother's clothes and dress like a girl.

Go put on a dress and be a girly girl.

What's wrong with you? Be a girl and not a tomboy.

Are you a lesbo or something? Get girly.

Put on some make up, you look like a boy.

Why did you cut your beautiful hair? Now you look like a wimpy guy.

What's wrong with you? Are you a tranny?

You're just confused, go pray some more.

GOD will hate you if you switch to a girl.

GOD will hate you if you switch to a guy.

GOD hates homos, fags and queers, you will burn in hell.

How can you sin against GOD? What's the matter with you?

Bullied, Bullying, Harassed, Harassment, Picked on, Teased, Teasing, Verbal Abuse, Terrorized, Belittling, Disapproving, Dissing, Disliked, Hated, Haters, Cursed, Bitched out, Yelled at, Screamed at, Hating myself, Racist, Cursing myself, Self-Harm, Self-Destruction, Self-Abuse, Self-Bullying, Self-Hating, Self-Disappointment, Self-Belittling, Self-Hatred, Self-Harming, Sexual Abuse, Rape, Molestation, Incest, Tried to kill myself:

ADD in: I've been called a, I've been harassed for, I've been, Done to me, I, I'm a, You are, We are, They are, And You Too, (insert any other before or after wording for your situation if necessary):

Hated for _____ (Race, color, religion, etc.)

Harassed for _____ (Race, color, religion, etc.)

Beaten for _____ (Race, color, religion, etc.)

Teased for _____ (Race, color, religion, etc.)

Picked on for _____ (Race, color, religion, etc.)

Bullied for _____ (Race, color, religion, etc.)

You're a skinny little wimp.

You're a fatty.

Stupid dickhead

Stupid bitch

You are a dumb shit.

You stink.

You think you are so smart.

You are an asshole.

We all hate you.

Just go kill yourself.

I hate you.

Get away from us, you dill weed.

Go bother someone else.

Nobody wants you.

Get off of our table.

Get lost, you fucking loser.

You are a nerdy little geek.

Stupid bimbo cheerleader

Nerd

Smart kid

Dumb kid

Jock

Freak

Cowboy

Flake

Goody Two-Shoes

Screw up

Tattle tale

Nark

Teacher's pet

Scholar

Outcast

Weirdo

Punk

Skater

Doper

Chosen one

Preacher

Churchy

Church mouse

Church boy

Church girl

Stupid bastard

Ugly bastard

You are damaged goods.

You are no good.

I HATE YOU.

I'll kick your ass because I feel like it.

I'll kick your ass 'cos you deserve it, you little punk.

I will make your life miserable.

I'll make you wish you weren't born.

I hate you and I will make your life a living hell.

Do us a favor and go kill yourself.

I wish I could just kill you and get away with it.

I wish you weren't born.

I should have aborted you.

I wish your mother aborted you.

You are nothing and you're worthless.

I hate my body.

I hate myself.

You hate everybody.

I hate you.

I hate my mom.

I hate my dad.

My mom hates me.

My dad hates me.

I hate my brother.

I hate my sister.

My brother hates me.

My sister hates me.

I hate my grandmother.

I hate my grandfather.

I hate my uncle.

I hate my aunt.

I hate my teacher.

You're nothing.

I wish you'd died.

I wish I'd died.

Oh, go kill yourself.

I want to kill myself.

You are a stupid fat ass.

Go dance with yourself.

You can't sit at our table.

Get away from our table.

Go find your own table, you loser.

Nobody believed me when I said I was raped.

Nobody believed me when I said I was touched.

Nobody believed me when I said I was molested.

Nobody believed me when I said I was abused.

I was raped by my dad.

I was sodomized by a priest.

A priest sucked on my dick.

I was raped by my brother.

I was raped by my uncle.

I was raped by my stepdad.

I was raped by the priest.

I was molested for years by my dad.

I was molested for years by my grandfather.

I was molested for years by a priest.

I was molested for years by a reverend.

I was raped by a reverend.

I was raped by a teacher.

My dad's friends raped me.

My mom's boyfriend raped me.

My mom's boyfriend touched me.

My mom's boyfriend molested me.

Nobody ever even listened to me.

I'm no good since I was raped.

Addiction & Addictiveness: Co-Dependency, Alcoholic, Gambling, Sex, Drugs, Procrastination, Anger, Rage, Fighting, Aggressiveness, Sarcasm, Putting People Down, Hating, Haters, Racists:

ADD in: I have been, I have to, I can't, I, I'm a, You are, We are, They are, And You Too, (insert any other before or after wording for your situation):

I can't stop drinking.

I need a drink.

My whole family drinks.

I need a beer.

I can't live without drinking.

I can't drink.

I want to drink.

It's everyone that made me full of rage and hate.

I have to insult people.

I have to insult you.

I have to cut people down.

I have to cut you down.

I get to cut you down.

So what are you going to do about it?

Just suck it up and take it.

HA! You're a joke!

I lost my car gambling.

I'm homeless because of gambling.

I'm broke from gambling.

I need to have somebody around all the time or I freak out.

I can't live without you.

I can't live without my boyfriend.

I can't live without my wife.

I can't live without my girlfriend.

I can't live without my husband.

I can't live without my mom.

I can't live without my dad.

I can't live without my daughter.

I can't live without my son.

I can't live without my grandkids.

I can't live without my children.

I can't live without my friends.

I can't live without my dog.

I can't live without my cat.

I can't live without my pet.

I can't live without someone to take care of me.

I can't live without my drugs.

I love drugs and I love the way I feel high.

I need my drugs.

So what if I hate everyone.

I'm angry at myself.

I can't get out of my own way and I hate myself.

I just can't get started.

I just can't finish.

I just can't start my projects.

I can't do my job.

I can't go to work.

I can't go out in crowds.

I can't go out in public.

I can't be myself.

I'm not good enough for you.

I'm not good enough for me.

I'm not good enough for _____

I'm not good enough for GOD.

I'm not good enough for Jesus.

I'm not good enough for anyone.

I'm not good enough for myself.

I'm not _____

NOTE: THIS IS NOT THE ENTIRE
Awful-Distressing-Stuff List

Please feel free to add any other negative issues or words that come up for you or add it into the closest one above and work on clearing it!

My Awful-Distressing-Stuff List:
(Add your Stuff here)

My Awful-Distressing-Stuff List:
(Add your Stuff here)

My Awful-Distressing-Stuff List:
(Add your Stuff here)

Positivity & Empowerment List

Words and Statements for becoming Happy, Healthy, Whole and Complete!

No requirement for any explanation of this list except to say, "Please make sure that you are strong to all of them!"

Also, please regularly check these via "The Art of Muscle Testing" to make sure that you are staying strong to all of them!

NOTE: The "Positivity & Empowerment List" is very small compared to the "Awful-Distressing-Stuff List" since this book and workbook were put together from focusing on and clearing the pain and suffering of those who have been helped by the information within.

Please feel free to ADD Any and All Positive, Up Lifting or Motivating words, thoughts, feelings, events, emotions, statements and sayings that encourage and build you up!

Use this Example:

I AM _____ *(Insert your own positives here. I recommend you keep searching and adding them to your list!)*

Use Muscle Testing to check yourself

(Do the test on yourself. Are you strong or weak for items on the list?)

Positivity & Empowerment List

ADD in: I AM, I, I'm a, You are, We are, They are, And You Too, (insert any other before or after wording for your situation if necessary):

I AM Happy, Healthy, Whole and Complete.

I AM Healthy, Wealthy and Wise.

I AM Blessed.

I AM Better and Better, Every Day, In Every Way.

I AM Loved.

I AM Loveable.

I AM _____ *(Insert your own Positives here. There are thousands so keep searching and adding!)*

Positive Self-Perceptions/Self-Talk to be strong to:

I accept being paid well for my talents and abilities.

I acknowledge my own choices, feelings, and desires.

I am clairaudient.

I am free of judgments.

I am paid well for my talents and abilities.

I am peaceful.

I am still while being mentally active.

I am wealthy and famous.

I have infinite peace.

I trust my senses.

It is time to open and release my psychic abilities.

It's an act of strength of love and generosity to receive love.

Positivity words to be strong to:

Able
Absolved
Accept
Acceptance
Accepted
Accepting
Accessible
Accurate
Acknowledged
Adaptable
Adequate
Admired
Adore
Affluent
Agreeable
Alliance
Allowing
Angelic
Applauded
Appreciative
Approval
Approve
Approving
Assertive
Assurance
At Ease
Authentic
Balanced
Belief
Believe
Benefited

Benevolent
Blameless
Blessed
Brave
Breathing
Bright
Built Up
Calm
Calm, Cool, Collected
Capable
Cared For
Carefree
Careful
Caring
Celebrating
Chant
Cheerful
Cheering
Cherished
Childlike
Choice
Cleansed
Clear Vision
Clear-Headed
Collected
Comely
Comfortable
Comforted
Compassionate
Competent
Composed
Comprehend

Concerned

Confident

Congruent

Connected

Constructive

Content

Cool

Cooperative

Coordinated

Courageous

Curable

Decisive

Decisiveness

Defended

Deserve Good Things

Deserving

Determination

Directed

Discerning

Discernment

Dutiful

Dynamic

Easy Going

Ecstasy

Edified

Elevated

Elevating

Embracing

Encouraged

Energetic

Energized

Enjoying

Enlightened

Enthused

Esteemed

Excited

Excitement

Express gratitude

Exuberant

Exulting

Favor

Fearless

Flexible

Flow With Control

Flowing

Forgive

Forgive Self

Forgiven

Forgiving

Fortunate

Forward

Free

Freely

Friendly

Fulfilled

Generous

Genial

Gentle

Genuine

Glowing

Good

Good Attitude

Good Natured

Good Humored

Graceful

Grateful

Gratitude

Happiness

Happy

Harmless

Harmonious

Helpful

Heroic

Honest

Honorable

Honored

Hope

Hopeful

Humble

Independent

Informed

Innocent

Insightful

Integrity

Interested

Invigorated

Invincible

Involved

It's Okay.

Joined

Joy

Joyful

Joyful Expectation

Joyous

Judicious

Just Cured

Kind

Know

Knowing

Laugh

Laughing

Laughter

Let Go

Letting Go

Liberated

Life Works For Me

Lifted Up

Light

Love

Love Life

Love Makes Me Strong

Loved

Loving

Loyal

Manage Successfully

Mature

Meet the Challenge

Mellow

Merciful

Methodical

Modest

No Blame

Non-Blaming

Non-Competitive

Obedient

Open

Open to Truth

Open-Minded

Optimistic	Provided For
Organized	Pure
Outgoing	Purified
Participating	Purposeful
Passion	Qualified
Peace	Quiet
Peaceable	Radiant
Peaceful	Rational
Peacemaker	Reassured
Perceptive	Reconciled
Perfection	Redeemed
Persistent	Rejoicing
Pleasant	Rejoicing in Life
Pleased	Relaxed
Plenty of Opportunities	Released
Plenty of Room	Releasing
Positive	Reliant
Power	Relieved
Powerful	Renewed
Praise	Repentant
Praised	Replenished
Praiseworthy	Reserved
Pray	Resolute
Precious	Responsive
Pride	Restored
Privileged	Revered
Prized	Revitalized
Productive	Rewarded
Progressive	Rich
Promoted	Sane
Prosperous	Satisfaction
Protected	Satisfied

Saved	Trusted
Secure	Trusting
See Clearly	Trustworthy
Self-Assurance	Truthful
Self-Assured	Unassuming
Self-Confidence	Unbiased
Self-Confident	Unconstrained
Self-Determining	Understand
Sensitive	Understanding
Serene	Undisturbed
Sincere	Unequaled
Singing	Unique
Solace	Unprovoked
Spacious	Unrestricted
Spiritually Awake	Unselfish
Stable	Unshaken
Stalwart	Up Building
Steadfast	Upheld
Straightforward	Uplifted
Strong	Valiant
Sufficient	Validation
Supported	Valuable
Sustained	Valued
Sweet	Victorious
Teachable	Vindicated
Thoughtful	Virtuous
Together	Vivacious
Tranquil	Warm
Transformed	Welcomed
Treated Fairly	Wise
True	Wizard
Trust	Wonderful

Worthwhile

Yielding

Again, Please feel free to ADD Any and All Positive, Up Lifting or Motivating words, thoughts, feelings, events, emotions, statements and sayings that encourage and build you up!

Use this Example:

I AM _____ *(Insert your own positives here, I recommend you keep searching and adding them to your list!)*

My Positivity & Empowerment List:
(Add your Empowerment here)

My Positivity & Empowerment List:
(Add your Empowerment here)

My Positivity & Empowerment List:
(Add your Empowerment here)

PART VII

Glossary

Clearing – Energy Clearing:
Our thoughts, feelings, emotions and words are made of energy, everything is made up of energy. Practitioners use multiple energy modalities and techniques to provide clearings or removals of stuck energy. They may also provide blessings or ceremonies as part of their service in removals and clearings.

Emotional Freedom Techniques (EFT):
In 1995, Gary Craig developed and released his own tapping techniques which involved tapping all the meridians without concern for their order. He called these Emotional Freedom Techniques. He was a student of Dr. Roger Callahan.

Energy Medicine:
Energy Medicine is both a book and a simple practice that works with energy as a vital, living, moving force that is at the foundation of our well-being. It was developed by Donna Eden.

Energy Tapping and Meridian Tapping Techniques:
These were developed by Dr. Joseph Mercola and involve using tapping of one's fingertips, emotional relief and physical healing procedures to help break free from negative emotions and noxious feelings that drag down your life.

Gestalt Therapy:
Psychotherapeutic approach developed by Fritz Perls (Friedrich Saloman Perls 1893–1970)

Holographic Repatterning:

Chloe Faith Wordsworth developed this process through working with clients to transform the painful areas of life to create extraordinary outcomes for greater potential for health, relationships, and well-being. It was the early beginnings of Resonance Repatterning.

Kinesiology and Applied Kinesiology (AK):

Applied Kinesiology was founded by Dr. George J. Goodheart, Jr. a Michigan Chiropractor in 1964. He is known as the "father" of muscle testing and for using it as a diagnostic tool on his patients. It is a popular diagnostic and therapeutic system used by many health care practitioners. Many of the components in this method were discovered by serendipity and observation.

Mason, Masonry or Freemasonry:

A Mason or Freemason is a member of a fraternity with more than six million members worldwide. Freemasonry has been a cornerstone of fraternalism for centuries and is the world's oldest and largest fraternal organization. Members have included kings, presidents, prime ministers, politicians, justices, titans of industry, movie stars and probably your grandfather! The Freemasons are always open to good men of moral character who strive to be better husbands, sons, fathers and members of their communities. Freemasonic roots date back to as early as the beginning of King Solomon's Temple, roughly 820 BCE.

Masonic Lodge:

Local organizations of Masons are called lodges. A Masonic Lodge is a basic organizational unit in Freemasonry. There are over 13,000 Masonic Lodges in the United States of America.

Meridian Tapping Techniques (MTT)

A generic name that also covers multiple energy and meridian modality-based techniques being used today:

✓ Emotional Freedom Techniques (EFT), Gary Craig
✓ The CHOICES METHOD, the late Dr. Patricia Carrington
✓ Energy Tapping and Meridian Tapping Techniques, Dr. Joseph Mercola
✓ Simple Energy Techniques (SET), Steve Wells and Dr. David Lake
✓ Thought Field Therapy (TFT), Dr. Roger Callahan
✓ Tapas Acupressure Technique (TAT), Tapas Flemming
✓ Whole Health Easily and Effectively (WHEE), Dr. Benor.

Modality:

A type or method of therapy, energy work, combined techniques, process, style, way of doing or any combination of them together.

Psycho-Neurology:

"The Art of Eliminating All STRESS, FEARS, PHOBIAS & ADDICTIONS" and "Psycho Neurological Repatterning" developed by Virginia Dunstone, M.S.

Simple Energy Techniques (SET):

Simple Energy Techniques are a collection of simple, user-friendly energy techniques, which can provide significant relief for a wide range of emotional and some physical problems. Developed by Australian Energy Psychology pioneers Steve Wells, Psychologist, and Dr. David Lake.

Sedona Institute:

This was founded in 1974 by Lester Levinson (1909 – 1994) to help others improve their self-awareness. Led by Hale Dwoskin, the institute's motto is 'Transforming Minds – Transforming Lives Worldwide through The Sedona Method and the Holistic Releasing Process'.

Shriner, Shriners International:

All Shriners are Masons however, not all Masons are Shriners. A Master Mason is eligible to become a Shriner. Shriners International is a fraternal organization of men who are dedicated to brotherhood, compassion and service to others. Shriners are a brotherhood of men committed to family, engaged in ongoing personal growth, and dedicated to providing care for children and families in need. Shriners Hospitals for Children admitted the first patient, June 1922 in Shreveport, LA. Through the remarkable foresight, commitment and fundraising skills of the Shriners, nearly one million children have been treated at one of the 22 Shriners Hospitals for Children across the United States, and in Canada and Mexico.

Tapas Acupressure Technique (TAT):
Tapas Acupressure Technique is an alternative medicine therapy to clear negative emotions and past traumas. Developed by Tapas Fleming in 1993, it incorporates elements of, and builds on, other acupressure techniques.

The Choices Method:
The Choices Method, developed by the late Dr. Patricia Carrington, combines basic EFT with Choices affirmations, which has proven much more productive than just saying or thinking an affirmation without EFT.

Thought Field Therapy (TFT):
Dr. Roger Callahan discovered that tapping meridians in certain sequences could alleviate fear. His complex system, known as Thought Field Therapy, uses muscle testing to determine tapping sequences. From Dr. Callahan's work, other meridian tapping techniques, known as energy psychology, were developed.

Vocal Vibrational Toning:
I use my own voice, energy and vocal vibrational tones to give sound and energetic clearing while working with individuals in person and around the world via the telephone and the internet. By connecting with clients and their energy to bring through their vibrational sounds, often the sounds coming from me sound extremely painful however, I do not feel any pain and they give voice or sound for the client to release any stuck energies that are ready to be released. (Gary Niki)

Whole Health Easily and Effectively (WHEE):

Whole Health Easily and Effectively developed by Dr. Benor, takes the bilateral tapping from Eye Movement Desensitization and Reprocessing (EMDR) and puts it together with the positive affirmation style of the Emotional Freedom Techniques (EFT) to quickly remove negative emotions that block individual's happiness in their life.

zen-Zen-ZEN:

For purposes of this book, I use "zen" in lower case, NOT tied to a Religious or ZEN Religion, Zen Buddhism, Doctrine, long time traditions, Buddhists, Sutras, schools, literature, organizations, dogma or beliefs.

To me it's the *"zen"* my dad lived, demonstrated and the way he was: *aware; focused; mindful; spiritual; centered; present; attentive; meditative; calm, cool and collected; relaxed; peaceful; quiet minded; clear; self-aware; balanced; inner harmony to be himself.*

Final Note and Call To Action

Although there may be multiple roads that lead to the same destination, I believe there are a multitude of modalities, techniques, tools, ways and means of working and clearing ourselves. The *d.i.y. zen and The Art of Gentle Emotional Transformation* modality with the "Put Your Fingers on Your Forehead", "The Energetic Action Process", and "The Art of Muscle Testing" techniques are only three of them. The two lists: the "Awful-Distressing-Stuff List" and the "Positivity & Empowerment List" are power tools for us to use throughout our journey. Best of all, they have all been extremely effective and simple tools that WE are able use anytime in private!

So again, I ask you to continue on your journey. Explore all of the tools, techniques, and modalities out there that may resonate with you. There are hundreds of them.

I am only one example of someone who has used and experienced multiple modalities, techniques and tools to get to where I am now. I say Thank You Very Much to all of the brilliant, amazing and wonderful teachers, coaches, counselors, friends, and colleagues who have helped me through the dark and hopeless times in my life!

It has been an honor for me to share the information in this book, workbook and the two lists with you!

I send you best wishes with lots of love and good energy!

With my deepest respect and appreciation of you.

Mahalo! (Thank You!)

Sincerely yours, Gary Nobuo Niki

Mission Statement and Call To Action

My personal mission is to make a positive difference in the lives of millions of people around the world by sharing strength through inspiration, insight and caring. And to stand for a positive outcome!

It has been the same for me and never changed since the late 1980s! Maybe you could help me with my mission…

If you were helped, aided or assisted by this book and workbook, and you are willing to help me help others, please check out the questions below:

- ✓ **Do you want to help others?**   **If Yes…**
- ✓ **Will you please help someone else?**   **If Yes…**
- ✓ **Please share your story with us!** (People of the world)
- ✓ **Help donate or distribute this book to your group, business, organization; start your own study group**
- ✓ **I'd love to hear from you!**

Please help me make a Positive Difference in the Lives of Others by connecting with me and sending or sharing your story with me and posting on my Social Media links below:

Website:	www.garyniki.com
E-Mail:	info@garyniki.com
Facebook:	https://www.facebook.com/IAMGaryNiki
LinkedIn:	https://www.linkedin.com/in/garyniki/
Instagram:	https://www.instagram.com/garyniki1/

Suggested Format for Experiences or Testimonials:

- Start with your overall situation. Include how you were feeling at the time and how it affected your life.
- List other modalities that you used, if any.
- Describe how you found out about the *d.i.y. zen and The Art of Gentle Emotional Transformation* book.
- Describe how you have used the "Put Your Fingers On Your Forehead" technique.
- Describe how you have used "The Energetic Action Process" technique.
- Describe how you have used the "Art of Muscle Testing" technique.
- Describe how you have used the *Energetic Action Process 33-Day Workbook*.
- Describe how you have used the two lists:
  o Awful-Distressing-Stuff List
  o Positivity & Empowerment List.
- Describe YOUR process of identifying the emotions that affected YOU. What methods did you use? (muscle testing, knowing, guessing, someone telling you, psychic, etc.).
- What were your results? (How did you feel?)
  o Immediately
  o After a week
  o After a month
  o Longer
- Would you recommend the *d.i.y. zen and The Art of Gentle Emotional Transformation* book to others?
  o If so, have you shared it with others?
- Would you recommend the "Put Your Fingers On Your Forehead" Technique with others?
  o If so, have you shared it with others?

- Would you recommend "The Energetic Action Process" to others?
  - o If so, have you shared it with others?
- Would you recommend the *Energetic Action Process 33-Day Workbook* to others?
  - o If so, have you shared it with others?

Thank You Very Much for taking your time to share your story and experiences with me, and to potentially help the individuals that may be inspired by them around the world, and make a positive difference in their lives!

THX GARY...

Acknowledgements and Gratitude

Please know that I could have never, never, ever, ever accomplished this by myself. It really has taken a village to bring this book and workbook to you!

This project took 22 years of work from a lot of amazing individuals who have used the information and techniques. Then, they pushed me, kicked me, cajoled me, helped, guided, led and inspired me to get it done and out in the world. Now, it is available for those who may benefit from the information.

Physically, the original documentation was not nearly as clear and cohesive as it appears in this book. It literally started out on napkins, pizza boxes, Moleskine notebooks, steno pads, yellow legal pads and, yes, Post-It-Notes.

My Special THANK YOU with My Deepest Gratitude and Appreciation goes out to all of those dedicated and amazing individuals listed in this Acknowledgements section!

To all of the amazingly brave, dedicated individuals who contributed Anonymously On Purpose, Thank You. Because of you, we all have the Awful-Distressing-Stuff List that helped so many, and I was able to gain the experience with all of you, along with your stories included in this book and workbook!

NOTE: It would literally be impossible to list and name all of the thousands of individuals who helped me however, to anyone who contributed that I alone missed in writing, Thank You Very Much!

I express My Sincerest Gratitude, Appreciation, Acknowledgment and THANKs to ALL of those listed above and to the following:

GOD, Higher Power, The Blessed Divine, God, Lord, Jesus Christ, El Shaddai, Jehovah Jireh, YHWH, Mother Earth, Father Sky, Grand Mother Moon, Grand Father Sun, The I AM, Your Higher Power, Divine Providence, The Universe, The Highest Self, The Great Spirit, The Mighty I AM Presence, or by YOU.

My dad Carl Nobuo Niki and my mom Kay "Keiko" Niki, who valiantly raised me and put up with me for all of those years!

Also, to all of those dedicated, amazing individuals who provided the typing, reading, reviewing, editing, feedback, practice, and assistance that made this book and workbook possible!

Lynne Plante: The first brave typist and editor of this book in the mid-2000s, who took all of my handwritten notes, yellow legal pads and Moleskine Notebooks and magically turned them into the first workable eCopy, and the very first prototype book! You're a Rock Star!

Marlis McCollum: 2014 Final Editor and combiner of the two books and the lists to be able to bring to life the prototype in paper format! Thank you for your dogged dedication and persistence, Marlis. You showed me what was possible for this book, gave me hope and I certainly couldn't have done it without you. No one would be reading and benefiting from this book without you!

Linda Benko: The typist who sorted through literally hundreds of napkins, papers, and notebooks to make some sense of the original list before it was divided up. We wouldn't have the final lists without you!

Rosemarie Gresham McCormick: Second typist

Bill McNeice: Writing and initial book formatting guidance

Edmund Reynolds: Typist, editor and formatter

Mary 'Cricket' Coleman: Typist

Capt. Kathy Callahan, Ph.D.: Evaluation, guidance, editorial, coaching

The late Dr. Patricia Carrington: Reading, evaluating and working with the techniques in this book and workbook with her clients and colleagues, along with providing her wisdom, expertise, guidance and for generously spending her time writing the forewords for the book and workbook!

Thank You Very Much! To all of the brilliant, amazing and wonderful teachers, coaches, counselors, friends, and colleagues who have helped me on my own path to becoming as Happy, Healthy, Whole and Complete as is possible!

Virginia Dunstone: Psycho Neurological Repatterning

Dr. Roger Callahan: Thought Field Therapy

Sally-Jo Walters: Gestalt Therapist and CoDA Leadership

Don Haury: *I'm Not My Fault: The Why of Shame and Codependency*

Chole Faith Wordsworth and Lyndis: Holographic Repatterning

Alyson Reid: Holographic Repatterning

Mary Burmeister: Jin Shin Jyutsu

Hale Dwoskin and Lester Levenson: The Sedona Institute, The Sedona Method – Sedona Training Associates

don Miguel Ruiz, don Jose Ruiz, don Miguel Ruiz Jr and Heather Ash Amara: Toltec Wisdom Teachers and guides, *The Four Agreements*

Dan S. Kennedy: Teacher, Guide, Motivational Speaking Trainer, Strategic Advisor, Author, Business Coach and Great Mentor

Richard Gordon and Jennifer Noel Taylor: Quantum-Touch Healing

Rev. Kate Rodger Ph.D.: Institute of Modern Wisdom, Sacred Journeys

Bill Bauman Ph.D.: Center for Soulful Living (CSL)

Donna J. Bauman Ed.D.: Center for Soulful Living (CSL)

Dr. Rev. Debbi Brown Adams: Minster UNITY of Sun Lakes, Director CSL Minister Ordination program, Higher Consciousness Teacher Coach

Marcy Shimoff: *Happy for No Reason, Chicken Soup, Happy,* CSL

Debra Poneman: Yes to Success, Seeds for Your Soul, CSL

Rev. Dan Chesbro: The Sanctuary of the Beloved - The Order of Melchizedek; Author: *The Order of Melchizedek & The Gospel of Thomas*

Peter Lowe, Zig Ziglar and the late President Ronald Reagan: Preach Positive events/seminars

Rev. Victoria Melvin: Anger Management Facilitator & MST Therapist

Ihaleakala Hew Len, Ph.D.; Donna Ka`imana Clingaman; Michele Maika'I Raab; Josephine Moanaloa Diaz; Mary Koehler – My Wild Irish Rose; Regina Milano; Jean-Pierre Deluca; Linda Sunrise Dunatov Ed.D.; Constance Zhoku=Pana Webber; Deborah Haleiwa Mangis, Ph.D.; Patricia Leolani Hill: Self I-Dentity through Ho'oponopono

Stevan J. Thayer; Carol Armitage; Barbara Stepniak; Karen Puglia; Rev. Maria Kramer; Rev. Keith Horowitz; Edmond Carroll: Integrated Energy Therapy (IET)

Raymon Grace and Jeff Jones: The Raymon Grace Foundation, Author, Healing Energy Shamanic Work Clearings and Dowsing Teachers

Rev. Deborah Oleszycki: Everyday Angels Radio Show, Angel Messenger

Dr. Bradley Nelson and Jean Nelson: Emotion Code & Body Code

Mooji: Spiritual Teacher, Satsangs Fire of Self-Discovery

Lynn V. Andrews: Shaman Mystery School Teacher and Guide

Dr. Mike Murdock: Pastor of The Wisdom Center, author, singer, song writer, evangelist around the world

Bryan de Flores, Coralie Pedersen and Shelia Graham: Lightwave Energy Healing Teachers and Guides: Lightquest International

Alain and Jody Herriott: The Wonder Method & Quantum-Touch

LeRoy Malouf: Energetic Well Being Process (EWBP)

Joshua 'Doc' Kai N.D.: Author *Quantum Prayer*, Naturopathic Doctor at Makaio Light Medicine, Healer, Teacher, Coach

Sean Roach: Coach, Entrepreneur, Speaker and "THINK ENGINE"

Dr. Don Ka'imi Pilipovich and Sarah Simonis: Accunect healing

Sam Meranto: Hypnotherapy Past Life Regression

Gopal Rao, Alain Roth, Roger Smith, Colleen Hoar, Dr. Alan Weiss, Nancy Zapolski, Mary Artz, Donna Eller (All of my teachers and facilitators): Landmark Forum and all the Advanced classes

Jill Lublin: Radical Influence Coaching and Publicity Strategist

Ron Potter-Efron M.S.W., Ph.D. and Pat: *Stop The Anger Now Workbook* and Anger Management & Domestic Violence Offender Treatment Certificate Program Trainers

Dr. Wendy Luck: Internationally recognized flutist, vocalist, composer, A VOICE. A FLUTE. A MUSE. A MISSION.

Rachael Jane Groover and Datta: Groover Seminars, Coaching

Susan Taylor-Gol: The Healing Cooperative

Shoji Kameda: Music KaDON learn taiko and fue online

Rev. Bob Sima and Rev. Shannon Marie Plummer: Where The Light Gets In, Musical Consciousness Concerts, Healing facilitation workshops

Barbara Lane, Ph.D.: Clinical Hypnotherapist

Michael Meade: Mosaic Multicultural Foundation

Tom Tam: Tong Ren Healing

Masha Petrie Sue: The CEO of You & Toxic People

Rose Rosetree: Energy Spirituality and Empath Skills

J.J. Hurtak, Ph.D. and Desiree Hurtak, Ph.D.: Founders of The Academy for Future Science, an international NGO, Social scientist, futurist, author of *The Book of Knowledge: The Keys of Enoch*

Mignon Manin Erixon-Stanford: Shaman Manin, The Councils for their Attunements, Teaching & Healing. Photography Credits for the photos of me with Scarlet Hall and Scott (aged 6); Kyle (aged 8); Taylor (aged 6); (My Demonstration Team Buddies for the multiple technique photos throughout the book) Great Work everyone! Thank you very much!

Christel Libiot & Jim Wert: Sacred Cacao Ceremonies and Storytelling

Randy Peyser: Author One Stop

Didge Master Joe and Peggy Gentile: Didgeridoo Teacher, Healers

Elizabeth Pan, Wayne Hay, Dr. Sue Anne Lewine, Dr. Michael Milner, Carrie Vieira, Ellen Turverey, Tracy Hall, Lissette Thomas, Janet Will, Rev. Deborah A. Ozga, Ph.D., Judith Fox, Tracey Callendar, Joanne West, Margaret Joy Weaver, Kumarji, Tajasa, Krishnaji, Preethaji, Sri Amma, Sri Bhagavan: Oneness and the O&O Academy

Grant Connolly: The Transformational ZPoint Process

Rev. Gina Maybury: Intuitive Wellness Center – Energy Teacher, Healer

Rev. Miriam Hunter: Energy Teacher & Healer, Quantum-Touch

Ruth Kent: Success Together programs, Emotion Code and Body Code

JoAnn Parks: The Loving Guardian of Max The Crystal Skull

Rev. Nancy Fox: Spiritual Teacher Healer, Sam-U-EL The Crystal Skull

Shaman Mary Tyrtle Rooker: Teacher, Practitioner, Healer

Rev. Jennye Z. Johnson: Shamanic Priestess of Avalon, Healing Energy

Beverly L. Nickerson: Earth Light Promotions, Healing Energy

Yogini – Dr. Vanaja Reddy: Healing, Wealth & Abundance Poojas

Lobsang Kunga, Lobsang Paden, Tenpa Dhargyal, Tsering Norbu, Karma Sonam, Souam Dorjee, Lobsan Norbu, Geshe Tsering Dhoudup, Tenzin Nyima: Loosling Tibetan Monks

Douglas Bentley and Prema: Oneness Monk & Sacred Wisdom School

Rev. Wendy Wisner, Rev. Alice 'Alicja' Jones, Rev. Wanda Lasseter-Lundy: Rays of Healing Church

Catherine Scherwenka: Author of *PTSD A Drug-Free Me*, Oneness Teacher, Guide and Meditator

Mary Ann Winiger: Human Design – Jovian Archive

Lynn Waldrop: The Body Channel, Medical Intuitive

Daniel Bellone: Awakening Through Music, Spiritual Leader and Artist

Dianne Fanti: Friends of the Homeless – Reset for Wellness

Lynne Elektra Porzel: Intuitive Healing Center, Creation Institute

Diane Ruth Shewmaker: Creator Sekhem-Seichim-Reiki healing matrix

Rev. Paul and Rev. Terry Carruthers – Chaplains to American Indians also providing Healing with Amazing Therapy Dogs

Rev. Sylvia Sumter: Sr. Minister UNITY of Washington DC

Ken W. Stone: The Soul Archeologist, Healer, Coach and Teacher

Gregg Braden: Pioneer in bridging Science and Spirituality

Dr. Kenneth Harris: Author *Synchronicity: The Magic. The Mystery. The Meaning.*; Mind-Body Wellness Center, The Waldwick Wellness Center.

Dr. Coletta Long: Hypnotherapy Past Life Regression and Teacher

Tamara Green, LCSW & David Dachinger: LovingMeditations.com

Rev. Selina Mae Denny: Shamanic Story-Teller and Journey Leader

Father TommyLee Whitlock; Ac Tah; Charlotte Bushroe; Rock Ahulau; Deirdre Aragon; Jo MPowers; Kathe Preston; Carrie Pasco; Bill 'The Somber Sonneteer' McNeice; Twila Holbrook; Connie Nash; Erin Beckman; Holly Woodworth;

Christina Azores; Cynthia A. Rose; Kristin Dahl; Jody Hill; Kästle Olson; LisaMarie; Brian Gresham; Jeff and Vicky Howard; Bob Burch; Shaylene Robancho; Charles Wells; Nancy Hill; Trish Fortune; Goksin Carey; Rev. June Dillinger; Grayson 'Sensei' Zia; Deb Higgins; Scott and Keron Bowen; Terry Brooks; MaryJo Spencer Abbatiello; Steve Adams; Cathy McCue; Marty Moran; Claire Waltman; Chuck Goodwin; Steve Rodriguez Carrie Swearengin; Bruce Grotta; Ken Weeman; Dave Meade; Meg Sinclair; Cynthia 'CJ' Anderson; Bill Schlachter; Tamara Elassal; Nathalie Chapdelaine; Steve Carter; Catherine Mulligan; Patra Taylor; Cynthia Lane; Owen Lombardi; Natalija Weissmuller; Beth Stein; Rev. Angela Mandato; Cathy Galati; James P. 'Kimo' Cavanagh; Barbara 'Lakshmi' Carpenter; Mary Carnahan; Terri Spencer; Dante Baker; Robert Lee; Nora Nagatani; Carol Rose Duane; Glory Lane; Sandra Solomon; Molly Sullivan; Herb Ruplinger; Chris Hook; Darren Baze and Judy; Karen Coates; Yas; Jim Dilettoso; Terri Minnich; Jim Gerlach; Michael Boney; Jill Remmington; Theresa Smyth; Cheryl Smith; Stream Ohrstrom; Janine Smith; Bob and Linda Bennett; Georgia MacDonough RN; Heidi Hyson RN; Norm Barnett; Christine McCabe RN; Mary Duncan RN; Dr. Richard Thomas; Terrie Christine; L.A. Tony Sentif and Ginny; Steve Billings; Jeff Miller; Rohma Kellert; Stacia Hipkins; Cathy Hill; Ruth Masterson; Dr. Thomas Acklin; Debbie Takara Shelor; Rev. Star Deer; Kathy Maksymyk; Dan Dutters; Shaman Rose Khalsa; Patricia Mimbela; Eldon and Paulene Bradbury; Robin 'Mr Wizard' McCoy; Nora; Ellen Adams; Bill Wolf; Lisa Scacewater; Debby Lopez; Bob Torgerson; Sigung Leung Ting; Sifu Keith Sonnenburg; Sihing Phil; Ed Kurowski; Susan Magouirk; Rod Rego; John Burroughs; Carol Poserby; Scott Hodges; Kathy Williams; Sandy, James, Todd; Jeff Cournoyer; Pedro Ayala; Bonnie Wright; Alexandra Seals; Kelly Blount; Leslie Billings; Jennifer Shoup; Pat Griffiths; Nancy Susel; John Jay Heisse; Catherine Christy; SkyWolf, Susan Dreiband; Paula Smith; Shaman don Diego; Kim Leinberger; Riva Wine; Tara Morrell; Ingrid Saunders; Jerry Ya; Adrienne Eichner; Yvonne Howe; Stephanie Courtney; Arlene Crowley; Arielle; Shirley Ward; Ayo Handy-Kendi; Jannah Riemer; Becky Pettengill; Tarie Lee; Ben Perchik; Sue Conklin; Patricia VanValer RN; Dr. Bob; Josie Orr; Jennie Perdue Hege; Cathy Feder; Antone Thomas Richard de Herendez y Ontiveros Jr.; Heidi Hudson Bassett; Bette MozDzen; Cate Deckard; Dee Cisco-Yeater RN; Beverly and John Stephan;

Svitlana Tager; Ellen Anderson; Ron Cooper; Bonita Woods; Tim Warneka; Shaman Ken Wright & Erica; Bella Simons; Lee Brown; Bobbi Montgomery; Rev. Kerry Chinn; Halee Whitman; Margaret Gennaro MD; Debbie Young; Denny Unger; Sheryl Chastine; Rev. Genevieve Hogan; Rev. Bonnie Bankhead; Robert Fischer; Mona Posner; Larry Walz; Joe Barth; Terri Sisley; Ken Lee; Sage Leeson; Kristy Smith; Laura Freix; Marie Tasker; Rev. Susana Maria Cardosa; Mary Grace; Sifu Matthew; Jennifer Roberts; Mary Phelan; R. Neville Johnston; Tim Tablada; Piper Miles; Maryann Kilduff; Swan Ramachi; Meredith Davis; Shaman Paul Sivert; Rev. Mary Hubber; Tom McSherry; Micha Rhodes; Sacred Owl Quinones; Orlando Reyes; Todd Dean; Rev. Sally Ogden; Pat Munsil and Rick; Shaman don Zane Curfman; Susan Hamilton, PhD.; Pia Aip; Patricia 'Breezy' Santee; Lauren Spiro; Teddi Zia; Candace Williams; Teresa Morris; Rosanna Tufts; Dianne Eppler Adams; Chuck Adams; Alicia Korten; Lorne Epstein; Leo Eckenrode; Dia Costello; Nicole Ehrentraut; Carol Hexner; Terri Coleman; Kathlene 'Rosie' Johnson; Kate Baker; Teo Simu; Shaman Azurea Windwalker; Jennifer Adolph; Dorothy Corless; Laurie Timmermann; Leslie Sigman; Carol Stanley; Miri Klements; Keli Adams; Dann and Diane Terry; Carolyn Williams RN; Shaman Rune Wolf; Gary Ashkenazy; Rena Huisman; Linda Tello; Greg Brown; Eve Hennessa; Shaman Eric Weinstein; Pat 'Rod' Rodriguez; Susie Buckley; Bobby Kountz; Marion O'Meara; Patricia Divecchio; Russell 'Unca Russy' Kratzer; Keiko Ellis; Shaman Angela Blueskies; Thomas Booth; Katheryn Waggoner; Steve Adams; Greg Niki; Rande Young; Cheryl A. Maro; Robert Beasley; Bobbi Breo; Elise Fee; Kathryn Burton; Kristina Muller; Dr. David; Chris Allen; AnnaMariah Nau; Sergio Baroni; Amy Armaw; Bonnie Allen; Pamela Maraldo; Ken and Peggy Weiner; John Begg; Amanda Romania; Alice Sevivas; Suzanne Holt; Gary Larsen; Lee Brown; Pat Stacey; Elizabeth Santos; Carl Bieniek; Wayne Tripp; Andrew Carr; Charlie Zurenko and Steve; Frank Smoley; John O'Neil; Joe Lasch; Peter Van Daam; Steve Caplan; Linda Wilbur; Liz Myers; Pamela Alesky; Kelly J Howard Carter; Ken H. Bloom; Mateo Swan; Rev. Brian Grandon; Lia Sader; Isabel Archer; Lori Tiernay; Allison Johnson; David Gleekel and Steve; Terrie Christine; Abigail Cornish; Rev. Laura Bennett; Dean Shibler; Clayton Decker; Nancy Kay Wanha; Ricky F. III; Dové and Andy; Heather Sanden; Tiriq R. Callaway; Rev. Sharri Mackenzi; Betsy Lawson; Cindy; Emilie Mehmedovich;

Cynthia; Gina Mostafaie; John Melvin; Big John; Doug Leihbacher; Matthew Lundbeck; Joe Laird; Oliver; Justin Kapisak; Blake Kapisak; Ali; Donna Nabors; Joyce Mornigstar; Jim B.; Fran T.; Rev. Renee Keitzmann; Julie; Hira Gurung; Kristin H.; Lois; Stephanie; Gail Neiburg; Rev. Tim Taylor; Hanuman; Audrey Wartman; Bob; Giancarlo D'Alimonte; Shawn Hadian; Brian O'Connor; Mark Evans; Logan; Maureen O'Reilly; Rev. Tremayne Johnson; Suzanne Holt; Kelly Neylan; Shaman Jacke Schroeder; Pat Sousa; Gay Bird; Laurie T.; Joseph Frishknecht; Bob H,; Karuna Joy; Lee Brown; Carlos; Josh; Oscar; Rudy; Phyllis and Chuck Reynolds; Beverly B.; Chris Saeger; Karen Breslin; Michael Ma; Tony Gutierrez; Madhulika Jinsi; Jensy Scarola; Rev. Kelly Swartzlander; Mike Lansey; Don Berg; Daniel Berg; Ted 'Duck Man' Woynicz; Dr. Z; Scott Collinash; Chip; Walter G.; David Bradshaw; Ricardo; Jim Grapek; Charles Myers; Shahnaz; Carl M.; Ramona Murphy; Byron Harper; Mary Gayden; Richard Turner; Barbara Barrett; Keith Kayler; Coach Ong; Coach Oliver; Hila Jo Hawk; Rita Maloney; Wendy Polly; Rebecca; Kathy Grace; Elizabeth Cho; Jo Pitcher, Valerie; Ashleigh; Dr. Skip Mondragon; Tim Lisbon; Melissa Savory; Diana Allen; Laurie Timmerman; Elizabeth Eddy; Linda Roebuck; Mary Sise; Iva Nasr; Michael Overlie; Wilma Grobbelaar; Dr. Kymn Harvin; Shawn Mahshie; Betsy Conger West; Richard and Rosemary Bredeson; Grant Stewart; Jennifer Taylor; Tyler Jones; Pam Culley-McCullough; Lauren Murdock; Leslie Bridger; Wilfred Holder; Rosie Guagliardo; Lilia Shoshanna Rae; Joe King; Bob; Lori Kaplan; Desha Hall-Winsted; David Campbell; Cameron Ballantyne; Dorothy Baume; Reem, Heidi C, Gwen, Jane Austin; Bud Williamson; Debbie D.; Adriana; Melanie R.; Susan, Bethany; Dannette Z.; Bob W.; Agi H.; Sian M.; Scott and Estelle; Kathryn W.; Loren Anderson; Jeff Beare; Dr. Anna Moseley; Bob and Lis Haggett; Lynette Sprowls; Amanda Romia; Valeria Laticia Frances; MaryBeth Geronimo; Samuel Haines; Rev. Wendi Rose; Eric W. Jones; Rev. Russell Heiland; Rev. LeAnne Gioeli; Rev. Nina Gibson; Rebecca Whitecotton; Carol Elaine Lewellen; Ken and Lois Lewellen; Lynne Greulich; Jerry Moore; Jeff Lewis; Perry Fladager; Albert Chen; Rene Penny; Norma Crowder; Trevor Riggen; Frank Favila; Gregory L. Smith; Ed Finley; David French & Yessica; Bob and Wilma; Woody Woodson; Francisco Gonima; Sara Jones; David Rudduck; Janet Buckwalter; JJ Shepard; David Craig; Gary and Patty Gilham; Tony Coxx; Steve Haley; Barry Boyce; Paul Roeber;

Rick and Marilyn Rimer; Tim Jones; Chuck Cornfield; Jerry Cottington; Jayson Ferron; Teala Brewer; Mary S. Elcano; John F. McGuire; Gail McGovern; Lois Grady-Wesbecher; Terry Sicilia; Joe Becker; Jerry Krinn; Willie Clark; Al Vliet; Steve Tippit; Michael Lukpetris; Ceil Rostosky; Col. Walt Mikols; Elizabeth Dole; Dr. John Clizbe; Ken Deutsch; Douglas Kinney; Col. Bill FitzGerald; Colin Chapron; Dr. Phil Terry; Debra Yamanaka; Col. Jeanine Dahl RN; Abbe Keith; Mike Goth; Russell Clark; Michael Schlittenhardt; Chris Moore; Chuck Erickson; Mark Robertson; Col. Joe Moffat; Armond Mascelli; Carol Hall; Col. Dick Colson; Gen. Don Jones; Adm. Marsha J. Evans; Garrett Nanninga; Tom Wilmeth; Sheriff Joe and Ava Arpio; Dow Rigler; Bruce J. Gebhardt; Beverly Burns; Henry Fenn; Rocky Lopes; John Kappert; Steve Houser; David McCarthy; JJ McCarthy; Lonnie Stilley; Charles Blake; Steve Hailey; Ed Axman; Linda Bryce; Robert Spencer; Mike Austin; Jan Kimmel; Linda Mason; Frank Kriz; Morgan Hoaglin; Darlene Trammell; Chuck McHugh; Louis Trammell; Brian Fiffick; Cliff Jones; Craig Fugate; Suzanne Frew; James Lee Witt.

All of our ARC NHQ Safety & Security (SAS) Team; Life Safety and Asset Protection (LSAP) Team; Critical Response Team (CRT); ALERT Team and Aviation Incident Response (AIR) Team. The dedicated Red Crossers and Disaster Responder members and teams from all of the Emergency Management and Disaster Response Functions around the world. The dedicated Salvation Army Disaster Responders and all of the amazing, dedicated local, town, city, county, state, federal and tribal Emergency Management; Disaster Management; Public Safety; First Responders; National Guard; Armed and Uniformed Services, named and un-named, I've had the privilege of serving with over the past several decades, who made a Positive Difference in My Life! It was an Honor to have served with you! THANK YOU VERY MUCH!

All of my Anger Management Participants; Private Session Clients; Groups; Organizations; Businesses and Individuals that I have served.

President George W. Bush: Thank you for your presence in our American Red Cross National Headquarters Disaster Operations Center in Washington, D.C. during the Hurricane Katrina Disaster Relief Operation. I never thought that I would have the privilege of meeting a sitting United States President, let alone have the opportunity to talk to one about the importance of the Safety & Security of our Red Cross Workers and clients! Being there with just you and our Executive Vice President, Alan McCurry after he introduced me to you and you started asking me safety and security questions, was the longest seven minutes of my life! I certainly felt your genuine concern for our workers and clients, and I was happily surprised that you would take your time to talk to me pointedly about what we needed for our Disaster Response and how it was important for you, too. Then, you said for me to tell my Safety & Security Team on the ground that you asked about them and to give them your "Thank you for your service!" That was a huge morale booster. All of our team members would remember it for years to come! Thank You Very Much Mr. President!

To the following amazing authors, teachers and leaders that I have not had the privilege to meet in person however, your books, audios, videos and teachings have definitely made a positive difference in my life! Thank You Very Much!

Anthony 'Tony' Robbins; Les Brown; Nido Qubein; Tommy Hopkins; Pia Melody; Bill W.; Thich Nhat Hanh; Bruce Lee; Dalai Lama; Lau Tzu; Jim Rohn; Paulo Coelho; Carolyn Myss; Edgar Casey; Gary Zukav; Michael Beckwith; Neal Donald Walsh; Vishen Lakhiani; M. Scott Peck MD; Richard Bach; Ester Hicks; Lynne McTaggart; Donna Eden; Brian L. Weiss MD; Melody Beattie; Leonardo da Vinci; Donald Trump; Louise Hay; Eckart Tolle; Oprah Winfrey; Robert Kiyosaki; Earl Nightengale; Stefan Swanepole; Dr. Phillip C. McGraw; Bob Proctor; Shakti Gwayne; Deepak Chopra; Rev. Peter Poppoff; RHJ; Dave Logan; Steven Covey; Marianne Williamson; Helen Cohn Schucman; Dan Millman; Cesar Millan; Joe Vitale; Rhonda Byrne; James Redfield; Barbara Brennon; Lobsang Rampa; Joel and Victoria Osteen; Michael Newton; Cheryl Richardson; Pema Chodron; Joyce Myers; Chris Guillebeau; Lama Surya Das; Mara Altman; Robert Kriegel PhD; Yehuda Berg; Susan Jeffers PhD; Alan Cohen; Damon Zahariades; Dr. Joe Dispenza; Alice Miller; Brad Blanton; George Forman; T. Lobsang Rampa; Timothy Ferriss; Jack Canfield; John Gray PhD; Mark Victor Hansen; Brian Tracy; Warren Buffett; Dr. Daniel Benor; Matt Kahn; Michael A. Singer; N. G. Abramson; David R. Hawkins MD; Lee Harris; Dr. Sue Morter DC; Jill Bolte Taylor PhD; Joe Cross; Joel Fuhrman; Shawn Coyne; Steven Pressfield; Donald Middleton; Ryan Hoover; Tabitha Zalot;

Nir Eyal; Paul O'Brien; Eilat Aviram; Mark Manson; Alinka Rutkowska; Lady Gianne; Michael Heatherington; Derek O'Neill; Dr. Amir Levy; Dr. Wayne Dyer; R.J. Von-Bruening; Dale Carnegie; Karen Frazier; Mike Dooley; Rick Frishman; Katherine Sandusky; Maria Altman; Ed Bernd Jr.; Andrew Carnegie; Marc Fennell; Molly Burke; Francois Lelord; Shunmyo Masuno; Laurence G. Boldt; Guido Henkel; J.B. Rhine; Niki Elliott; Marybeth Wuenschel; Ryder Carroll; Gene Kranz; Melissa Mintz; Ken Mogi; George W. Grant; Roger James Hamilton; Mimi Emmanuel; Dr. Jeffrey Donner; Nick Pope; Elaine Roughton; J. D. Vance; Lauren Cassel Brownell; Angela C. Santomero; Matt Zagula; Prim Pattanaporn; Diane Stein; Patrick Rhone; Lysa Terkeurst; Amanda Lera; Kevin Flanigan; Tara Brach; Garbor Mate MD; Pete Walker; Mark W. Muesse; Tim S. Grover; Pierre Pradervand; Robert Plank; Som Bathla; H.P. Blavatsky; Raza Imam; Tucker Max; Zach Obront; Dan Davison; Eugene Kim; Zoey Arielle Poulsen; Luke Fatooros; Daniel Gilbert; Émile Coué; Dan Davidson; Kim Eugene; James Allen; Paul Reps; Nyogen Senzaki; Daniel Todd Gilbert; Eugen Herrigel; Marisa Moris; Cynthia Sue Larson; Britton Costa; Birister Sharma; Zinovia Dushkova; Lynnclaire Dennis; Andres Pira; Eiver Stevens; Richard Branson; T. Harv Eker; Ernie Zelinski; C.Alexander Simpkins; Eric Bergman; Julien Smith; Kevin Mit; Annellen M. Simpkins, Robert M. Pirsig; Jose Silva; Ellen Bass; Laura Davis; J.K. Rowling; Marsilus Ficinus; Robert Collier; Ramit Sethi; Shelle Rose Charvet; Marianne Cantwell; Cotter Smith; Thomas J. Stanley PhD; William D. Danko PhD; Steve Wells; Dr. Amir Levy; Dr. David Lake; Dipo Adesina; Wes Berry; Peter Hollins; Briana Henderson Saussy; Emmet Fox; Leon Logothesis; Tessa Cason; Wallace D. Wattles; Dawson Church; Mitch Horowitz; Dr. Joseph Murphy; Dr. Larry Nims; Kahikahealani Wight; Stanley H. Redgrove; Derek Sivers; Derek O'Neill; Devi Nambudripad; Marcos Aguinis; Tina Samuels; Dr. Steve G. Jones; Anthony William; Howard E. Gardner; J.D. Vance; Jackie Huba; Marianne Gracie; Aura D'Amato; Michael Bennett MD; Jason Heiber; Wallis E. A. Budge; Soraya M. Lane; Howard Falco; Michael Hetherington; Gabriela Pereira; Dr. David Jeremiah; Shad Helmstetter; Peter Ralston; George S. Clason; P.T. Barnum; Sergey Brin; Larry Page; Bill Gates; Steve Jobs; Lance Armstrong; Benjamin Franklin; Sun Tzu; Wim Hof; Jacquelyn Mitchard; Friedrich Nietzsche; John C. Parkin; Chuck Chakrapani; David A. Phillips; William Wynn Westcott; Cyndi Dale; Martin Goldstein; Elizabeth

Clare Prophet; Michael Talbot; Demian Vitanza; Jonathan Green; Hal Elrod; Aziz Gazipura; Kazuki Kaneshiro; Damon Zahariades; Joe Hempel; Max Lucado; Ben Holland; Thomas Nelson; Marisa Murgatroyd; Heather Alicia Lagan; Esin Eskiizmir; Sandy Gallagher; Manly P. Hall; Alixander Laffredo-Dietrich; Steven Pressfield; Chris Prentiss; Joe Hyams; Colin Wright; Jordan Gross; Debbie Drum; Karol K. Truman; Jen Sincero; Michael Newton PhD; John and Dodie Osteen; Laura Day; R. J. Banks; Jeff Bezos; Mike Murphy; Joshua Fields Milburn; Ryan Nicodemus; Leo Babauta; Wayne Froggatt; Holly Alexander; Tony Little; Burt Goldman; Eckhart Tolle; Charlie Morley; William Bridges; Joshua Becker; Genevieve Davis; Sasah Stephens; Hitomi; Brene Brown; Tammy Strobel; Jeffrey T. Mitchell, PhD; George S. Everly, Jr., PhD; Cal Newport; Chris Neibauer PhD; Dan Harris; Stedman Graham; Helen Schucman; Thomas Cleary; William W. Li; Jon Acuff; Amanda Owen; Inazo Nitobe; Joseph Benner; Ed Lewis; Dr. David Perlmutter; Yogananda Paramahansa; Michael J. Gelb; Chuck Norris; Ken Abraham; Pam Grout; Tom Kenyon; Jonathan Goldman; David Logan; John King and Halee Fischer-Wright; Jeffrey Gitomer; Shaman Durek; Jennifer McLean; Caroll Spinney; J. Milligan; Dr. David Hawkins; Aleister Crowley; Daniel G. Aman MD; Michael Hetherington L.Ac RYT; Peter A. Livine PhD; Toko-pa Turner; Tim Burkett; Carol Tuttle; Robyn M. Fritz; K. L. Randis; Robin Sharma; Guy Kawasaki.

Oops! Before, I acknowledge my amazing Publishing Coach and Team, this important acknowledgement did originally slip my mind!

Here it is, I Must Stop and Say This To YOU (if it applies!):

I almost forgot the individuals that I felt hurt me. I have to stop right now to acknowledge and thank all of you who I felt were the most awful, distressing individuals and groups, that ever walked the earth! I hated and wanted to destroy you!

However, now only in retrospect, can I say thank you for everything and all of your actions towards me. Through all of the inner work that I have completed and continue to work on myself, I have learned to forgive myself! It was not about you; it was about me! I have to acknowledge that you were my best teachers in an awful, hurtful way!

Only now, am I able to say thank you to you! Because, without you, I could have never accomplished everything in life. It would have been impossible for me to have helped the thousands of individuals through my work and I would not have been able to bring forth this book and workbook to assist all of those to come in the future! Thank You!

-- Gary Nobuo Niki

A Very Special, Thank You Very Much! To my incredible book coach and publisher Christine Kloser! Thank you, Christine. This book would not be the book that I wanted to publish without you! YOU are The Best! To her publishing team: Carrie Jareed, Jean Merrill, Julie Clayton and Penny Legg for all of their awesome, intensive personal coaching, assistance and guidance! To Director Carrie, YOU are The Best! To Jean YOU, too, for everything! To Julie Clayton for the original editorial assessment, suggestions and guidance! Thank you, Julie. You helped me shift the energy of the book to a more positive feel in addressing and dealing with horrible real-life situations! To 'The Amazing' Penny Legg for her final editing, her writing and book process coaching! Penny YOU are Amazing and The Best! To Ranilo Cabo, the front cover and book designer, every one of my colleagues, friends and pre-readers who has seen it, love the final book cover! And it's way better than anything that I could have come up with on my own or even imagined. Awesome work! To David Kloser; Geoff Affleck; Derek C. Doepker; Karen Everitt; To The Get Your Book Done (GYBD) Program and the whole Capucia Publishing Team, YOU are The Best! I literally could not have done it without you and this book would not be here without you! Thank You! Thank You! Thank You!

And THANK YOU VERY MUCH to My Linkedin; facebook; Twitter; Instagram; YouTube; actually ALL of YOU who are Connected to ME as My Social Media friends, colleagues and family or Ohana (Hawaiian Extended Family of CHOICE we may not be able to choose our biological ones, WE can choose each other!) Even though YOU may not hear from me personally or regularly, PLEASE KNOW that EVERY MONTH, I included YOU and Your Loved Ones in lots of love, blessings, prayers and good energy because WE are Connected through the ethers!

Again, this is My Special Thanks to YOU! My Deepest Gratitude and Appreciation goes out to all of the individuals listed and not listed above (on purpose however, I still remember you in private!) and to anyone and everyone who has contributed to and made a positive difference in my life and in this book!

And to YOU who were brave enough to pick up this book, look at this book, buy this book, read this book and make it through this book to read this SPECIAL THANK YOU for making it here all the way through to The End, I hope it made a positive difference in your life too!

With my deepest Personal Gratitude, I AM Sending YOU lots of XTRA love, blessings and good energy!

THX GARY...

Praise, Endorsements and Testimonials for *d.i.y. zen and the Art of Gentle Emotional Transformation*

This book, *d.i.y. zen and the Art of Gentle Emotional Transformation*, is an outgrowth of a desire to help people improve their lives and attain a higher level of spiritual development.

Rev. Gary Niki gives of himself in many different ways for the benefit of others and is generous with his blessings and healings. I've had the privilege of knowing and sometimes working with Gary for well over a decade. In that time, he has worked with the Red Cross and taught Anger Management classes in his career. I've gotten to know him as a caring person who has a genuine, burning desire to improve the condition of all humanity.

Many of us have enjoyed watching Gary grow and develop spiritually and professionally using the techniques that he shares. His circle of friends has known for years that there was a book within him waiting to be published. I am delighted that Gary has completed the long process of writing and publishing this book and am sure that it will be a source of help and inspiration to all who read it.

— Fr. TommyLee Whitlock, OSM
Celtic Christian Church.

We often walk around unaware that we are carrying so many negative emotions that are ruling our lives. Gary has done a marvelous job of putting each of these emotions in front of us, and, in a gentle non-threatening way, has shown us how to release them. I have worked with Gary on my personal issues and had amazing results. I am excited for all the people that Gary's book *d.i.y. zen and The Art of Gentle Emotional Transformation* will help because it holds the gentle, supportive, loving energy he uses to help people in person. Now, anyone can benefit from this work. It is great to have that loving "Niki" energy and be able to use it in the comfort of your own home. Best of luck on your spiritual transformation.

> — Lynette Sprowls
> Holistic Health Coach

I had no idea that Gary Niki's *d.i.y. zen and The Art of Gentle Emotional Transformation* would have such a profound impact on my life! The first time I met Gary was via a phone call when we both worked for the American Red Cross Disaster Services. Within the first few minutes, I realized what a special man he was. His kindness, positive energy, enthusiasm, and compassion were so tangible even though we were over 1,000 miles apart and this bond remains unbroken and solid to this day.

Gary and his techniques helped me through some difficult times in my life, especially during the back to back deaths of my two four-legged children Smoke and Molly, two black labs who consoled me through a devastating divorce, sick and dying parents and the most difficult journey of all, sobriety from alcoholism. When it was time for them to cross over the Rainbow Bridge, I was devastated and alone. I immediately called Gary. He helped me ride the waves of emotion through to become calm and coherent. He guided me with putting my fingers on my forehead and more, to be able to function and do what was necessary while pushing through extreme pain and suffering. I cannot express my gratitude enough for my life preserver, kindred spirit and one of my most cherished best friends, Gary Niki. I am blessed to have Gary in my life.

His clear instructions and techniques for helping us navigate the trash in our minds, body and spirit are simple (Not Easy) to follow and will change your life for the better. I encourage you to read this book with an open mind. Do the hard work, take it slow as he says and invest in yourself. Thank you, Gary for persevering on this journey to helping us help ourselves.

> — MaryJo Spencer Abbatiello
> Former Public Safety and American Red Cross Disaster Manager

Gary Niki's book *d.i.y. zen and the Art of Gentle Emotional Transformation* is truly transformational! His experiences and wisdom are an inspiration. I have seen first-hand how Gary has helped people transform their lives with his techniques, just as he has transformed his own. This book is a must-read, a timely treasure chest of gems for every one of us!

> — Tamara Elassal
> MS, NCC, LPC resident

Gary Niki is a being of light in this sometimes-crazy world! He has extensive experience in helping others, which he captures in his book *d.i.y. zen and the Art of Gentle Emotional Transformation*. He is very sensitive to others and shares his wisdom, helping others to address whatever the needs are in the situations they face. Gary gives examples and stories of how his work has helped others that demonstrate the effectiveness of his modality. He is well rounded and strongly grounded, open to listening to others and willing to hear more than one side of things, which enhance and expand his own beliefs. *The Energetic Action Process 33-Day Workbook* is a practical way for the reader to apply the work to their own life. Through this, he helps people grow stronger and enables them to fulfill their purpose. Those who do so will no doubt reap the benefits that others have described. I am honored to call him a wonderful colleague and a true friend!

> — LeRoy Malouf
> Founder, developer and owner of the Energetic Well Being Process© (EWBP©), an energy clearing process that enables clients to get stronger and more fit in all ways, and to make ongoing dramatic and positive differences in their lives.

Gary Niki is an impassioned truth-teller, shaman and healer. He is a powerful yet lovable warrior living deeply in the present moment. In a practical, yet profoundly loving way, Gary, in his book, *d.i.y. zen and The Art of Gentle Emotional Transformation*, offers us a well-organized protocol, which streamlines an otherwise lengthy healing process. He reveals what it takes to cut to the chase, while still going deeply into the depth of the issue. If you are lucky enough to spend time with Gary, consider yourself blessed with something special that catches you off guard. He IS true warrior spirit with that extra twinkle in his eye. We are lucky at last to have a profound healing experience with Gary anytime, through the inspired pages of his masterful book and workbook.

— Wendy Luck, Ph.D.

Flutist, vocalist, composer, and sound healer. Her solo flute CD, *The Ancient Key*, was recorded inside the Great Pyramid in Egypt. The author of *The Therapeutic and Healing Effects of Music* and *Sound, and Flute, Voice, Muse, and Multimedia: Creating a Work of Performance Art.*

Give yourself a blessing and experience the new global healing shift of *d.i.y. zen and The Art of Gentle Emotional Transformation!* The Shamanic Samurai Medicine Man, Rev. Gary Nobuo Niki, ushers in a simple, easy to understand, healing process with the potential for you to take charge and to make change!

Gary is a remarkably gifted and compassionate healing arts professional, able to identify the pain of others and help them create opportunities for true happiness. Over the years, I have found miraculous healing through Gary's facilitation of multiple techniques and I have personally used the "The Art of Gentle Emotional Transformation" process to eliminate traumas, minimize phobias and to neutralize the devastating pain of losing my parents just weeks apart. It's now my go-to technique to address immediate stressors and trauma.

In this book, Gary gets real and shares authentically about his life experiences and traumas that resulted in stuck patterns of self-sabotage and limiting belief systems. He then takes you along on his insightful journey of transformation through valuable life-lessons and the rich teachings of family, friends, colleagues and mentors.

He wraps up the journey by generously synthesizing his decades of experience and work into a 33-day workbook offering the potential to transmute your pain into peace. I highly recommend Gary as a healing-arts professional and I strongly encourage anyone ready to have a life filled with joy to embark on the amazing journey of *d.i.y. zen and The Art of Gentle Emotional Transformation!*

    — Terri Sisley, CHT

    The Non-Ordinary Trauma Release Specialist

The techniques in his book *d.i.y. zen and The Art of Gentle Emotional Transformation,* especially the "Put Your Fingers On Your Forehead", really work! Gary shares the journey of how he has helped hundreds, maybe thousands of people release trauma at the toughest moments of their life (i.e. personal disasters to 9/11, Hurricane Katrina).

I've witnessed how "Put Your Fingers on Your Forehead" releases emotion-laden, traumatic memories on three separate occasions when Gary was speaking and demonstrating them at the Rays of Healing Church in Falls Church, Virginia. People loved the healing experience he gave them!

You can also use this release technique on life's little gnawing irritations, too. Thank you, Gary, for sharing this fast and easy way to let go and live life more fully.

    — Rev. Wendy Wisner

    Rays of Healing Church, Energy Restoration Healer and Spiritual Coach

Gary Niki's book adeptly, poignantly, and humorously portrays his early family life and career in the emergency services, and his own gradual healing evolution. The book is a heroic, courageous recounting of his difficulties, woundings, and healing work on himself and others. It gives a candid portrayal of how he began to find deep emotional, spiritual, and physical healing for himself and others. Kudos to Gary, and to all of the people he has helped.

The healing techniques in his book *d.i.y. zen and the Art of Gentle Emotional Transformation* are very straightforward to use on your own or with a friend. They have been tested and developed over many years by Gary, with real people in real-life situations. They are very practical and powerful practices to help clear any negative emotions and blockages. These methods, along with many examples of people's success, inspired and empowered me to try them. You will find that the book will be a very practical and effective tool on your own journey.

 — Charles Myers
 Parkville, Maryland

I love books. I value most a book, a practice, and a message based on the integrity and character of the author. In his book *d.i.y. zen and The Art of Gentle Emotional Transformation* Samurai Shaman Gary, as he is fondly known amongst friends, brings an impactful combination of real-world experience as a Red Cross rescuer, peacekeeper, and anger management coach. Teachings born of experience are the most trustworthy. Even if I did not know and love Shaman Gary and his goofy humor, exuberant, and generous presence, I would read and believe his teachings.

I have known Shaman Gary for a decade, as a special, and gifted spirit. He is a rare combination of professional crisis experience, as with the Red Cross, and a gifted healer who has devoted himself to absorbing and manifesting the best of truths and healing modalities. Blessed is the one who has an origami-folded, gratitude and abundance heart dollar for prosperity blessed in her wallet (I have many). Lucky is she who has been attuned in the deep vibration of his digeridoo. He exudes joy and healing with his robust presence.

He embodies what he is teaching in this book, through his compassionate life story, and through his teachings and practices. He is sought out as an anchor in shamanic ceremonies, including the installation of my Medicine Wheel, and at the same time, his humor and Light shines through, lifting the energies!

Readers of his book will also be lifted by the energy and light that infuses his well-earned teachings.

I have been a promoter in the self-help book business. It's not simple or easy for an author to break through the clutter of our busy world. Therefore, I highly recommend that you read and use the teachings of this book to experience the blessings and transformation offered.

> — Jennivette Roberts
> Medicine Woman, Yogi, GF Fleet Commander, Poet

As a complementary medicine practitioner, I can say that Gary Niki's book *d.i.y. zen and The Art of Gentle Emotional Transformation* is a must-read for anyone who is looking for greater knowledge and gentle, soul-created healing techniques taught with much love, compassion, and humility. His approach to healing trauma is a thoughtful and comprehensive journey to self-discovery, acceptance, and forgiveness that takes us from pain to relief, and from despair to joy.

Through his book and workbook, Gary takes his readers into a path of self-discovery while sharing personal stories he holds close to his heart with the wisdom of a Shaman and the guidance of a Spiritual Leader, always with humility and respect. Thank you, Gary, for presenting us with the gift of more than 20 years of your life gracefully wrapped with that very unique love so characteristic of you.

> — Rev. J. Garbellotto
> Complementary Medicine Practitioner and Spiritual Counselor

I thought that it was no accident that just when Gary sent a copy of his book over for review, a number of things in my life were converging and I was feeling uncharacteristically upset. I am very aware that we have a choice as to how we respond to things that come up, and I was allowing myself to feel traumatized and saddened. So, as I read, I was reminded how powerful it is to place one's fingers on their forehead, and I did that. Then I came to the section on the Energetic Action Process with the hand clapping and the statements, and I took myself through the exercise.
I could feel the dark and sad energetic knots coming undone. Gary Niki's book,

d.i.y. zen and the Art of Gentle Emotional Transformation is a tremendous REMINDER. It is a beautiful and simple, straightforward teaching manual and reminder that we CAN nurture and heal ourselves. How wonderful to be able to have and take that kind of control for ourselves!

— Carol Rose Duane

Masters in Music from Peabody Conservatory, National Scottish Harp Champion, Certified Music Practitioner, Emotion Code Practitioner

I highly recommend Gary's book *d.i.y. zen and The Art of Gentle Emotional Transformation* for everyone wanting and willing to lighten and remove anxiety from their life. Gary has traveled extensively to some of our most traumatic events and disasters. With his simple techniques to calm those in distress, he has helped bring almost immediate relief. If these techniques can help calm victims of major disasters, think how you can be helped through many of life's challenges. A very helpful workbook to reinforce his teachings is included in the book. The tips and processes to relieve anxiety and fear are life-changing tools that I wish I had known about sooner.

— Phyllis Reynolds

I've known Gary Niki since the early/mid 2000s. I've been aware of the "Put Your Fingers On Your Forehead" for years from Gary. I've never practiced this technique before, maybe out of a habit of avoidance. As I read Gary's book *d.i.y. zen And The Art of Gentle Emotional Transformation* I began to realize just how many issues I've allowed to build up in my brain and psyche. It occurred to me that maybe this request to read and review Gary's book arrived in my life at a serendipitous time. Was it an opportunity to "clear" out some old and useless baggage? I read on to continue my journey of discovery. As I have mentioned, I've known Gary Niki for some time now. In reading his book I discovered details about his life that I never knew. I've always considered Gary to be a friend and mentor. Even though we only actually see each other once in a great while, I have always found him to be a constant source of positive inspiration. So, I was determined to find out just what these techniques were all about. Right on schedule a nagging, uncomfortable thought from my past popped up in my mind. I immediately tried the "Put Your Fingers On Your Forehead" and I have to say that almost right away this distressing thought lost its intensity. I followed through with instructions to relive the incident several more times and each time I did, the unpleasant memory faded away until I felt calm and at peace. I can't thank Gary enough for introducing me to this healing and powerful tool to clear my mind and spirit of years of clutter! I've yet to incorporate the muscle testing and Energetic Action Process, but I'm working on it. I've got a lot of work to do! Thank you, Gary!

— Leo Eckenrode
Retired Federal Employee

In the sciences, solutions sometimes appear which present fundamental answers — they can be reduced no further. These solutions can be recognized by a characteristic called "the elegance of simplicity", and they stand out for their inherent beauty as well as their simplicity.

Gary Nobuo Niki has discovered and formulated such a fundamental answer. The "Put Your Fingers On Your Forehead" technique, born from practical observation of human behavior in high-stress circumstances, contains both necessary characteristics — simplicity and elegance. It will help to reduce stress in thousands, if not millions, of people, and it is a wonderful contribution to the rising tide of humanity.

Gary's book, *d.i.y. zen and the Art of Gentle Emotional Transformation*, couples the "Put Your Fingers On Your Forehead" technique with other longer-term emotion-clearing processes, and he provides a workbook and other tools to help you apply and implement what you have learned. The book contains wonderful stories of Gary's own unique life, and descriptive experiences from many others. It's a fun read, and I recommend it to everyone!

— Rev. Dominick J. Gibino
The creator of the MINDSTEP multimedia presentation on science and spirituality, and the author of *Messages from Mom: A Remarkable Story of How Love Transcended Time, Space and Death* www.mindstep.us

Gary Niki is a rare combination! He is a spiritual warrior; is strong and artistic; is results oriented yet is a loving, gentle and compassionate shamanic laughing Buddha! His *d.i.y. zen and The Art of Gentle Emotional Transformation* book and workbook are both timely and urgently needed tools for all of us who are intentionally shifting our energy from 3D to 5D methods of self-care! Gary's intensive and wide-ranging experience in emergency preparedness gives him a unique perspective on the D.I.Y. process he has honed to an art. I've been lucky to share and co-create opportunities to learn, and teach with Gary, and offer all our abilities in service to humankind at this auspicious time. THE TIME IS NOW!

> — Bette Mozdzen
>> Energy Practitioner/Sound Healer - Light Living Energy Consulting for Business and Personal Goals. 30-year Practitioner - the Art of True Light

The *d.i.y. zen and the Art of Gentle Emotional Transformation* book by Gary Niki couldn't have come at a better time. With all the horrors, stressors and triggers that we are subjected to daily, both personally and globally, the techniques Gary talks about are incredibly effective and simple (not easy). I find myself using these techniques naturally and easily because they are instinctual. Thank you, Gary, for spreading your wealth of knowledge and helping people cope with trauma in a healthy and natural way.

> — Suzanne Holt
> Way Shower and Energy Healer

This book is life-changing and as such should be read by anyone who has had the feelings, emotions and "awful, distressing stuff" which Gary describes. I am referring to everyone, because each of us has had depressing, sad and difficult life events or situations which have stayed with us and then affect how we continue to live. I and many others wasted much of my life allowing these feelings to hold me back and weigh me down.

I was very happy to find what I will call a self-help book that included the 33-day workbook! I know this is a DIY guide, but I felt as if Gary was with me every step of the way! Going through this process and learning techniques to heal and improve have allowed me to look forward and to not allow these past hurts to hold me back from enjoying the rest of my life.

Gary is such a real and down-to-earth person who introduces us to his own life experiences with family and friends. The 33-day process was not a chore, but was fun and enlightening!

We can apply these techniques and improvements to our personal as well as professional life. This process has improved my relationships and my performance at work. Especially in these troubled times, I can't think of anyone who wouldn't benefit from it!

— Dorothy "Teddi" Zia
District Sales Manager, Maryland

About the Author

Gary Nobuo Niki continues to work in person with clients throughout the Washington, D.C. Metro Area, East Coast and around the world via phone and internet, working with a number of energy practices, modalities and techniques. He is the Shamanic Samurai Medicine Man; Diplomat of Pastoral Science (D.PSc); PMA Licensed Pastoral Provider; Priest - Order of Melchizedek; Minister - Center for Soulful Living; National Anger Management Association (NAMA) Diplomate and Anger Management Specialist-I; Domestic Violence Specialist-I; International Critical Incident Stress Foundation (ICISF); Association of Traumatic Stress Specialists (ATSS), Usui Shiki Ryoho Reiki Master-Teacher, Transpersonal Hypnotherapist (CHt) & Hypnotist; Integrated Energy Therapy Master-Instructor; Seichim Reiki Master-Teacher; Oneness Blessing Giver; Oneness Meditator; Founder of Good Finder I AM and the NIKIDO International Ministry of Service; Anger Management Facilitator; Spiritual Counselor; Healing Energy and Shamanic Practitioner and a professional speaker/trainer/motivator since 1983. He studied oriental healing and martial arts, along with multiple energetic healing modalities including: Holographic Repatterning; Psycho-Neurology; Jin Shin Jyutsu; Quantum-Touch; ZPoint; Yuen Method; Energetic Well Being Process; Accunect; Emotion Code; Body Code; Ho'oponopono; Tong Ren Healing; Shamanic work and Journeys; Vocal Vibrational Toning. Gary is the designer, inventor and maker of Riggi's Didges Non-Ordinary Spiral Didgeridoos.

Gary retired after serving as the American Red Cross (ARC) National Headquarters (NHQ) Disaster Services (DS): Senior Advisor, Safety, Security and

Investigations; Senior Associate, Safety & Security Weapons of Mass Destruction Terrorism Program Lead in the Washington, D.C. Disaster Operations Center, where he developed and led the Safety & Security (SAS) and Life Safety and Asset Protection (LSAP) Teams into a seasoned, effective group of over 1660 members from across the United States and the Territories, responding to large scale National Disaster Relief Operations.

Gary served on the Department of Homeland Security (DHS) Federal Emergency Management Agency (FEMA) Headquarters Interagency Safety and Health Committee; Liaison DHS FEMA Headquarters Security Office; Liaison DHS FEMA Headquarters Safety Office of the Chief Occupational Safety and Health Federal Interagency Working Group on Emergency Preparedness; FEMA DHS Instructor-Trainer and Instructor for a number of courses; ARC NHQ National Disaster Instructor Trainer; ARC NHQ DS National Critical Response Team Instructor-Trainer-Member; National Disaster Response ALERT Team; ARC NHQ DS Advanced Public Affairs Team (APAT) Safety & Security Spokes Person. He was part of the Aviation Incident Response (AIR) Team; an ARC NHQ National Human Resource and Diversity Instructor; Community Disaster Education Instructor and an Instructor of multiple Disaster Services Training Courses.

Gary was Adjunct Faculty Arizona Division of Emergency Management (ADEM); Arizona State Fire Marshal's Certified Fire and Life Safety Educator; ARC Grand Canyon Chapter Disaster, International, Armed Forces Emergency Services Volunteer Resource Manager; ARC Central Arizona Chapter Disaster Services Training and Preparedness Manager; Health & Safety: Emergency Response, CPR & First Aid Instructor-Trainer-Educator, Corporate Instructor-Trainer; held twenty-six Red Cross Instructor ratings. American Heart Association CPR, AED & Basic First Aid Instructor and Instructor-Trainer.

Gary still enjoys making the Origami "Heart Dollar Gratitude and Abundance Blessings" to share with individuals of service that he meets while he is out and about on his travels. Since 2002, he has made over 10,000 of them that are literally around the world. He has taught a number of individuals how to make them and now has D.I.Y. videos on his YouTube Channel to make and share the blessings. He is also known as "The Samurai Poet." His poem *I'm Always Here* was published in 2006 and has been embraced multiple times to offer comfort/spiritual care and hope at funerals and memorial services.

Gary is an Amateur Radio Operator: KC7TNU (1996). He is the owner and qualifying party for NIKIDO an Arizona Private Investigation agency (Lic #1001665) founded January 8, 1990.

Gary loves meeting people and road trips in his Shamanic Land Rover. Since 2016, Gary and 'Rovie' have covered over 76,000 miles together, on two cross country trips from the Atlantic to the Pacific and back. Then, as far North as Upstate New York and down to Key West, Florida, which was as far South as 'Rovie' could go to land's end. Gary continues to travel around the United States, taking and participating in training classes, sharing his Vocal Vibrational Toning, speaking, giving blessings at churches, events and workshops. He loves meeting, connecting and exploring with amazing individuals wherever he goes...

Rovie and I would love to see you on the road at events!

Bell Rock in Sedona, Arizona with 'Rovie' The Shamanic Land Rover.

Contact

Website: www.garyniki.com

E-Mail: info@garyniki.com

FaceBook: https://www.facebook.com/IAMGaryNiki

LinkedIn: https://www.linkedin.com/in/garyniki

YouTube: https://www.youtube.com/user/GaryNiki

Instagram: https://www.instagram.com/garyniki1/

Twitter: @GaryNiki

THE SAMURAI POET

ONCE A WARRIOR AND NOW I'M FREE
TO BE ME.

A POET HAPPY WITH GLEE.

I AM GRATEFUL FOR MY HORID PAST,

THAT LETS ME LOVE THE PEACE
I HOLD FAST,

FROM HACKING HEADS AND
VANQUISHING FOES,

I AM AT PEACE WRITING PROSE.

AND SHARING INSIGHTS FOR THOSE
WHO CARE.

I AM OPEN TO ALL WHO SHARE.

05.13.05C90IA

G. NIKI

THE SAMURAI POET

The Samurai Poet

THE SAMURAI POET

G. NIKI

THE SAMURAI POET

Please freely share my poem with anyone who has experienced the pain, grief and loss of either a two-legged, four-legged, winged or finned family member, loved one, friend, colleague, companion. . .

"Shared with lots of XTRA love, blessings and good energy!"

I'm Always Here

We're only here for a glint in time
And when we leave a love behind
There may be pain that in time will wane
But never forgotten on this earth's plane
So think of this as you miss a kiss
And think of me in eternity
I may be gone from my earthly shell
That at times may have been a living hell
And you were there to help me through
And find some heaven just for two
So as you sigh and start to cry
Remember dear I'm always here
Although I walk another plane
I'm here for you and that won't wane
So dry your tear give up your fear
Just think of me I'm always near
In spirit to give you comfort and cheer.

Gary Nobuo Niki, The Samurai Poet